The NOTEBOOK GIRLS

Ju

FOUR F

ONE

RE

WARNER BOOKS

NEW YORK   BOSTON

This is not a work of fiction. It is the real life group diary kept by four girls at a New York City high school. Their real names are used, but all other names have been changed to protect the privacy of their friends, classmates, and teachers.

Warner Books

Time Warner Book Group
1271 Avenue of the Americas, New York, NY 10020
Visit our Web site at www.twbookmark.com.

Printed in the United States of America

First Edition: April 2006
10 9 8 7 6 5 4 3 2 1

Library of Congress Cataloging-in-Publication Data

Baskin, Julia ... [et al.]
   The notebook girls / Julia Baskin ... [et al.]
            p. cm.
            ISBN-13: 978-0-446-57862-2
            ISBN-10: 0-446-57862-2
 1. Teenage girls—New York (State)—New York—attitudes. 2. Teenage girls—New York (State)—New York—psychology.
            HQ798.N68 2006
            305.235/2097471 22

                                                                    2005045662

Thank you to

Our parents
Miriam and David Baskin, for allowing me to publish this book, for their unconditional love, and for teaching me to be a good person.

Stephanie and Harvey Newman, for giving me love and support in everything I do, especially in publishing this book, because I know it wasn't always easy.

Katha Pollitt and Randy Cohen, I love and admire you for your honesty, courage, and humor (sometimes).

Pamela and Norman Toombs, and my sister, Allison: You are the most important people in the world to me, I love you more than anything, and may nothing ever change.

Those who helped us professionally:
Our editors, Caryn Karmatz Rudy and Emily Griffin, and everyone else at Warner Books who supplied us with advice, patience, and free *Gossip Girls*.

Our agent, David McCormick, who never gave up on us. (If he wanted to, we thank him for not saying it out loud.)

David Rakoff, with admiration for his writing and appreciation for his encouragement before any other adult saw the notebooks.

The fifth notebook girl.

And to everyone who inspired material—you know who you are (or you think you do).

Everyone likes to think she started the notebook. Sophie claims she stole the idea from two girls in her math class. Courtney still has a death grip on the theory that the notebook was her invention. Lindsey doesn't really care; she's just along for the ride. And Julia never knows what's going on anyway.

What we do know is that we started the notebook in the middle of our freshman year of high school. The four of us had known each other since middle school, but it wasn't until high school that we became friends. We devised the notebook as a way to keep in contact when our conflicting schedules denied us one another's company. The notebook also served as a much-needed distraction during double period Bio at 8:00 a.m.

As it evolved, we added geeky pictures from middle school (you never realize just how nerdy you were until it's too late), lengthy entries, and pages in the back such as "Words of Wisdom," dedicated to ever-funny phrases said by our teachers, friends, and yours truly. The notebook allowed us to express ourselves and our views of the world in a tone of complete sarcasm, obscenity, and blind honesty. Through it, we connected in a unique way by expressing our frustration at the unfairness of adolescence by cracking down on our parents, teachers, society, and most frustrating of all, teenage boys.

Even though this book is just a journal of life stories, within it is also the saga of a few boys we just can't get out of our heads, a tale of drugs and alcohol, trials and tribulations with parents, conflicts involving political beliefs and religions, and the menace that is high school. We are four girls each with our own issues that plague us, such as self-confidence, acceptance, obsession, heartache, sexuality, and loneliness. When you take away the jokes, pictures, doodles, and anecdotes, you have the growth of four best friends over two insane years of their lives.

The notebook provides an atmosphere of totally uncensored thoughts and feelings where we help each other deal with life through advice, responses, and the most effective remedy, laughter. Through poking fun at ourselves, the people around us, and those stupid marijuana prevention ads that make *no sense,* we bond in a hilarious way that we want to share with the world. We've spent a significant portion of our adolescence trying to figure out who we are. The notebook is the closest we've come.

We don't claim to be anything we aren't. We aren't on crack; we're not pregnant; our parents don't abuse us; and we're not failing out of high school. We are just a group of normal girls with normal lives. Our notebook isn't meant to make you depressed or make you feel sorry for us; it's meant to make you laugh and to make you remember.

All right. That's all we have to say on that subject.

PLACES

Stuyvesant High School: Our high school, a place we love and hate (but mostly just hate). It is a specialized high school for math and science (which just means that the science and math departments get way more money than they should), and is also considered the best public high school in NYC. Twenty thousand NYC kids take an SAT-style test to get in, only 750 – 800 are accepted. (But this test is *not* an accurate portrayal of brilliance, as the test is generally a measure of how much prep your parents can afford to pay for, or their hardworking immigrant work ethic.)

The Wall: An actual wall. A dingy, gray . . . wall, right across the street from Stuy. We hang out there after class, during our lunch periods, etc. Lots of drugs go down there, and a few too many acoustic guitars.

The Senior Bar: A high concrete slab about fifteen feet long. Defines the area where most seniors have their lockers on the second floor, near the school's entrance. Also where seniors hang out, cut class, and bask in the glory of senior year. The pinnacle of senior privilege at Stuyvesant, totally *taboo* if you do not belong to the senior class. Judging by how much alcohol and illegal substances are housed in these lockers, it could be an actual bar.

Upper West Side: A middle- to upper-middle-class, Liberal/Democratic, NYC family neighborhood in which we all grew up. Even though it is now gentrified to the *max*, there are still some lower-income areas. Lots of babies and lots of Jews.

The Globe: The "Wall" of Environmental/Beacon/LaGuardia high schools. It is an actual globe outside of the Trump Towers in Columbus Circle.

Joan of Arc: Statue (guess who it's of) in Riverside Park, near Sophie's house. Secluded area where we smoke weed.

The Monument: Huge monument to soldiers and sailors on the outskirts of Riverside Park, near Lindsey's house. Used to be *the* place to smoke, drink, and chill, but ever since it got overrun by lame sophomores, we prefer Joan of Arc. Sad but true, Sophie and Lindsey used to play there when they were babies.

Delta: An Upper West Side public middle school supposedly for "gifted and talented" students. Where the Notebook Girls and many of our friends attended middle school. Most kids go on to the select public high schools, including Stuyvesant, Bronx Science, LaGuardia, Beacon, and Environmental.

Bronx Science: Like Stuyvesant, but bigger and less intense. You take the same test to get in, but need a slightly lower score. Same douche bags, lower test scores.

LaGuardia: School for the artsy lost souls (basis for the movie/TV show *Fame*). Students are not as academically oriented, but love attention. You must audition to get in (music, dance, drama, and art). Many of our friends go there.

Beacon: Alternative public high school. Instead of statewide standardized tests, you submit portfolios. Like LaGuardia kids, Beacon students are more laid-back than Stuy kids, but again you find a lot of posers and a lot of druggies.

Environmental: Like Beacon, another alternative public high school.

Martin Luther King Jr. High School: Big zone high school in the middle of the Upper West Side, next to LaGuardia. Many metal detectors. Sometimes people get shot.

GLASS: Gay Lesbian and Straight Spectrum, the gay club at Stuy. Filled mostly with awkward kids and a few cool ones, all at different stages of coming out of the closet. Lots of talk about giving head. Surprisingly elitist.

The Speech Team: Competitive acting team at Stuy made up of eccentric performers, including Sophie and Courtney. They compete in tournaments, and Stuy has the best team in the country. Sometimes the team is awesome. Other times it's just painfully lame.

Villiger: The big sleepaway speech tournament in Philly, where everyone parties.

SING!: Stuy's drama competition. Each grade writes/produces its own play. A big school spirit event that everyone gets into, but somehow the same people always end up being the stars.

NFTY: North American Federation of Temple Youth, where Reform Jewish teens go to pray, argue, be outdated hippies, and get with one another. Julia's reason for living.

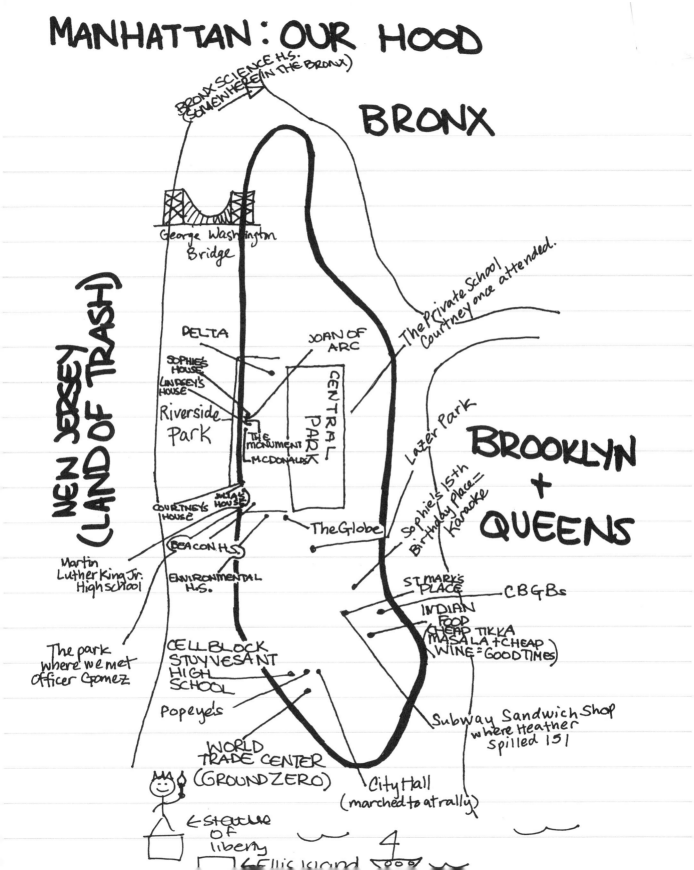

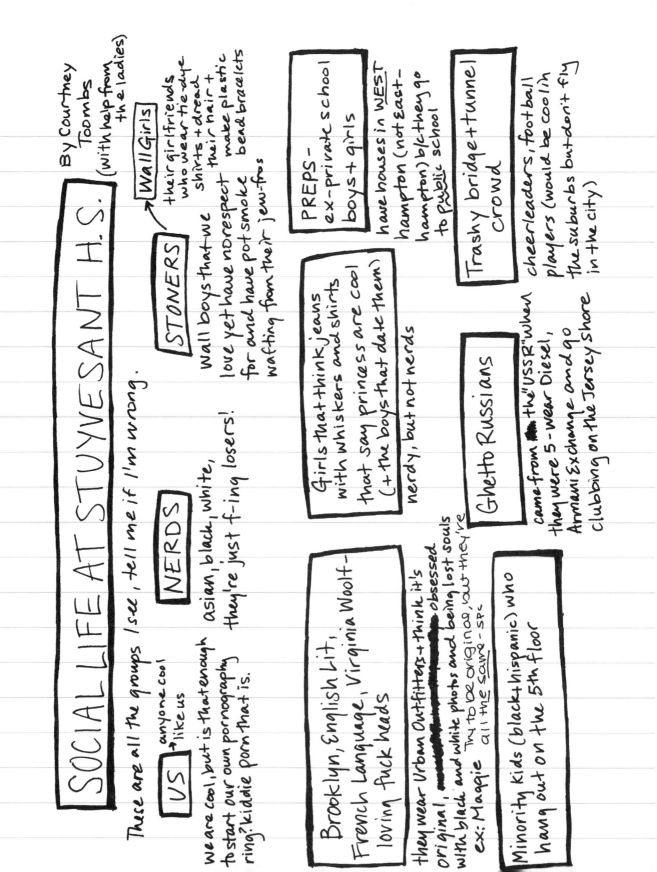

SOCIAL LIFE AT STUYVESANT H.S.

By Courtney Toombs
(with help from the ladies)

These are all the groups I see, tell me if I'm wrong.

US → anyone cool like us

We are cool, but is that enough to start our own pornography ring? kiddie porn that is.

NERDS

asian, black, white, they're just f-ing losers!

Brooklyn, English Lit, French Language, Virginia Woolf-loving fuck heads

they wear Urban Outfitters + think it's original, ~~obsessed~~ with black and white photos and being lost souls
ex: Maggie Try to be original, but they're all the same - sPc

Minority kids (black + hispanic) who hang out on the 5th floor

STONERS → **Wall Girls**

Wall boys that we love yet have no respect for and have pot smoke wafting from their jew-fros

their girlfriends who wear tie-dye shirts + dread their hair + make plastic bead bracelets

Girls that + think jeans with whiskers and shirts that say princess are cool (+ the boys that date them)
nerdy, but not nerds

Ghetto Russians

came from ~~the~~ the "USSR" when they were 5 - wear Diesel, Armani Exchange and go clubbing on the Jersey Shore

PREPS -
ex - private school boys + girls

have houses in WEST hampton (not East-hampton) b/c they go to **Public** school

Trashy bridge + tunnel crowd

cheerleaders, football players (would be cool in the suburbs but don't fly in the city)

4th floor Indian Bar

You know, the other side of the fourth floor

Ghetto Asians AZN

6th floor bar (like the senior bar but on the 6th floor and for sophmores)

4th floor kids from GLASS. who are really liberal + wear raver Jewelry

6th Floor Magic Card-playing nerds

a special kind of nerd (the new Dungeons + Dragons)

PPL WHO YOU DON'T KNOW EXIST BUT WILL ONE DAY COME AND SHOOT UP THE SCHOOL.

Example: go to a meeting of the Robotics club. You'll see

Julia as GOD looking down on US at the beach.

watch out, she might see

↳ Drool-in-i.CT

P.S. We are so beautiful.

RULES OF THE NOTEBOOK

1. NO taking like 30 days to write one entry!! (Hmm...who could I be talking about?) FUCK YOU! -LN

2. If you don't have anything nice to say, DO NOT use Julia as a tester for your new insults. She doesn't like it. DAMN THAT JULIA -LN

3. Put the mad MULTIMEDIA in the notebook.

4. NEVER listen to Courtney

5. Only kill yourself on days that end in "y."

6. If you're Lindsey, you are beautiful

7. Only put FUNNY things in the WORDS OF WISDOM (sophie)

8. Your mom

9. your mom's mom

10. Your mom's mom's hairdresser's mom.

3-5-02

Hey ladies! WOW, I get to write the 1st entry—I feel very special. (but you aren't :-) CT)

Alright, I know I shouldn't be all mother-ish or nagging, but don't you guys think it's so uncool when people do drugs or get drunk alone @ home? YES! CT

It really bothers me, because it's one thing to do on a saturday night w/ your friends (that's a social thing). But last night, Hunter was just high alone @ his house. That's so dumb. I kinda feel like he lame -w only does that so he can tell everyone about it + feel all cool and hard-core. He's my friend and all, but I think he makes some really bad choices. (like being your friend-CT)

SUCK IT. -SPC

Lindsey's surprise party was so awesome! We surprised the shit outa that girl. And the cake was so buttery and sweet...MMMN...

So speaking of buttery goodness, I gotta go do my History Homework. Gotta love that Ottoman Empire! Big ups to World History!

—Sophie

PS—The Ottoman Empire was in Turkey, right? oh god, I'm going to fail...

← is this drawing smoking a cigarette-CT
yes. -SPC

I AM AN
F ARTIST!!

(ha!)

3/5/02

What's up guys?

First notebook entry! I guess I better make this an awesome one! Sophie, Hunter is so weird. Is weird spelled wierd or weird cuz it looks right either way. Anyhow, ciggs and pot are only fun if you can enjoy them with company, otherwise you have issues, like being a loser.

idiot. -SPC

god use of abbreviation. -SPC

Anyway, I've realized something really sad lately, telling the truth makes everyone upset. When people tell the truth about anything, esp. cheating, it just fucks things up. Everyone should just ~~~~ be ignorant and pretend that things are ok. ■ Blah, bio is boring and I need foood. 🥣 spaghetti w/ meatballs!

Sophie's right, wasn't Lindsey's suprise party the shit!? Grandma's (aka Lindsey's) hair was mad messed up and it was really funny. All frizzy and shit! And funkmaster something (Sophie) looked like the ghetto shit in that "cat in the hat" hat. It's true -SPC

YES. -LN

courtney dumbest

Moving along, isn't ~~Ryan~~ the ~~cutest~~ boy at Stuy?! He is always at the Senior Bar before we go to lunch 5th period and he goes to lunch too. Anyway, he's really cool

It's so wierd that they call the senior locker/hangout area a bar? Actually, not that weird, since the seniors store so much alcohol in their lockers, and it looks like a bar. I should just pop over there 3rd period and order a dry martini w/ a twist! —SPC

and we all want to be in his pants now. So Julia, what's up with Joe?

Sophie and I were talking and wee need some mad hot boys right now so we can date em, mess with their heads, and then leave them. Don't you just want some play!

Love the ~~woman~~,
Cartney

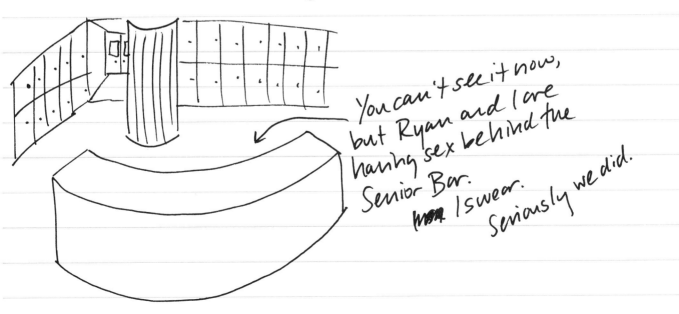

You can't see it now, but Ryan and I are having sex behind the Senior Bar. ~~I~~ I swear. Seriously we did.

3/6/02

Hey! This new notebook thing is so exciting. It's going to be so much fun to write to you guys. At least it'll give me something to do while I'm in school. I know we just came back from vacation, but I can't wait for the next one. *we really do just live vacation to vacation don't we—CT*

Ewwww, I hate having to go back to school now. After we have finals, it's always so hard to get back into the rhythm of this prison cell... I mean, school. Right now, I'm sitting here in English, doing nothing, woo hoo. Bored to te-ars, boo hoo (Hey, it rhymes!). But at least I have my new friend, The Notebook to keep me occupied.

Yes, just like you guys, I too would like some ass. Not just any ass, but a tight, luscious... um, right. But let's try not to let the lack of ass get us down. Be strong, girls!!

This is kind of random, but now that I see the pictures from my SURPRISE party (awesome, by the way. Thanks guys), when Grandma's hair is "mad messed up," you could let a sister know, ya know?

Oh yeah, guys, I learned a new word today in Music

Appreciation class →Glockenspiel← C'mon say it, just say it, you won't be disappointed.

After all the talk about people getting high, I think I'm high. That Dr. Pepper at lunch was a little too bubbly. Well, this has been fun, kiddies, but I've got places to go, people to see (I wish).

Big ups to Big L (raise the roof)

~Lindsey~

A pretty picture:

3/7/02

Hey dudes 'n dudettes,

I know everyone wrote really funny ~~some more than others~~ _LN_ letters to start off the notebook, but mine isn't gonna be funny cuz I'm actually really sad at the moment. I didn't make the hiphop tryouts for SING! and I'm really sad. Not even first cut! It really sucks, because SING! is like this huge play that all the grades compete in, and I'm totally not a part of it. I was so excited to go on stage, u know, wearing a cool hiphop outfit and be all slick with the dancing like "Oh yeah, you know I'm hot." Well, turns out I just crashed and burned instead. The judges didn't even glance at me. It's such an ego-buster when you're so confident about something I was really good at, you know, like Courtney can draw well and Sophie does that whole horseback riding thing and draws the pretty squiggly design, and Lindsey plays bball like a mean machine. I mean, if I love it so much, shouldn't I be good at it? I'm so sick of just not being able to do anything well. And hiphop dancing is supposed to be really attitude-y and smooth, and the fact that I missed 1st cut means that, along with talentless, I am none of the above. Well poopie. I'm just so tired of being plain. I feel like I have nothing to offer in life. I'm so regular. I'm not even great at sports. I'm just 0-fucking-K at everything I

right, the doodles I do in math class will get me far in life. -SPC

you would think so. -SPC

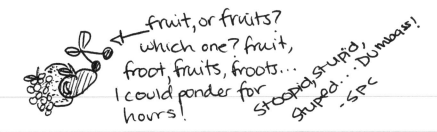

fruit, or fruits? which one? fruit, froot, fruits, froots... I could ponder for hours!

stoopid, stupid, stupd...Dumbass! stupid. -SPC

do, good enough to play but not good enough to make the team. I have tryouts for the tennis team 2morrow. We'll see how that goes. I can see it now, the coach avoiding eye contact and shaking her head as she says she knows I have some talent, but they just don't have enough room on the team and ....bullshit. Good but not good enough.... alright, I gotta end this, it's too much

Sorry to bring y'all down.
Peace in the Middle East.
Julia

Cool Design:

```
        J
        U
        L
   S O P H I E
   O    A
 C U R T N E Y
 L I N D S E Y
        E
        Y
```

See Julia, you do have talents!
-SPC

SURPRISE!!

HAPPY BIRTHDAY LINDSEY!!!!!!

Oh my lord (my amazing camera work!)
Lindsey, you kind of look like the grinch here.
-SL

looks like she
has no teeth!
(but beautiful)
-JB

Let the fun begin!

Why is Grandma wearing a shawl?

Do it... do it...

Yummy.

HAPPY BIRTHDAY LOOSE

My Beautiful Birthday Cake!

FART

Ewww that was a wet one. YOU love it!

ghetto booty! thanks, Jules, I thought my ass was flat! —JB

Hmm, should I comment about the phallic suggestion in the placement of this toy?

FRIENDS!
FOREVER!

and ever, and ever
and ever and ever,
and ever
(god I hope not)

AWW...FUCK

PARTY FUN ↙

It's your Birfday!

3/7/02

You guys!
 I TOTALLY get what Julia is talking about.
I danced ballet for 8 years of my life, and I lived
for it, but it's a world of extremely skinny people and
once I didn't fit into that mold anymore my talent
didn't matter, so I quit. How can you look graceful
and beautiful when you are putting on weight.
As a girl you are defined only by how sexy and
attractive you can be in front of an audience of
men. And even though you do want to be sexy, it's all at
the sacrifice of your self-esteem. Do you guys understand
what it's like to be 5'2" and 93 lbs. and be told that
you are fat? Or to see a 12 yr old girl vomitting blood into
the toilet in the dressing room bc she doesn't think she's tiny
enough. It kills me that I let myself subscribe to that brand of
bullshit because I wanted to be perfect. I should have been
proud to get breasts and hips when I was eleven, but I never
was because they came as the begining of the end. But
now when I see other girls doing it, I envy them bc
now I'm on the other side. Funny thing is now,

if you looked at me, you'd never guess I used to be one of them.

Julia, don't worry about the girls that got on the crew. Most of them take dance classes after school, so they just get more practice than you do. Trust me, I've seen you dance, and you're really good. Court speaks the truth. Amen.

-W

Peace Guys,

♡ Court

Thesmourt.
Bourt.

Wow. I look butt ugly. -JB ← TRUTH.

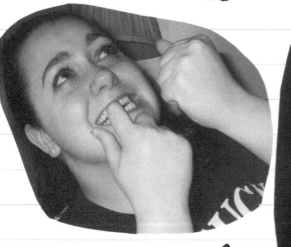

Julia and I seemed ↑ →
stressed about our
skills. We'll live.

3/8/02

Courtney, Lindsey, Julia: Hey guys. I'm listening to Weezer here in Italian class.

We don't do shit here, but sometimes my teacher hits people w/ his cane. Anyway,

it's the song Only In Dreams. I love it so much, but it makes me sad... it reminds me

of New Years, so it's all bittersweet and really good memories @ the same time.

Anyway, fuckin' terif! As the wannabe English punks in SLC punk say,

what a good movie.

Jewbah (my awesome nickname for Julia. It's amazing ~ it's Julia + Baskin,

and it's also a pun b/c Julia is Jewish... God I'm so lame...) I know it sucks/about not

↑ yes you are - CT

making SING ~~thats,~~ but don't worry. Also, you have a man (15 year old boy, same thing),

Joe, which none of us do. Lucky! Anyways, I gotta make like a basketball and

bounce, because I just got to art class, so in like 5 minutes I'll be giving this to Julia

herself. Actually more like 25 minutes, b/c she's always so late. And then fucking

Ms. Lloyd always acts like it's my fault and gives me evil deathstares. But she can

never manage to keep me down, b/c her Caribbean accent is so jolly and sweet,

so even when she's giving me the old fish-eye, she's still a nice piece of candy.

Actually, more like a giant donut, because Ms. Lloyd is kind of a wide load.

much love
- Sophie

Julia, look @ the following photo montage: we all have talents,

even you.

→▷

3/10/02

Dear CoCo, Jay Jay, and S-man, [See, I can make
up clever nicknames too]
Big L here, comin' atchya from the
'hood on Chambers. Question of the day:

WHY Ya'll GOTS TO BE
HOLDIN ME DOWN YO?

Anyway...   oh it'll be worth it - CT
I gotta see this hot guy, Ryan.
Ahhh, senior boys, thank god for them. If he is anything
like what CoCo's been saying, then he must be a sweet
potato. And I do mean sweet. You mean a yam? - six

Speaking about crack whores, Julia- it's okay if you suck at
everything, or you're just okay. Not everyone can be a winner.
Some people are just born special, and others just exist to run
things while the special ones are on vacation. Just think- if everyone
was great at stuff, then we wouldn't know what it meant to be bad at
something and everyone would be the same, and it would make a pretty
dull world. And remember, if there's ever a time when you're courtney
feeling particularly suckey, just look at ~~courtney, sophie~~, and thank the
heavens god had pity on you.   ~ Lindsey

3/11/02

YO! I'm back! I still have the Notebook, so I'm adding a little to my entry. I just wanted to write about something that's kind of weird to think about: today is six months since 9/11. Does anyone else feel kind of weird about this? I mean, there's been all the hype around it, I even watched a 9/11 thing on t.v. last night. It was a film by these two French brothers who had been making a film about a fire company, and happened to be with them on 9/11. They captured ~~this~~ lots of stuff on tape, like the planes hitting the towers, the firefighters inside rescuing people, and walking around after the towers fell. *I saw that. It was really emotional -JB* Watching it was strange because I was sort of reliving that day. Every time I see a replay of the planes hitting those buildings, or the towers collapsing, I get a weird feeling in the pit of my stomach. I watch the scenes play out and its like watching it in the moment, and knowing what's going to end up happening, but no matter how hard you try, you can't stop it. *I always think it will end differently -CT*

Having something happen like September 11th is so hard to process. It happened six months ago, but it feels like it was just yesterday. I can remember everything I did that day so clearly. It's hard to forget something like this, especially if you see it everyday when you go to school. I mean, who could ignore the barges next to the school carting the debris and maybe it's just me, but it's hard to believe the administration when they say that there are no health risks about being next to ground zero, and the next minute reminding you, under NO circumstances should you drink the water from *i did anyway. I swear it was fine -CT* the water fountains, and having the ventilating system blast full-on during the winter months, because we can't open the windows, but we need air from SOMEWHERE, so why not crank up the air conditioning and keep the school practically the same temperature as the winter air outside. Yeah, that makes sense. *And those guys in the suits w/ the air tester things... -JB*

Everything is so ridiculous and surreal right now, and it feels like nothing will ever be the same. It's like there are two worlds: pre-9/11 and post-9/11. But, I guess we'll just have to get used to the post-9/11 world, and the sooner the better.

Peace Out,

Lindsey

Stuyvesant High School

New York, NY

```
TO THE PARENT(S) OF:
LINDSEY NEWMAN
```

September 14, 2001

~~~Remember when we had to go here b|c our school was being for triage after 9-11~~~

Dear Parent:

Beginning on Thursday, September 20, all Stuyvesant students will report to Brooklyn Technical High School, located at ███████████, Brooklyn, NY. Students are to report at 11:00 a.m. to the first floor auditorium. A seating chart will be available. Classes will begin after a brief meeting and distribution of new program cards. Our normal school day will be 10 periods, from 10:55 a.m. to 6:11 p.m. Students should bring their Stuyvesant ID card everyday.

Sincerely,

Stuyvesant High School

SOPHIE SEZ: did you know that Congress acts as a check/and a balance? WOW! Piss on me! PS. Julia smells. ~~Fuck~~ you you're cross-eyed. True NO I'm not!

~~I'M AN ASSHOLE!!~~

3-12-02

NO, she says, did ~~someone~~ _LN_ shit themselves or did ~~Lindsey~~ _JULIA J_ walk by? AAH I HATE PERIODS!! Just thought I'd start out w/ something -SPC

special. But seriously, I hate periods, and I hate PMS. I spazzed @ all my
↳(which ones besides us?)-CT
friends today for no reason—I'd get mad or upset @ the dumbest shit, and

yesterday I had freaky mood swings. Guys need to understand the pain we

females go through. Let them go just one month of ①cramps that feel like a

rabid wolverine is trapped in your ovaries + is trying to claw its way out.

②Periods. I wonder how they'd react to blood coming out of... ahem... And

you KNOW that whenever a guy celeb got his period it would be like the

national fucking news. {THIS JUST IN} ASHTON KUTCHER IS HAVING HIS PERIOD. ALL

FILMINGS OF "THAT #70'S SHOW" WILL BE POSTPONED DUE TO MR. KUTCHER'S BLOATING

AND CRAMPS. (Read "If men could menstruate" by Gloria Steinem, that shit
                                                                    shit.
is the ~~shit~~). What the fuck, man? ③Pads. Tampons are a gift from Jesus/Hashem/Allah,

but let them go through hours of sitting in their own nastiness feeling like an infant

wearing a diaper that could withstand nuclear holocaust ④Tweezers.

Coming from the queen of tweezer pain. Because you know you want those

brows to look pretty + perfect, but then again WHY AM I PULLING HAIRS OUT

OF MY FACE?! ⑤PMS that makes you feel like shit. ⑥CONSTANTLY

being compared to bleached, implanted, lifted, tucked, injected, liposuctioned

celebrities. It's SO fuckin' frustrating how boys feel that just being male
                          authority
gives them the ~~right~~ to comment on/compare + contrast (just like

in history homework) girls' bodies. Guys in my classes are always

I take you seriously as a musician. Especially when we ROCK OUT:

mullet → 🎵 Sweet Home Alabama 🎵   tie: cooler than Avril Lavigne
cool guitar →   — acoustic looove
puffy ass vans →   — skirt over pants
SOPHIE   ME (Julia)   → converse

looking at stupid magazines like FHM and Maxim, saying shit like

"oh her tits are so small" or "she's too fat." who the FUCK are these

guys-they're like 15 years old w/ acne up the wazoo. Who gave

them the right to comment on girls' bodies like that? OK, those
                                                    like that
girls are in a magazine, but they talk/about girls in our

school too. But, of course, who cares what these guys look like,

how flat their abs are or how much they weigh, because there will

always be some girl to suck their dick no matter what (what they think,

maybe not true, but sad to say it just might be). ① Not being taken

seriously about anything that's been named "guy" stuff, ie. electric
                                                    WORD.
guitar, any good music, or just life in general.

   Lemme tell you, guys could NOT handle being a

girl. (yeah they'd miss their penises too much - CT)

Yes, yes, we all want boyfriends, esp. me. But I don't know any guys I'd

want to date. The stuy guys I'm friends w/, like Hunter or Tyler, I couldn't... ew.

And it'd be hard to date someone @ another school... though I'm

not in a position to be picky like that.
                    eating warm apple pie
   Happiness is watching Courtney take showers.

         - Sophie

PS- I read this on a desk in my math class: "crack makes ya healthy

like milk!" so true

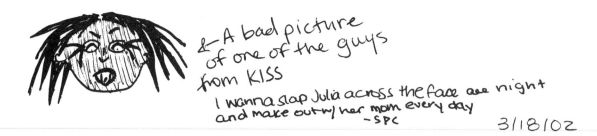

← A bad picture
of one of the guys
from KISS

I wanna slap Julia across the face one night
and make out w/ her mom every day
—SPC

3/18/02

So much to talk about!

So first of all, I didn't make the tennis team either. aww—CT It was really embarassing actually, because the coach told this one girl who was really good that she could leave and they'd call her, and then she told me I could leave, so I naturally thought it was because I was good too. But when I got outside, and people asked how it was, and I responded with "Great! They told me I could leave!", I realized just how ridiculous that sounded. whatevs, there's always next year. I'm not all sad anymore like I ~~was~~ was last entry, so the tryouts didn't get me down.

↳ isn't that "cow" in Spanish? —spc

So anyway, we all gotta chill over vaca. First spring break of high school! We should chill with both Globe and Stuy people. Gotta see our middle school posse, but also gotta bond with the school homies, fo shiz and fo real, from the nos to the homies. Sorry guys, that little part of my brain that made me remember I'm white just went haywire for a second. Yea. know the feeling. —SPC

↳ Best part of your entry —SPC

OK, 1st order of business: OMG I agree with Sophie sooo much on the 7 things that piss her off that guys should go through too. Especially the one about being compared to nipped and tucked celebs. I mean, come on, what gives? Damn straight we don't look like Britney, but it's not like we're paying muchos dinero to shove our

↑ like nipple
LN
↑ like tuckle —CT
not me —CT

plastic self at 12 years old boys and to have our voices run through synthesizers at a speed of 5 bad covers of rock songs per hour. Dudes gotta stop comparing us and like us because, for girls who get their looks and style and personality from no one else but ourselves (and of course the conforming demands of society and pressure us into being molded into the teeny-boppers we are), we are PRETTY DAMN **HOT**. Whew. OK, that's my shpeil (for all of those goyim out there, that means little lecture or speech. And goyim means people who are not Jewish — on to live through such pain! Just kidding.) I guess I can't really complain though cuz I got myself a man. But more on Joe later.

Well, I'm out and about, givin' a shout to ma S-DOGS, Cocos, Big L's. Buh bye y'all.

hey! -cT

*Julia

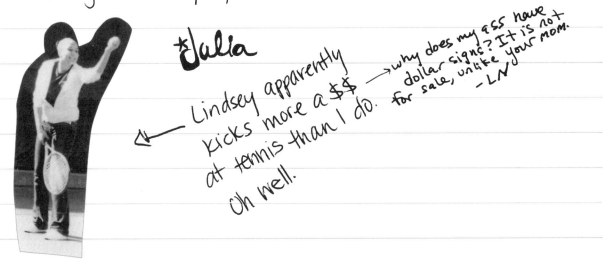

← Lindsey apparently kicks more a $$ at tennis than I do. Oh well.

→ why does my ass have dollar signs? It is not for sale, unlike your mom.
-LN

3/21/02
(Second Day of Spring)

Are ya'll ready for some JESUS? Yes! —CT Well, good for you.
What up in the promised land? Before I begin my entry, I have
a few things to get off my chest: →Announcement← Ummm...
It has come to my attention that certain ~~people~~, not mentioning any
names (hint: think everyone) have gotten a little upset at the length
of time it takes me to write my super cool letters. Well, I am sorry
that I ~~take~~ my time and write thoughtful letters, instead of just
writing some shit on the page, like some people (again not mentioning any
names). I'm not saying that your letters are ~~horrible, retarded peices of~~
~~mindless crap that don't even deserve a place on the ass of a~~ ~~sick~~ ~~constipated~~
~~llama with herpes...~~ not good, I'm just saying that they... might lack the
great insight and maturity that I have presented in my own brilliant peices of
work. Thank you. I am done. →End of Announcement← Lindsey, sometimes I
wish you were dead. Just kidding. maybe. —PC

And now on to bigger and better things, for instance, MY ENTRY!!
Well, as you may have noticed from my heading, today is the second day
of spring. You know what that means, yes, that's right, SPRING BREAK is
coming!! I can't wait, I'm so excited to have our sleepover at Sophie's
house. We should set a date soon because you know I have such a busy
life. I am very popular with my fans. {☺☺☺} ← Lindsey's one (dorky and
ugly) fan. —JB

I'm so excited I just might have to use some of the new slang
I picked up from a magazine. One of the terms I saw that was

supposed to be "cool" is "amped." Who the fuck says "amped?" And why do these magazine writers think I need THEM telling me how to sound like a cool teenager. Yeah, like I'm going to listen to some middle aged writer who's on a deadline and probably just makes all this shit up anyway. I mean c'mon, who writes that stuff? In all those magazines, they probably make up all the "trends" and beauty tips they have. Like putting your face in the freezer for a quick facial pick me up? What the fuck?

But I don't have enough time to rant against the mass produced, hollow American culture that we love so much because I have a math test right now. I hope I don't fail, maybe I should study. Hmm... I think I'll just sit here and do nothing. Yeah, that sounds good.

here:
2+3=5 and O.K. Wish me luck. I know you'll miss me.
that should help - CT
          Love, Lindsey
P.S. I'm going to that project greenlight movie today. I hope Matt Damon is there so I can ~~have mad passionate sex~~ say hi.
  P.P.S. THIS LETTER ONLY TOOK ME <u>ONE</u> PERIOD TO WRITE. thank god - CT

3/21/02

Yo.

Lindsey, don't worry, we value quality over quantity. Unless your entries suck, in which case we yell at you for keeping the notebook too long and wasting our lives. I love you. How was your math test?

So we have to introduce a new and REVOLUTIONARY term to the notebook: oob. Now for those LOSERS who don't know what an oob is, (which is the whole world besides me and Sophie), it stands for order of business. Like if you wanna talk about something that you think is probably really important but we don't care about, write "the first oob is...." and so on and so forth. I know. It's genius. And now for something completely different. Yeah, Monty Python! -SPC

Ok, one oob to discuss (note: first example of the proper use of oob in a nbk entry): when are we gonna have a girls' sleepover at Sophie's house? Speaking of houses, has anyone ever been to Cartney's house? It's like the mystery place of the world.... no one's ever been there. Maybe she's some kind of evil villain whose secret ambition is to repopulate the world from a llama farm in New Mexico.... or maybe her house just smells bad or something. Right. well then, I'll be going. Ups to the outs.

Ta ta girls! ↳Excuse me! I would like to clarify that my house

Like Boobies! -LN

Julia is merely the local bordello and unless you want Madam Barney to eat you out then you're not welcome in my house! -CT In that case, Sophie's definitely welcome. -LN
↳ I'd like it...uh...I mean...Lindsey would like it....-SPC

What's Poppin', Poopsies? ⚡ 3/22/02

Sorry, but I don't think we can have the sleepover @ my house.

`OK, 1st oob:` "Hot Irish Guy." "For those of you who don't know, there is this senior @ our school. I don't know his name, but it doesn't matter. He is HOT, he looks Irish, + he is a guy. Hence the name Hot Irish Guy. Today on the wall, for reasons too complicated to explain, H.I.G. took off his shirt. All I can say is he goes to the gym.

HIG, not a very hot name. -LN

`oob2` My Rancid CD came! It's so good, and one of the few CDs I have on which I like every song. Gotta love "...And Out Come the Waves," that shit is the shit. Shit.

`3rd oob:` Julia smells. Really bad.

`4th oob:` I'm kinda pissed about the Tyler drama. Basically that girl Donna loves him, the completely acts like he has this huge crush on her, even after telling her he didn't. He's leading her on + I think it's pretty horrible. Maybe b/c so many girls like him, he doesn't get what it's like/how much it sucks to like someone, think they like you too (yay!), but then find out they don't (oh no!). Oh, I've been there, and it's a sad time. I really liked this guy once, we'll just call him... Dave. He acted as tho he really liked me, + everyone was always telling me how much Dave liked me. But they were WRONG, b/c then it turned out he didn't like me. I felt sad + also hella embarassed. The End.

Jealous much? -CT

That sounds like the guy Julia's in love with... oh wait, it IS. shit. That's b/c it is him. I was too lazy to think up a pseudonym. -LN

good story, not!

`oob5` The Spring Dance. It was actually fun. Julia you are a really good dancer. You got your freak on. I started a Mosh Pit w/ that Hottie McCutie in our grade, Paul. He is HOT... like when my mom makes a baked potato + I burn my tongue... I mean... what the fuck am I talking about? Anyway... @ the dance, I crossed the

Thanks!

A sad, drunk monkey
WTF?!

border. No, I didn't take a Mexican vacation, but I did smoke weed for the 1st time. It was OK, I guess, which probably means I didn't get high (if I don't know if it was fun or not). ~~That guy~~ That guy Andrei (or however you spell his name) said it was crappy weed. He pretty much seems to be a weed connesiour, so I trust him on these matters.

COCO → Responding to Coco's earlier entry about ~~the~~ ballet + girls being pressured to lose ~~all~~ that weight: I can't say I totally understand, b/c I haven't experienced the intense stuff you described. But I can relate to feeling stupid for "subscribing to that brand of bullshit." All the movie/TV/magazine/media ingeneral shit hyping celebrity/"perfect" bodies sometimes gets me feeling really bad about ~~myself~~ myself, b/c who doesn't want to look like that? I feel really stupid, tho, b/c I know I should be smarter than that, + I shouldn't buy into it, but it's so hard to escape it.

NEW TOPIC There is the funniest guy in my Italian class named Rob. He is out of his mind. For homework, we had to write 5 interview questions (in Italian) about the time of day you do things. Everyone did stuff like "Quando vai a scuola?" (when do you go to school?) or "Quando fai i compiti?" (when do you do homework?) His was (I don't know how to say it in Italian, but he looked it up) "when do you abuse the hunchback?" Clearly he has serious damage. Last week we had ~~he was~~ to write autobiographies. His was called "Mein Kampf."

I don't know whether to laugh or cry. me neither
— Scott ?

LINDSEY + SOPHIE THROUGH THE AGES

A PORTRAIT OF THE ARTISTS AS FUCKIN AWESOME!

nice hats
you guys.
Really in style.
Really.
JB

THEN →

I ABSOLUTELY LOVE THIS PHOTO!! -CT

Dinosaur + Bird strike again!!! -CT

early wrinkles + brace face! JB

NOW →

← That date is all wrong. -CT

Almost too sad to laugh at. New si...

{HEY GUYS, I'M BACK FOR MORE}   3/23/02

My life is over. It has ended. It is no more. It has joined the chior invisable (big
ups to monty python!) Ok, I'll just cut the cheese. I mean to the chase. *ewww* *It's spelled ChOIr.* Stuyvesant
Highschool has confiscated my cellphone! Just b/c I was sitting in the hallway, talking on
the phone... ok, I guess they have a point. (omg what are you going to do?)
                                                              — CT

Anyway, I need to do "community service" @ school to get it back. At first I was like oh
no, am I gonna have to paint a mural or something? But ~~I~~ I have to help out in one
of the dept. offices. So I'm working in the English dept. office for none-other than
our favorite Stuy High ~~xxxxxxxxxxxxxxxxx~~ cutie boss man, the head of the dept. ~~xxxxxx~~ Mr. Klein! maybe he'll
be like "oh Sophie, the way you ~~file~~ those folders + organize those books just sets my
heart a flutter. Lets run away to the sandy beaches of Jamaica and dance to the reggae
beats all night long." OK, or not. So until that happens, I'll just be pining for my phone.

In other news, today was cool. I chilled w/ Sam from Delta, which was nice, b/c I hadn't seen him
in a while, and you can't forget those middle school friendships. He invited me to come jam w/ the
band he has w/ Andre from Stuy + that kid Jimmy. I felt so awesome, like the tough girl who
can hold her own w/ the guys, cause I was most def rocking out w/ my guitar ~~xxxxx~~ solos.
I also smoked up... thru a shower head. I'll never look @ one the same. I actually felt something this time. We were getting chinese food + I was being so crazy. I was laughing so hard, which
lead to troubles trying to dunk my fried meat dumplings in the sauce. They kept falling in. IT
NEVER GOT ANY EASIER!

          my pupils are quite large.   👁 like this?
                                              — JB
          woah. — Sophie   Are you still high or something? — CT

← You're just
jealous.
— SPC

That would
never happen
sorry. CT
← WORD.

Hey Guys,

SPRING BREAK THIS WEEK □ woo! -JB 3/25/02

<u>1st oob</u>: I'm glad Sophie isn't a weed virgin, but don't act like drugs are your best friends just yet, bc they're ultimately just a way for us to escape our problems, which is kind of messed up→ but hey, I've done drugs so I guess I should shut my fucking trap! All those assholes who smoke cigarettes yet say, "Anti Corporate America! Anarchy!" are lame in the first place and then also b/c CIGGARETTES ARE CORPORATE AMERICA—and those people really need to check their beliefs. word, they are major hypocrites -SPC

<u>2nd oob</u>: speaking of corporate America I can't believe they are making us dial **1-212** before everyone's since when is that what NY is about? -JB phone # now! What the hell is that? I mean that is part of what New York is about, be people being too fucking lazy to dial area codes for Manhattan bc there are so many #s. Wasn't the point of having 718 area codes for Brooklyn and Queens to make us all dial 1-718 to call them, thus making us hate them and call them creepy rejects and put them in their place across the river? I mean honestly what does it all mean anymore?!! By the way, It means 3 fucking numbers! -SPC don't expect any calls from me now you 1-212 bitches!

A "1-212 Bitch"

It looks like she's holding half of a doughnut. -LN

3rd oob: Everyone should put multimedia into the notebook, basically that's photos and scrap book stuff like this.

where the CRACK is -LN →

Speaking of ciggs, I bummed this cigarette on Friday and I forgot about it but I found it this morning broken in ½ in my wallet and took the half I could smoke and put the other half in here.

4th oob: Awesome about the Rancid CD, Sophie. They had this interview in Spin Magazine about the first cds all these famous artists owned and when I thought about it my first cds were Green Day-Dookie, Weezer- Blue Album, Sublime, and Yours Truly: ~~Rancid~~ Rancid- Out Come the Wolves. They are from like 1994 so the cd is about the thickness of a Sackajewaya dollar. Fuck, I hate those things. I always forget they are dollars.

Good choice! -SPC

Well love ya, byes,

Court

for a while, I thought they were Sequoya (sp?) dollars! Sometimes I amaze myself. Slap -JB

Julia →

WIDE
LOAD

The government makes her wear that sign.

shutup!
my mom says
i'm shapely...
right.... HA!

4/9/02

It's 1st pd-yeah, world history! uh oh...Mr. Linus is checking our homeworks...

All of them! And he wants us to hand in #19-the one I didn't do (of course)!

Whenever he hands our HW back, they always smell like a certain someone

named MARY JANE. He's an old hippie + he loves to talk about the good

old days. Also, the other day when he was teaching us, he was playing w/ a

pack of matches in his pocket (he smokes like 2 pack a day) + he

accidentally set himself on fire. Man, Stuy is so wack.

so 1st boob The museum. For art class, we have to visit a museum +

take photos of certain paintings. Since Julia + I are in art together,

we hit up the met. It was kinda sad, b/c whenever we'd pass particular

pieces of art, we'd remember stuff. Julia's memories were all like "oh, this

is one of my favorites," or "I LOVED this when I was little!" but

mine were all "in 4th grade I ~~accidentally~~ almost knocked that over + I set off

the alarm + the guards came + my teacher yelled @ me." I

felt so uncultured. (b/c you are)-cT

isn't that everyday?-cT

2nd boob Yesterday. It was the day of embarassment. First of all,

my mom came to classes w/ me for Open School Week. Horrible! Every

period she'd be like "HI, I'M SOPHIE'S MOM!" It wasn't anything specific

she did that was so embarassing, but you know as a teenager, everything

your parents do in public makes you want to crawl into a whole and

TRUE die. But it was also sorta fun ~~showing~~ showing her around + having her

if he's smoking a cigarette, wouldn't he be on fire? That would also hurt for the girl using it! —CT

OUCH. —LN

—Hi!

see what my day is like. she looked so cute in class, sitting @ her little desk w/ her hands folded all primly and shit. THEN, during 10th pd, I was hanging out on the 10th floor w/ Tyler + Maggie. I was talking to Maggie, + when I looked over, Tyler was taking a tampon out of my bag. He yelled "EW! DIRTY!" really loud + threw it across the floor. what an idiot. ♡ Sophie

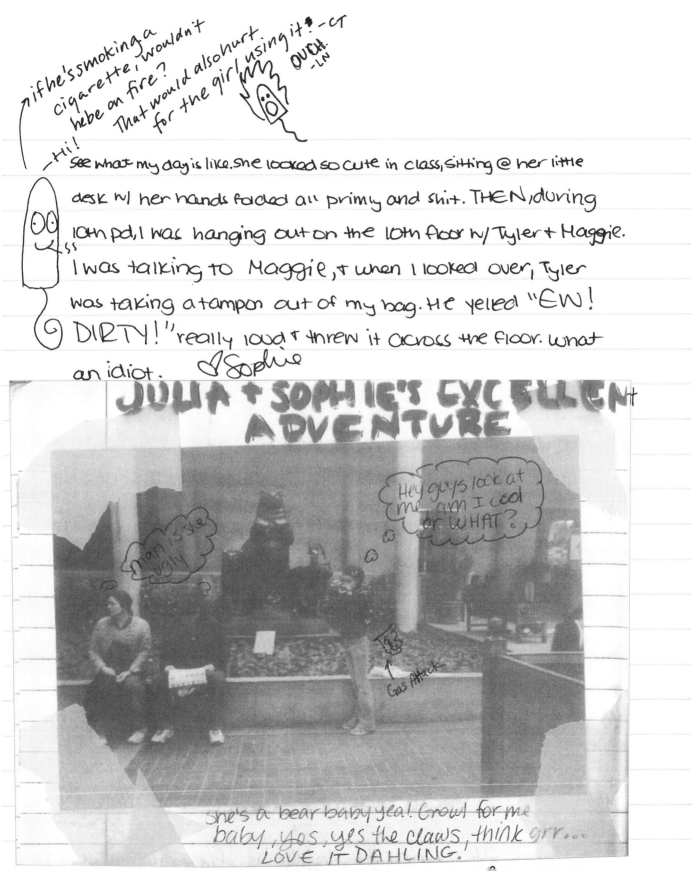

JULIA + SOPHIE'S EXCELLENT ADVENTURE

Maggie's ugly

Hey guys look at me... am I cool or WHAT?

Gas Attack

she's a bear baby yea! Growl for me baby, yes, yes the claws, think grr... LOVE IT DAHLING.

4/10/02

Hey it's Julz again,

SHHH! -LN

First and only Boob: Day of Silence. So the Day of Silence is when you don't speak for a whole day in order to represent the silence that many gay, lesbian, bi, transgender, questioning (from now on referred to as GLBTQ) people feel when they're not allowed to express who they really are in terms of their sexuality in their schools, homes, communities, etc. Being silent is really powerful. I mean, this little deed I'm doing seems to affect so many people. When they realize what I'm doing, even if they don't agree with it, they suddenly open up to me and tell me all their beliefs and ideals and opinions. My silence is somehow a sign that I'm more ready to listen, and people are really willing to express their views, maybe because I can't respond to them. Some people told me I was being stupid, and that I can't accomplish anything by just not talking. But in my opinion, the Day of Silence is a personal thing. Not talking for a whole day is not easy. In fact, it's really frustrating. If I myself can feel a fraction of what people who have to live in real silence feel, then this day is a success. And if someone is so moved by it that they begin to talk about their issues with the subject, then the goal of this day, to raise awareness, has been accomplished.

It's really powerful to be silent, cuz you really have to think about what you're being silent for. I mean, discrimination against gays and lezzies (and BTQ as well) is a really big issue. I mean I'm not gay or bi or anything I don't think, but I always feel responsible for any acts of discrimination because I feel like I have the power to stop them. I feel like that's the whole point of America (besides imperialist arrogance, but more on that some other time), you know, to be able to step up and change things that are wrong. And if every person relies on someone else to step up, no one ever will, so isn't it up to me? Deep feelings. I'm trying, but no one can be superman I guess. Or superwoman. Or supertransexual. Hehe.

Fight for the Right, (to paaartay!)

Julz

I promise I'll fill you guys in on Joe sometime.

JULIA GOOLIA

CRACK ATTACK!
-LN

DAY of SILENCE
GLSEN
USSA
www.dayofsilence.org

Speech/labels in drawing: "And Lindsey is all alone", "Kitty?", "I hate you.", "-SPC", "Julia CCM. soph. 4/13/02"

Dear Everyone,

PLEASE DON'T KILL ME! Sophie kept asking me about the notebook and I kept telling her that Julia had it (sucker). She thought someone lost it, actually it was pretty funny. Why does everyone believe me? I can play you guys like a fuckin cowbell, **MANIPULATION IS THE KEY TO LIFE.** But everyone chill out, 'cause I always knew where it was.

First OOB: On Friday people came over to my house and we watched, get ready for it, yes! THE PATRIOT! (Best movie EVER!) Question:
I agree! Ohh Heath Ledger... -JB
What's with boys and playing with destructive stuff? Hugo had some lighters with him, and of course it was only a matter of time before someone thought of the brilliant idea to break them out and start playing with
what losers. Why was he there in the first place? -CT
fire in my living room! Whenever someone would pick up a lighter and start to play with it, my whole body would go tense and I could just imagine my whole couch setting on fire. That would be fun to explain to my parents. But despite my occasional seizures of paranoia (sp?), it was fun.

ME → (labels: "Kitty?", "why are you bald? -SPC", "couch ↑", "raging fire", "MEOW!", "black fire? -JB")

OOB #2: Silencio

hey I did it too! -CT

Julia, I'm proud of you and your new found power of silence. Woah, that sounds deep. I think that it's awesome that people actually show that they care about stuff like that I mean there are so many people in this country who are repressed and can't be themselves because they face discrimination and are not accepted by society, their communities, families, etc. But if we had a day of silence for each one of these groups, we'd probably never be able to talk. *—I'd be so glad if you couldn't ever speak again. —spc*

OOB#2.5: Even though I support the cause, I think that a lot of those kids in GLASS seem really stuck up and exclusive. They *YES!! —ct* just get into "socially conscience" things and groups because they think it's the "cool" thing to do. Because, let's face it, most of those kids are white, upper-middle class kids from Manhattan or Park Slope who *plus they're gay.* never understand what real oppression is. The vibe I get from them is "I'm too cool for you cause I dye my hair, make my own clothes and *so do we! But we're cool... right? —spc* *assholes (jk) —ct* like to smoke pot. I'm ALTERNATIVE." What the fuck does that really MEAN anyway? I mean, I don't have anything against kids who really, genuinely believe in this stuff (although they will soon have to come to terms with the fact that the world is just screwed.) But the ones who are self centered and too cool for everyone else and in it for the wrong reasons really annoy me cause they're the total opposite of what they say they are.

WHY ARE PEOPLE SUCH DOUCHES?
(a disgruntled) Peace Out,
Lindsey

Lindsey, that is the unsolved mystery of life. I don't think the answer will ever be known. —SD

Hey homeslices→ Ha! ♥♥ NO.

4/16/02

So Julia + Joe! How's the big crush going? Do you loooove him? Do you want to fuuuck him? Maybe just a little bit? OK, enough about you...

OOB! me + Paul. We've become pretty good friends since the dance, talking on the phone a lot, hanging out after school, etc. Then, a bunch of us (me, Paul, some Stuy friends, + more) went to Lindsey's house to watch a movie (God I _hate_ "The Patriot"). Paul was being all flirty + touchy + I was def. enjoying the vibes. It became pretty clear that we both liked eachother, + he asked me out the next day. But guys, now I'm having some doubts. The more I spend time w/ him, the more he annoys me, + I wonder if I only probably like him for his looks + semi popularity. I tried to imagine his personality on an ugly person (TV ugly, not real life ugly), + I'm not sure if I'd like him so much. Also Paul is SO intense. He has an online journal + he wrote in it all paranoid ~~about~~ saying "Sophie, ~~nooooooo~~ I love you, not in a casual way, I really love you...what if I'm not good enough for you?"

AAAH!   yeah Paula always acts like he has so
many problems, it's really not true -ct

So I told Tyler about Paul's crazy intensity (intensity = $\frac{Power}{area}$. I'm smart! ~~sooooo~~), b/c they're becoming pretty chill + I thought it'd be better for P. to hear it in a casual guy to guy way than if I were like "You're freaking me out! Stop!" But my plan backfired, and P. just got upset that I hadn't confronted him. He bitched me out online, and signed off in a huff. Then I realized how DUMB and SAD it is to have important conversations online. Teenagers are so lame.   no that's just
you -ct

But to Coun, who says you can't have deep conversations w/ Tyler, he's been a mad good friend.

LATER

Because I live life in the fast lane!
-SPC

THAT WAS FAST! -CT

Paul + I just broke up. The relationship was ridiculous, + I'm glad it's over. I think I was just so excited that [Paul] liked me, so I didn't stop to think about how little we knew eachother. Anyway, I hope we can be friends, so probably not. Oh FUCK. I just realized that the ENTIRE Sophie/Paul relationship is in this one entry, beginning, middle, + end. I'm so embarassed right now.

Oh, this notebook is there through all the good + bad times.

I'm out.
~ Sophie

PS - my hands smell bad. Should I be concerned?

Where have they been? On second thought, I don't want to know.
-LN

The corner where Sophie sells herself (for apple pie)
-LN

4/17/02

Hey Homeslices (a cue from Sophie),
　FIRST OOB: Sophie, I never said you couldn't have a ~~serious~~ deep conversation with Tyler. I just meant that sometimes it's hard to talk to him because he likes to be silly, but when he's chill, he's really cool. Getting him alone is the key to understanding him. I mean look at him w/ the girls he's interested in, he's so much different + more serious. But I love Tyler (almost) whatever way he is.
　SECOND OOB: Right, so what the hell was that shit with all those wall kids fucking each other? When I came to Stuy, Karyn's (Delta buddy) older sister told me that if you wanted to hang out on the Wall you had to be an official "wallie" which only the seniors could declare. Their determiner for a true "wallie" = a "punk rock" kid. So I said, that's the fucking lamest thing I ever heard in my life and fuck them, I'll hang out there if I want to. So basically now us freshman have taken over the Wall and made it cool again. Anyway, so now all those dirty, grimy heroin kids who hang out on the wall are having sex with each other.

WORD-SPC

Once upon a time, not too long ago, when people wore pajamas and lived life slow... (Slick Rick) —LN

STORY TIME.... kids gather round....

Trent is dating Alina (former JAP, current wallie). Trent went to a party, got wasted, and had sex with Katie (Alina's friend!) while this other girl was giving some guy head right in front of them. (Ha, then that other girl threw up on that guy's dick while she was blowing him b/c she was so drunk.) True! I swear! Ok, then everyone found out about Trent + Katie having sex so Alina broke up with him and won't speak to Katie and hates her guts now.

The worst part is that most people aren't even mad at Trent who should be taking a huge chunk of blame. Katie's really upset about everyone finding out about it and she was talking to me about it in homeroom. It's weird because she seemed so innocent but now she's all like having sex and shit and I was like whoa, how did that happen. She said she fucked him bc it didn't matter to her. She said, "relationships in h.s. don't matter." But even if that's true, people shouldn't fuck around. She also thinks sex can mean nothing, which I can't understand. She's no virgin, but is it really not a big

what assholes!!

That's b/c girls are always sluts, and guys are pimps. Why is this world so fuckin fucked up? -SP

deal to her? Back to this whole cheating thing, if she fucked Trent while wasted then she could have gotten pregnant—she said there was no condom and she did it like 3 times—then she'd be so fucking screwed. I mean that's what scares me the most, a baby. The 15 min of pleasure (and come on it's not like it even lasts that long or that most teenage girls have orgasms all the time) isn't worth fucking up my life forever.

+ point for using Yiddish. -LN

↳★ Sorry about that long schpeil, but that story has been passed around school so much I thought I should set the record straight. ★

THIRD OOB: Joe and Julia! What is with this dude, he gets all the mad hot chicks! (Julia) So are you guys gonna go out or just be fuck buddies, cuz either way it's pretty cool. Julia get that boy some new clothes b/c he is a nasty Wall boy whoever does laundry.

FOURTH OOB:

SOPHIE ❤ PAUL

ON THE ROCKS!
he's a nice guy,
but you can't be with
someone that you don't like
(except for his hottness)

sophie Paul
ROCKS -JB

Julia, there are no words. -SP
wait... how bout STUPID?

what? You never said that when I was going out with Dave and Dave wore his bro's old clothes but yes I agree. -JB

Day of Silence!

Abortion Day! (just kidding!)
↳ the day you got an abortion? WHAT?! -SPC

FIFTH OOB: Julia, the Day of Silence was great! Classes were boring without my astute comments, but seriously it did make an impression on a lot of people. At the end of the day when I could finally talk, when I was coming home on the train w/ you and Rosie, I had been wanting to say stuff all day, but I didn't, and then when I could finally talk I was like wait, no, don't say that...wait...fuck! I _can_ say that! And it's soo hard not expressing yourself all day, esp. when Sophie and Lindsey are being really stupid (haha). And then this stupid girl asked me if I was gay, and I was like dude it's not just for gay people, it's also for people who _support_ gay people. I feel that gay people are just like anyone else in the world, trying to find love and happiness in the best way possible.

SIXTH OOB: THE GLOBE SUX!! Everyone is realizing that now, and I said it like a zillion years ago! This always happens! Damn bitches got no respect for me! It's just a lame place where all the Upper West Side kids hang out. It's no wall if you ask me. And the other non-Delta people there are mostly (not all) really exclusive + judgmental — and I don't want to bother being friends with people who are always fighting + hating each other /everyone else) (okay, I know Sophie and I ~~kinda~~ hate everyone, but still, we only hate people who suck.)

SEVENTH OOB: Parents suck too.

Courtney

Wall Story: This is the ultimate wall Urban Legend. Guy + girl hook up on the wall. Then he talks out his fingers, licks them, another guy + girl hook up on the wall, she has skirt on, he fingers her. Then he takes out his fingers, licks them. Cops come + bust the wall for drugs. That shit is nasty yo! I just threw up.

Hey guys, it's me, and God, I am ~~cool~~ Lame and FAT.   4/18/02

Court, your ~~story~~ fully encompasses just how stupid Trent and co. are. But let's not

dwell on them. You said (why am I only writing to Courtney? she's not that cool) you

feel weird around me + Tyler. Why? I'm sorry if I'm making you uncomfortable, but I don't

know what I'm doing wrong. I feel bad, so please tell me.

OOb#Whatever-Even tho I didn't participate in the day of silence, ~~it seemed~~ it seemed like

a really powerful thing to do. But we all know I couldn't keep quiet for a whole

day. Power to supporting gays, lesbians, transexuals, transgenders, etc. But I agree w/

Lindsey, a lot of people in Glass are really exclusive + stuck up. You'd think they'd
                                                                          TRUE
be the most accepting kids @ Stuy, but they just look down on everyone.

   And now I have a question, speaking of pseudo-diversity: do any of you

find it strange that we have an Asian club @ Stuy? I mean, the school

is 60% Asian - why is there a club?

   Speaking of Asians, Paul + I talked last night + decided to put

the arguing behind us + try to be friends. that's good.
                                       Yeah right.
          Love, Sophie   -LN

PS - We'll see how long that shit actually lasts!

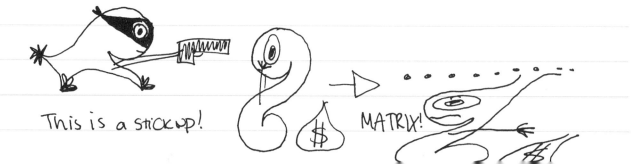

This is a stickup!   MATRIX!

What up Notebook lovahs,   4/19/02

    1st OOB: Sophie + Tyler.

       I can see what Courtney is saying about you two. Sometimes

this looks like Julia writing we become more similar everyday -CT

when you guys are together you do stuff that's exclusive to only you two,
yeah those are really lame! -CT
things like your spitting matches or fights. It seems like you guys get into your
own little world and people around you feel left out or really grossed out,
although during your spitting matches, it's mostly the later.

    OOB 2: What the f-bomb is up with Paul? When I first met
him, I thought he was really hot, but after getting to know him, I'm ~~really~~
realizing just how annoying he really is. He's kind of fucked up... way
too needy. Sophie, at first I thought you were really lucky to get Paul,
but then I realized that god actually hates you and this is probably
a punishment for something you did in your past life. You know, when
you were that three toothed circus freak who would rub the elephants
the right way.
       Those were good times...
           -SPC

Guys, I wrote a poem ~~about~~ at Julia's house while we were talking
about... who else... DAVE! (of course) Will Julia ever be able
           Nope.-SPC no way -ct uhh, no. -JB
to get over Dave... I think not. But I took the liberty of
writing a song about her deep felt love.

Dave: To the One I Love

by: The Beautiful People (a.k.a. Lindsey + Julia)
illustrations by Julia

We're the ill poets -JB

Dave is the Sun ☼

He makes the flowers grow in my heart

But then I remember him and I just fart   PFFF!

He was a boy and now he's not

Sure was the word he said when I was hot

We were together, now we're not   ♡ →

Man, he smokes mucho pot

And I like him a lot ✓

This is a hit

when you're so smitt-

-en like that kitt-

-en Dave Sucks

— bongos end —   I love bongos -CT

Hmmmm.... that was beautiful. Julia, we are true artists.   wow. There are no words to express the beauty -SR

Alright, that's all my huge IQ can squeeze out.
Honky Tonk Hell Yeah.
Bigs UPs to Big L

The Greatest Notebook Entry Ever Written: [↗] By The Biggest Asshole. Ever Born. -LN   4/22/02

1st oob: So Tyler and Sophie shit. It's not like you guys are a couple we have to put up with, but you do things that are only fun btw the two of you, and not for the rest of us. That makes us feel like shit. I mean it's supposed to be the four of us and Tyler, not you and Tyler. But then again, what's gonna change on that front. -JB Aww, kind of harsh. -JB It's just hard But true. -LN to get used to the fact that even though the four of us go to his house almost every day after school and smoke up, there's still inside jokes between you guys that we aren't in on. —ME TOO!!!! -SPC

2nd oob: Paul is pissing me off! God Sophie, I'm so glad hey... I'm not you! First he called me fat, by accident, which wasn't cool. I wouldn't call someone like that a "sensitive guy." And then he apologized for it, but I think that he didn't even know it was mean when he said it. You don't joke around with someone and make fun of each other and then whip out an insult that's true. And he's just a little too obsessed with Sophie, even though she is great. Thank god you assholes broke up b/c that boy sucks.

Peace and hair grease.
Courtney

Excuse me, I believe HE is a porky bitch. -JB

4/23/02

✭ ✭ ✭ ✭
✭ Hey guys- I'm in 8th period, scary math w/ Mr. Puerta from
✭ ✭ ✭
Bolivia! He's always telling us to be like Barbra Streisand-when.

everne explains a new way to do a proof or something, he'll say

"if you do it this way, you will be as sophisticated as the great

Barbra Streisand!" Damn he's being such a bitch -he's yelling

@ us because he didn't get to eat lunch. That ~~sucks~~ sucks, but

why is it because we don't understand the rule of Modus

Tollens? This guy is so insane. He has a new "game" now,

where he randomly freezes in mid-sentence t won't move

until you throw change @ him. He says he picked this up

@ a square in Rome. He always says that "The Nanny"

has problems, but math has solutions. Oh, and you must

attack a math problem the way Bruce Lee attacks his

enemies. And unlike "Escape from New York," there is

NO escape from math. So true. It's hard to concentrate

w/ Mr. Puerta shrieking 6 inches away from my face.

When he gets all riled up, he starts to froth @ the mouth, and

guess who sits in the front row t gets all that spray-spray? That's

right, ME.

Speaking of teachers, you know what always cracks me

up? Teachers always think they know what's going on, but they have NO idea. In 8th grade, Ms. Gompers prided herself on her ability to spot kids chewing gum. But I chewed gum every day, and she never knew. The one time she caught me, she was like "see? YOU REBEL! -LN I know EVERYTHING that goes on here!" Then, when teaching us about cleavage in rocks, she showed us her BOOB cleavage! It was as long as my arm, I swear.

← Courtney   ← Dave   ← Tyler
                ↳ drum   – I only wear
                  stick   2 shirts!

– Sophie

PS- me + Tyler. Guys, I'm sorry I make you feel like that, I don't mean to, but I don't know what to do. We've just become pretty close friends, but I get that we can get into our own little world, or some-thing. I'll try to work on that. Thanks, bitch. -LN

PPS-Paul (of course) is being a DOUCHE! I don't like him in any form, as a friend or more. He imitates Tyler all the time, esp. if it's something he does to me, like an inside joke. Ugh life is so dumb. I should be a philosopher. what?!? -LN

Yo Ladies! Last day of April!   4/30/02
   So basically this week was uneventful except for SING! The
seniors did rock and deserved to win, and the mosh outside
in the hallway was so fun! Wish you guys could have been there.
   So we didn't do much hanging out this week, except for the
Walkout this week. I didn't think that anyone was really going
to go, but I guess some people do care about protesting budget
cuts for public schools. Everyone who was walking out from our
school met at the senior bar and then we all cut the rest of
the day to march to City Hall. It was really boring at first, even
though everyone I knew was there. We were walking for a
really long time carrying signs and chanting. But I did feel like
we were making some sort of a difference. I mean, people were

let's hope so. -JB

hanging out the windows to see us. And coppers (what my parents
call cops) were mad protecting us. *oh shit it's the popos! -JB*
   Once we got there it was weird to see people like Brody and Karyn
who were there with people from their schools. And Tyler ditched us.
~~Booper~~ Suprise. I know he has other friends that he doesn't get to see
as much, but I feel like it's us or them. But whatever, he should
be happy with whoever. Like Sophie and I were saying, we feel
like our group always does what Tyler wants, not what we
want. People always treat him like he's fucking King of
one day i'm gonna be Queen of the ~~world~~ -JB the world. →

We always do what he wants, smoke up when he wants, hang with the people he likes. I also feel like our happiness or fun is compromised by what HE wants us to do. I mean I love him and all, but a lot of people follow him around and I don't want that to be us.

uh oh...

COURT

"ON THE RUN FROM JOHNNY LAW, ain't no trip to Cleveland."
- Bottle Rocket

Grandma. panties!

Hey! Those are my leopard print panties from victoria secret!! -LN

delicious!
-SPC

Sophie
~~Lindsey~~ eats 🐱

(not that it's a bad thing) -SPC

What up notebook homies    5/1/02

Wow that was a boring hello. I need some more pep in my step. How about this: yesterday I stapled my thumb! Yes, it is possible!! Props to the L to the I to the N-D-S-E-Y!! I love that I have a medium to share my incredibly brilliant moments. I know you guys appreciate my stories.

But on to OOB#1: SAY NO TO TYLER!

Courtney (and everyone else) - if you're so fucking upset about always doing what Tyler does - than JUST DON'T! You don't have to follow him around if you don't want to. Here's the thing, whenever our group is gonna go do something, just lay down the facts. We should be like "we're going here" and if he come or not WHATEVER! You'll see him tomorrow. Everyone seems so attached to Tyler, but come on, we're cool enough to not have to wait around for HIS decisions... I hope.

OOB #1.5: In case no one has said this already: Paul fucking sucks!

And now for OOB#2: Sex Books

On Friday Courtney, Sophie and I had a bonding experience in Barnes + Noble. We picked up sex books and magazines - it was fun. After reading the joys of Kama Sutra it was on to sex for dummies ↑ by the really old lady who looks like the kid from Jerry McGuire. Sophie's favorite part was the Ben-Wa vaginal balls. Courtney's favorite chapter was the one on sex for seniors. (She loves

↳ you mean Dr. Ruth! ⊚

Lindsey's tambourine — JB

sad clown! —CT

← *Lindsey's stuffed animals*

penis pumps and old people smell.) no I don't! —CT *do you do? —SPC*

OOB#4: This weekend was fun. I ROCKED OUT with my tambourine. I set up all my stuffed animals up and had a concert for them. The crowd was very pleased, though they got a little hostile towards the end. After the concert, I just tried to relax. You know, music is my life and all, but it's hard work and can be a little draining. To chill out, I jammed with my cat. *stupid and then you —JB*

Hey! It's my cat!

your finger

ROAR   ME + MY CAT

← AWW what cuties Lindsey + Bo! —CT

OOB#2: I mean OOB#3? : Score another one for Lindsey:

I RULE. I told all of you guys I gave Julia the notebook, and you believed me; on the day she was absent. *maybe b/c we don't notice when Julia's gone —SPC   snickers —JB*

But don't be too upset, I need extra time to craft my letters. I guess this letter isn't gonna be that long, but oh well. The only reason Courtney's letters are so long is that she writes so goddamn big and her greetings take up like 10 goddamn lines. Julia just makes all her letters up, but whatever, I don't read them anyway. And Sophie, well her letters are long cause — don't get me started, don't even get me started. By the way, if you're gonna write a letter in the goddamn fuckin fuck beans notebook, DON'T WASTE A PAGE writing your ever so intriguing invisible thoughts. I need those pages to write my very interesting (shut up Courtney) letters, that yes-use more than a page... sometimes.

WORD.

Big Ups to Big L

↑ tambourine

chair

meow! knockin' on heaven's door...

By Sophie

why is the cat playing? - CT

ME at halloween!

is this a triangle because Paul is also in love with Tyler? -CT

"the Paul, Sophie, Tyler love △"

By the artist formerly known as Sophie who now goes by POOPIE, BREATHE -LN

5/5/02

Oh man I haven't seen this lined lover in so long!

So many things to talk about! Where to begin? Here goes.....

OOB #1: The Paul, Tyler, Sophie love triangle. Paul is so whiny and *see above -rpc* annoying! I mean, yea he is hot, but he's a little drama queen-y for me. And apparently for you too. As for Tyler, well, it just makes things more complicated that he's in the situation. It's tough to decide who Paul wants to bang more, you or him. *So true -LN* We just have to focus on not being the Tyler fan club, of which Paul is the President. I mean granted Tyler's a cool guy and he's funny, but we, me included, have to work on |not| doing whatever he says. *def -CT* Grr! Boys get whatever they want!

OOB #2: So I told you all I'd tell you about Joe.....we're "together" I guess, it was never really defined. He's a really cool guy. I'm feelin' the guitar playing. and of course the jewfro, and yes, hooking up with a pot head means getting to smoke up for free. Excellent. The "fling" (I guess that's what I'll call it) started when we were hanging out one day and we went to the park and were lying down in the grass, having a really interesting conversation, and we just ended up hooking up! It was really nice. & I mean, it's not very serious, we're not staying together for the summer or anything like that, but I'm having fun. And it's nice to think about someone besides Dave. God knows I have to get over that boy. But that's my love life in a nutshell. *b/c of course it fit into one. ya know cuz ... small. forget it -CT*

OOB#3: You guys I really miss Tom. We used to be best friends in middle school and now we never talk. I don't even know him anymore. I want to call him and talk to him again. We used to be such good friends and it's all my fault that we're not. I mean, granted, when I cheated on Dave, it was a little obnoxious that Tom took so much offense to it, and sided with Dave instead of me, but I'm over it. I'm just pissed that we never got to re-bond, and we've kinda lost that best friend vibe.

totally -CT

I think he was jealous of you and Dave that's why he was mad -CT

It's weird, I still know so much about him, even his cats! (One is named Paula and the other is Chubbs, Paula looks like Fidel Castro and Tom once told me she had genital herpes but I don't believe him. Chubbs is fat. Like sit-on-top-of-a-newspaper-and-the-entire-thing-dissapears fat). I know his sister, her best friend, his parents, I mean, I went to his country house with him for christ's sake! Allright, time to stop. But I mean really, ya know the saying friends come and go? Well that's not supposed to be true. You can't just give up on a friend right? I mean, I was so stupid to let our relationship go and now I'm really jealous b/c he thinks Zoe is really hot and wants to spend time with her, but he doesn't have any reason to spend time with me. I just looked at a picture of him coughing and I got really sad. The memories all came back, and I realized I've just been trying to forget him this whole time. And now it's too late to go back. Grr I'm so angry with myself!

aahhh -CT

haha. b/c he was coughing??-ct

Ⓞ Julia... boolia... schmoolia Ⓞ

✡︎✡︎ Hey guys-same day just later-i'm not nearly as blue as I was when I wrote this, I just missed the T-man. I called him and we had a cool convo. It's not like we're best friends again or anything, but it's nice to know that the friendship isn't totally dead. And he said I was welcome at the Globe anytime. So yay.   what is he, the king of the Globe?-CT

-LN

5/9/02

Hey buddies-

Before I get down to the oobs, I gotta say something about those vaginal exercises we said we [we? -JB] were gonna do (all the better to orgasm with, my dear? Ew what if your grandma actually said that to you?! OK, moving on...). I was about to do one the other day in bio because class was so boring, + it seemed like a good way to spice things up. Then someone started jiggling their leg up + down while resting their foot on my desk, thus causing my whole chair/desk to shake. I didn't realize it was b/c of the kid behind me, + I thought I was having serious vaginal problems. Anyways...

OOB #1 - A crazy thing happened today. You know that girl Rosa in our grade who always wears the I♡NY shirt? Well she's in my English class, + we've become pretty good friends. 9th period I saw her as I was going downstairs to my locker + she was really drunk, but I didn't know -we all know how I can be pretty oblivious to people. So I, w/ my "pea-brain" as Coco likes to put it, suggested we race down the escalator, each sliding on a banister (i'd be on one side + she'd be on the other). All's going super, I'm wizzing along down the banister, when I hear this {CRASH}. I look over and Rosa is all sprawled out on the escalator, bleeding all over the place, + laughing like an idiot w/ these huge scratches down her face from the escalator steps. All I could think was OH SHIT I KILLED HER! But I took her to the nurse + she was fine. But I'm so dumb!

NO, wait.

She's dumb.

OOB #2: So the school year's almost done. So much has happened, but you know what the best thing was? ~~Me getting a 99~~ on my history test!

I mean...us all becoming best friends! loser -CT

OK, I only have a few lines left, so lemme break it down for y'all gangsters. Though we've been through some hard times together (not at all, actually, but shhh. don't ruin the moment). I'm so glad we're

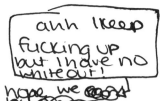
anh I keep fucking up but I have no whiteout!

hope we could

friends. I love you all so much, and I ~~could we could~~

stay friends for a long time. Please let me marry

a rich man so I can afford whiteout. And a

new face. yes, please. -CT

　　　　　-Sophie

PS- Does anyone else have ZERO motivation? I

YES!! -CT ·hardly do any work anymore except for studying

for tests. I wish I could be better, but I can never

bring myself to do homework. Even though in my

head I'm like "Sophie, go do your history

homework NOW. It's important." I can't, even though

I gotta. I just end up playing guitar or talking

on the phone. It sucks, b/c I have like six hist.

homeworks to make up. *It's called amotivational syndrome. That's Right Sophie, you have a disease. -JB*

PPS- Julia, I'm glad you called Tom. He's one of

my close friends + ~~too~~ its good you're staying in

touch. But check this out: we were really drunk

the other night, and he told me his "brilliant"

That is so lame! -CT theory that the universe was created by drunk

people, so that's why you feel it spinning when

you're wasted. He also wants a tattoo of Buddah

hmm...my glue stick kinda smells like almonds.
Yum?

Playing an electric guitar surrounded by flames.
That is so lame i can't write anymore.
PHOTO TIME! WE ALL ♡ to stuff our
faces, especially LINDSEY NEWMAN!
Yum!

court eats sand-
witches slower
than anyone
on this planet.

mmm eat that cookie, Lindsey!
It was mad good. -LN

HEY GUYS!   5/9/02

School is a bore. I realized that if we went to one of those cheesy suburban schools, Tyler would be like the "most popular guy in school." SO LAME.

<u>1st oob</u>: Speaking of h.s. in general, today my teacher told us that we are all supposed to be "really ~~smart~~ smart" kids. Just because ~~we~~ we're the top 750 out of 20,000 means that we should understand matricies? Ok, maybe we should, but still the teachers always rag on us and expect so much of us b/c we took a test and did well on it. But then again, there is something about Stuy that makes it different than other places. You guys have to understand that when I went to private school back in the day, everyone was so stupid. They all went to school there b/c their parents were really rich and they could afford it, but I was the only remotely intelligent person there and I was on financial aid! That's fucked up! And then I came to Delta, and for the first time in my life I was sitting in a room with kids who thought the same way I did. I didn't have to wait 15 min anymore for the class to finish the math problem I did in my head. And the weird thing was, at Delta, it was ok to be smart. People didn't think it was weird that you →

wanted to get As and not Cs and it was known that everyone was "gifted and talented," not fucking braindead.

I think we are all lucky that we came to Stuy like Sophie -LN because it's just a continuation of the kind of place Delta was. One time I was talking to my friend and she was saying how she used to hate it when she was a freshman because she thought all the kids thought they were so smart and amazing when they weren't. But then she spent a lot of time with kids from other public schools and she realized it was fun to get wasted with them, but ultimately, deep talks were never quite as deep as the ones she had with her friends from Stuy. I guess it sounds pretty elitist, but there is a respect I have for everyone at Stuy that I don't always have for people at other schools. People at Stuy are on some other plane of thought. Wow, now that I've become a total asshole, I'm out.

                    Courtney

Horray for self realizations! -SPC

WOW! Yay for me!!   Fatty: JB   5/14/02

O.K. I'm down at the bakesale (COOKIES GALORE!!) for the basketball team, right now, 3rd period. Since I was the only one with this period free, I get to sit here all period. Lucky me. No one's coming by here, which is kinda sad. Half our stuff is gone, and MAN I really want a cookie. **EAT IT.** -SPC A guy just came by, he was annoying. He was all like "soooo... if I help sell this period, can I get stuff for free?" "NO! Now get the hell out." MAN. I get no respect.

5/15/02   The Next day.   hmmm... now for my oobs. Whenever I see Boob, I ~~think it says boob~~ froth at the mouth. That wasn't my first Boob, or was it? no it wasn't, but whatever! -CT

<u>2nd OOB: MOTIVATION:</u> I find it hard to get motivated too. I go home, determined to do all my work, but then I don't start anything 'till like 6:30 and then I only do an hour of work, cause, duh! the simpsons are on... gotta love that Millhouse. I get scared sometimes that I'll never grow out of this "phase" of non-motivation.

unfortunately that's probably what will happen -CT I mean, what if I get to college and it's still the same thing — you know, no motivation, not doing shit when it matters, then I'll be SCREWED. I don't want to be a screw up, I just hope that I'll grow out of it soon.

<u>3rd OOB:</u> I feel as though I should comment on what Courtney said about Stuy. OK, here's the deal. Sometimes I'm glad that

I go to a school that has such high standards and everyone is on the same mental plane. I mean, even though there are some kids who are just screw ups in our schools (need I name names?), even the slackers are smart, they just choose not to try or do work. Sometimes I feel like it's good to be in such an intellectually stimulating environment, the atmosphere in school has some drawbacks. Sometimes it's hard to establish yourself and not get swept away by the crowd. With all the competition and caring if you get a 99 instead of 100, sometimes I feel so turned off by it all and and think it affects me in a bad way, instead of motivating me to do well. I also hate all the school politics and having to get caught up in stuff, that really in the end, doesn't matter. I mean, it sucks to have to pretend to care about all these people who are really just douche bags.

~Lindsey~

P.S. My back hurts again... I really think I might have menopause. I got it last year and I really don't want to get it again.

This one time at the airport, speaking of menopause, this older woman turned to me and was like, "is it warm in here or am I getting hot flashes? Gosh I can never tell these days." It was weird. —JB

did you get it from Sophie's mom? I did. —CT

1. You can't get it twice
2. You can't get it at our age
3. You are an idiot
—JPC

5/16/02

Wutup girls???

How's it all hangin' on the upper west side? Right to the oobs... _toward the river_ -CT

Chillin in the (Sun)~ with OOB#1: OH MY GOD THE MOST EMBARASSING THING →you realized how ugly you are?-LN
JUST HAPPENED!!! OK so right now I'm in Art Appreciation class (which is really like Haiti appreciation class cuz everyday my teacher talks about how she's from an "island in the sun" and blah blah blah) and so me and Tali and Sophie are fooling around as usual and for some reason, Tali raises her hand and says "Andy Warhol" (don't ask me why, I never listen in this class anyway). So the teacher goes "who?" and I say "Andy Warhol, ya know, Campbell's Soup, Marilyn Monroe..." and Sophie's like "DAMN THAT'S SOME GOOD SOUP!!" and I know that this girl is never ever funny EVER in her life but this time she was just hilarious. So I burst out laughing (and here's the embarassing part) all the snot that had been camping out in my nose just flies out and it's like a booger ERUPTION right in the middle of class. Tali is hysterically laughing, Sophie is just hanging her head in shame and passing me a tissue, and our teacher is talking about Haiti. WHY GOD WHY do these things happen to me??? And Joe _cause you're going to hell. -LN_ is in my class. Fuck me. _Omg that was hillarious!-SPC_

OOB#2: OK, so I'm over the gravity-defying booger issue. Now about Joe. I'm getting a little freaked. He's like "I wanna spend more ~~fun~~ time talking to him than doing stuff with him. And Court, u know how you're always like, "I need a guy who's bigger than me?" Well, yea it's true. I need a guy who's taller! Joe has muscles and all, although you wouldn't expect it, but he's not the big, I-can-wrap-my- _YES!_

arms-around-you type of guy. Not that this really makes or breaks our relationship, but I have to ponder over what I really think about him.

OOB#REMORSEFUL FEELINGS: OMG, I'd like to apologize to Coco for not being at her chorus concert last night. I'm really sorry, and as a friend I should have been there and I feel really bad because I wasn't there to cheer you on. If it helps, I got caught being **high**. I went to Brooklyn to chill with Joe and I thought for some reason that it would be really inconspicuous to come home at 10:00 on a Thursday night with really red eyes cuz I was "tired." haha Needless to say, it was really pointless for me to deny my state and the parentals got it all out of me. They know I smoke weed, it doesn't mean I'm irresponsible or a failure at life. Grrr, I just hate not living up to people's expectations. Anyway, point being, if I was at your concert Court, I wouldn't be in the deep shit I'm in now. So don't be mad PWEEEZ??? haha, you got yours! -CT

L♡ve,

Julz

eating ice cream b/c I'm depressed (and maybe still high?)

Me in my room sad and grounded

The phone w/ spider webs on it b/c no one calls me. true, but that's nothing new. -CT

ICE cream

5/17/02

What up man? As Julia says, straight to the Boobs!

Ist oob: Work!!!! It sucks, but if you don't do it, you're screwed anyway. And staying home for a day from school is so so much more work than just dragging your ass to school and sleeping in every class. I think I've only actually fallen into real sleep like twice at school, all the other times were just half asleep. I've just been doing so much work lately, I mean I haven't even hung out after school in a week, and I don't really care. Also, when I do get to hang out, it'll be really special cuz it hasn't happened in a while, like how water tastes so much better when you are thirsty.

2nd oob: Wow Jules, I'm suprised Joe is so deep. He wants to talk with you more (or he wants your sweet lovin... or he just wants to talk). But as you said, I totally get why you aren't attracted to him. I mean there are all these mad scrawny guys that look like 14 yr olds and ~They are 14 year olds... But I get what you mean. -SPC~ make me feel huge. So I like the older guys who make you feel mature ~yeah! cuddling/spoons!-SPC~ and protected, like a girl! He seems nice, but he should have tried to talk to us, your friends! ~WORD: in~ You know the saying, if you wanna be with me, you've gotta be with my friends? I guess it's just the balance of friendship and hooking up that makes a relationship work. See, with your best guy friends everything is perfect except the chemistry, and with guys you just hook up with, everything is perfect except the →

friendship part. But all you need is that balance and then it's perfect! I realized I use exclamation marks all the time, check it out!!!!!!!

3rd oob: I was thinking about the way girls process their feelings about relationships, so just hear me out. There are maybe three different feelings you have in a relationship. In the begining it's all air because your feelings float above your head and you don't look at anything analytically or sanely, you are just floating with your new found love and make mistakes and shit. Then you're in your head and you finally step back and look at your relationship and your feelings and analyze them and think about what the hell you are doing. This is the part where you break up with the losers and decide if you want to stay with the good ones. I guess after that it's all in the heart. I don't think many people get to that place, but I think it's the best place to be. When you're in the heart you finally know what you want, you know your feelings are real and you know the guy is right. I don't know if I'll ever get there, but I hope I can because I think that's love. Wow that was the biggest cheese factory ever. Sorry.

ACME CHEESE ← a cheese factory

Courtney

5/28/02

whatup ladies-

Guys, I've been thinking: do you remember a while ago, we were @ McDonald's, + me + Tyler were joking around + pouring water on eachother, + it was like the first time he + I acted all crazy together? Anyway, then Coco was like "woah, soph's the newest one!" Now I think I get what she was saying, + she's right. It's like I was the newest best girl friend, there was one before me, and they'll be many more after me. We became close really fast, going over to his house like every day afterschool, talking on the phone, blazing together afterschool. But now I feel like we're growing apart. I hate that I care about him more than he cares about me, because I feel so stupid.

K Boobs... or eyes?

Body Issues: I've never felt bad about my body. I mean, I never thought I was the hottest person in the world, I just thought I was pretty regular looking: not amazingly good looking, but not a circus freak either. But recently, I've

just been feeling so...ugly, to put it bluntly.
Like today I had my hand on my ~~waist~~ dumbass-CT
(read: lovehandles) + I felt fat. Like physically,
(as in my hand held fat) + also ~~also~~ (also) 2 emotionally,
(as in I thought I was fat). I don't know
why, because this has never happened to me
before, but suddenly I find myself so totally fixated
on my body + how much I'm eating + planning
out bullshit exercise routines that I don't end up
doing. I feel guilty when I eat, + everytime I see my
stomach, I'm like "oh, I'm gonna do 25 sets of crunches
every night." What keeps me from overdoing it is
I totally know what you mean!-LN
my complete lack of self control or motivation. At
the same time I'm feeling this way, though, I feel like
an IDIOT. Cause for like 5 years, I've been running
from people saying I'm too skinny, but now ~~this~~ I've
become their exact image of some girl obsessed
w/ her weight. I know I should be stronger + be able to
resist the bullshit that is the popculture media
crap, but I feel like I can't escape it, + it's so much easier
to succumb + be what they (the man, esp. the whiteman

who is holding me down) want you to be, even if it makes you miserable, than to resist all the time. Everywhere I look is Britney Spears + 10 billion other celebs' half-naked bodies, magazines being like "20 new tips to get that superstar body!" (why can't I be a superstar in my own body?), or fashion mags saying if you don't have super-flat abs + tiny thighs you can't wear a bikini - but of COURSE guys aren't held to this standard.

On a lighter note, Julia said my boobs looked bigger today. Horray!
—Sophie

I did? Oh yea, sure, I remember....

PS-Don't forget to make the ~~notebook~~ multimedia!

PPS-I schooled another history test today! Gotta gives props to my moms, cause she helped me study mad much, even when she had a lot of work to do, and she <u>is</u> a busy girl. Plus, she knows so much about history - you can see where I got my smarts from.

What a kiss-up!-CT
As Mr. Greenberg says, "FRONTING=AUTOMATIC ZERO!"

Yo guys! Time for a Courtney-speech: 5/30/02

So I was thinking about the times we've been drinking lately. Let me set the record straight about something. Alcohol may be great and all, but I feel like it's a lot worse for you than weed. With weed the only health effects are on your lungs (like ciggs) and you CANNOT get physically addicted. Yes, it may be a gateway drug and it's illegal, but you can keep it under control. On the other hand alcohol damages your liver and your heart and is also illegal (under 21) and is HIGHLY (no pun intended) addictive. Also, is there a Potheads Anonymous! No! Only AA!! How many people die a year in drunk driving accidents (1000s), and how many die doing something stupid when they were high? (not nearly as many I believe) And alcohol is not only putting you in danger (passing out and getting raped) but putting others in your destructive path. I mean I enjoy drinking and smoking weed, but you can't underestimate the power of alcohol. It also has a lot of carbs in it! Just remember these things the next time you drink. So back to things that aren't depressing! Wait, actually I have to go back.

Sophie, GOD DAMN you are NOT fat! If anyone knows, it's me! I'm gonna be honest, when you say that you are fat, it makes me want to scream. If you are fat, then what the fuck do you think of me? I mean all these little girls, ~~with~~ who think they have it so hard with a little stomach ~~~~ flab have no fucking clue. And they probably never will. I'd rather be ~~starving~~ and too thin than be too fat. I just want to grab them and scream, "Live my life for _one_ day!" You have no idea what it's like to wake up everyday and hate yourself and feel like you are in someone else's body. You think ~~~~ "flab" makes you sad? I'm sorry but that's pathetic to me. Now, I'm sorry I blew up at you because it's not you personally Sophie (I love you more than words can say) but I'm _not_ sorry I said any of this and you have to understand how this is. There are some things in your life that you take really personally and can cut you very deep and this is one of those things. You know me, I'm never going to think things and not tell you how I feel. I will always say it out loud. If it hurts then we'll work through it. I hate lies and talking behind backs.

~ Courtney

Wasssssssup?   5/31/02

OH... MY... GAWD

SAT II tomorrow! I'm so nervous, actually, not really. I've
spent a pretty long time preparing, so I BETTER do well. Does
anyone else think it's ridiculous to have to take these tests
that determine the rest of our GODDAMN lives at **16**?!?!?
Everyone tells you "don't freak out about SATs too much, blah,
blah, blah. It's not the end of the world." But that's <u>total</u>
bullshit. Especially in ~~our~~ our school, where you're only defined by your
                        true-CT
scores or your average. Sometimes I'm glad that Stuyvesant is so
rigorous, or puts emphasis on acheivement, because it does motivate
me sometimes, and it's good to have high standards, but other times
it just makes you feel shitty about yourself if you <u>don't</u> have a
98 average, or get a 1600 on the SATs, and that's pretty ~~WHACK~~.
                                                     See! I can be clever too!

<u>OOBie #2bie</u>: Another speech about Weed.

didn't
someone
do that
already?
-CT

I don't want to sound motherish or annoying, but I have to respond
to CoCo's speech. I agree with some of the stuff you were saying,
but we also need to keep in mind that weed is bad for you also. Between
alcohol and Mary J., alcohol is probably worse for you, but they both
fuck up your body in worse ways than we probably know. And
don't underestimate the power of weed — it can cause bad stuff too,
like brain damage (permanent memory loss), and it's bad for your lungs

shut up! you smoke like a chimney anyway!) (now anyway!) -cT

(It destroys the membrane in your lungs). But then again, I look forward to lighting up soon. You guys could help me pop my weed cherry. YES! -cT

OOB#3: Another response to the Notebook gals: Sophie, everyone has body issues. I never really feel happy about my body either, and I too make false promises to myself about doing crunches. and stuff. Sometimes I feel bad and depressed about it, but other times I feel like it's ridiculous for me to care so much and play into society's pre-conceived images of what's "beautiful," or what size girls should be. But I also know that no matter what I look like I'll probably find something that I don't like about myself, and that's kind of scary. PLUS carbs are in EVERYTHING and I just love bread and cake way too much. ohhh me too. -JB

So FUCK those Atkins bitches.

4th oob: I don't really have one, I just wanted to write that down.

5th OOB: BYE!!

Big L

don't forget these friends:

cookie bowl of spaghetti

-SPC

my bra bunny
By the artist still known as Sophie a.k.a POOPIE BREATH LN

ridiculous amount of padding

10/3/02

Well hello ladies!

La premiere (B)Oob du jour: I got <u>another</u> padded bra at Victoria's secret. It's turquoise and shiny. I need to face the facts. Being an A is cool, I don't need padding! My boobs were lost in a sea of cotton-y shininess. Ohhh but it's so pretty. you're an addict! You need to go to padded-bra rehab - SPC

Oobalah # 2 balah: the oob that speaks Yiddish. So I'm having 2nd thoughts about Joe. Not that there's really much to rethink, I mean how can you tone down a relationship that was never really defined to begin with? "Umm, hey, I think we should stop liking each other?" No. Oh the twisted web we teenagers weave with our ambiguous chain of hookups. What? Story of my life? Oh well I guess. Joe's just so, well, stonerish. I mean, we all knew that from the start (when a before-meal blunt became a ritual, what else can you expect?) but it just seems like I can't get through to him unless we're talking about weed, sex, or people in Stuy. Welcome to Joe's mind. I feel like we have good conversation potential, I mean I know he's an intelligent guy, it just seems hidden beneath some kind of haze. Purple haze! Don't you hate it when you <u>know</u> you can have a really good conversation with someone, you just can't get it to start?

Also, Tali's mightily doubtful of him. Not that I'm gonna strictly follow her advice but she's a bit more objective than I am and I wonder if she's seeing things from the outside that I'm not. Sometimes the most obvious defects are sooo easy to miss when you think someone is really hot. Or maybe Tali just has like super good perception to make up for her extreme lack of intelligence. Just kidding! are you though?

TTFN, I'm out son!

stop using AOL language! what does this mean -LN

Julia

TT?. is this math? -SC

* Oh, funny thing happened: Me and ma familia went out to sushi tonite and my brother proved his intense ~~culinary~~ ignorance. You know how people use <u>soy</u> <u>sauce</u> on their sushi to make it saltier? Well my brother gets his and goes, "yo, son, lemme get some salt?" Oy.

Julia you're the horse b/c you weren't there -CT

OK, pop quiz, which one doesn't belong? JULIA BASKIN -LN

and 'cause you have a really <u>BIG</u> DICK! -LN

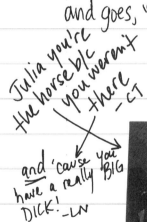

Fun game: match the shoe to the Notebook Girl. (Answers on top of this page) -SPC

what is this crap?

- PUT UP your dukes!

This fish has large teeth AND can read in the dark. Double whammy!

6/8/02

whatup bitches—

Here I am at Tyler's country house, but he blew a fuse or something, + now none of the lights work. Tomato ass bitch.

When I got to Tyler's house (NYC) to drive up to his country house, all the guys were over playing videogames (I'm not even going to go into the lameness), so I was allready to feel a little left out, but then I saw JULIA there! And that made me SO happy. She'd been feeling kinda left out, + was just as excited to see me. Then, when everyone was leaving, we went to kiss on the cheek, but we missed + kissed on the lips, which was AWESOME. But then I looked over and Tyler's dad was chuckling @ us in that "oh ho ho I'm a middle-aged man" kind of way. never fail to embarass yourselves—CT

Sooo, my friday wasn't too exciting. Went to lunch w/ my kickass 7th pd lunch crew. we ate @ China Red, gotta love that cheap gooey goodness that is the chicken + broccoli. I love it, but I always come back to school feeling a number of things, namely greasey,

YES —LN

nauseous, and gassy. That garlic sauce just gets my stomach all jumpy. But I'm an addict, and I keep crawling back week after week. DAMN YOU CHINA RED!!

In other news... WORD—so many people have sex in the bathroom at China Red! —CT ewww.

   I blazed afterschool w/ couth Tyler, and two of our lovely friends from school, Jessica and Manny. It was cool, but then I horribly embarassed myself in front of some senior guys. I don't remember what I did, all I know is I was really high + then they were laughing at me. as usual —CT

   Julia, don't feel bad about your ta-tas. I'm the queen of flatulence, and I don't mean farting. As you saw today by our "accidental" kiss, you are really not + I want you. OK, no I don't, but I do love you.

   I'm exhausted. Tyler + I are gonna go watch a movie. G'night jokers, smokers, midnight tokers.

                              —Sophie

(next day)
Hey guys! Aren't you just so thrilled to be

alive?!!?! (I'm trying out some positive thinking).

Anyway... about that entry I wrote awhile ago all sad + body issues + poop. I'm OK now. I dunno, I guess it was just a bad time in the life of Sophie. It was just such a stressful time w/ standardized tests — I agree w/ Linds, fuck those people who say these tests don't matter. That's like blasphemy @ Stuy-school, parents, boys, LIFE. I felt like everything was so out of control in my life, so I started obsessing over the one thing I could control, which is food/my body. Court, I'm sorry I made you feel bad, but you gotta know I didn't mean to. Plus I can't hide anything from you guys, gotta write what I feel. I know, it's all good :-CT

OOb# YOU SUCK: A while ago, Julia was writing about liking when a guy is bigger than you. Not to sound superficial, but big strong boy is the BOMB. cuz c'mon... cuddling is so nice, even if it's w/ just a friend or some random homeless guy on 47th street. Even though we're empowered women who make our own rules, it can be nice to feel protected by a boy too. Ok, enough of that.

I ♡ ALL YUYS! -CT

600b # I hate my life: Yes Julia, I hate it when I know I could have a good conversation w/ someone but I can't get it started. I wanna get to know that guy Stuart Woordsworth, b/c I've read some of his stuff in the school paper + he's hillarious. Plus w/ a name like Stuart Woordsworth, he's gotta have a good sense of humor. But we only end up talking on afternoons when I've just blazed + I'm chilling on the wall, so I'm on another planet + have no clue what he's talking about.

you are an ass-et

Oh the trials + tribulations!

    -Sophie

F—

write neater, I can't read your fucking handwriting! See me after class.
—Ms. Pollitt, your ~~favorite teacher~~ ugliest, fattest, hairiest, ~~dumbest~~ 6/10/02

Hey Guys!

1st oob: Julia, I know ~~him~~ Joe is this great hook up and all, oh wait by the way, Dave said he saw you hooking up with Joe on Friday all crazy! Ha, he noticed! I can't believe he finally started paying attention to your boyfriend, but don't start liking Dave again. Come on, we've all liked people because they liked us first or something on that line, but that won't keep you happy for long because Dave and you have such a history.

2nd oob: Tyler was at the kissing booth at GAYDAY at our school on Friday. He's not gay at all, I think

Kissing Booth
⊕ Tyler
5¢ french

people vomiting after they've kissed Tyler

we can all vouch for that seeing as he's conquered many a vagina, but he still was going to kiss boys to make $ for the Gay/Straight Alliance. That's really cool of him, esp. to put aside his sexuality to do something good. *I don't think he actually ended up doing the booth. —LN*

3rd oob: Cuddling is the best thing ever! Tyler is the best cuddler ever. *why don't you just marry him? LN* On the bus to a field trip we were really snuggly. (It was a nice change from the physical abuse. Sometimes that boy plays a little too rough.) I had my hair down and he was lying on my shoulder and he was playing with it and I said, "ugh, my hair looks like crap," and he said, "no it looks really pretty." That was just a small compliment, but it was really sincere and genuine, which meant a lot coming from him. I guess it was nice to finally think that Tyler could see me outside of a sisterish friend and notice that I am damn sexy to boot.

LOCO for the COCO

"choo-choo"

P.S. Stuart is so strange. Really **Soph**, he isn't as cool as you think. It's just the lore of his popularity. And it's wrong to hang out with someone just b/c you know that if he was your friend, everyone would be like "oh, there's Stuart's friend Buttface."

TRIPPY! -JB

OH...MY...LN

NOAH A
OPL

What up my Homies?   6/15/02

OOB #1: The good old days: Yo, I was just thinking, isn't it weird
how long we've known each other, and how we kind of all became
friends separately and then decided to do the notebook together?
It's mad weird, what a kawinky-dink. 'Cause if we didn't all meet
each other, the world would be a different place, and we wouldn't
have the notebook. Soooo here we go from the beginning...

    I met Sophie in sixth grade at DELTA (the place where it
all started). It was sixth grade, the beginning of school and we
broke up into map making groups. I was in the group with
Sara, Bobby and Sophie. Everyone seemed normal except that
fucking ugly ass girl named, what was it again? Suphie? Smoop?
Oh well, I forgot. Anyway, I could tell that she had NO
talent and was fucking up our map so I decided to kill her.
It's been a beautiful friendship ever since.   AWW Linds, love you
                                                   too spc
≡ FaSt FoRwaRD≡ I remember the first day of seventh grade,
all the girls, it seemed, were crowded around one table. I, the
last one coming in had to sit at the table in the corner, by myself.
                                                   ha you suck
                                                   -JB
Later that day, we were working in Physics, and I had a huge
fat ass pencil case for the first day of school, with everything
in it. I could possibly need. Of course it fell and broke, with everything
splattering everywhere!! No one helped me pick it up either!! I had to

walk all around the room picking up all my shit all by myself. So I guess I didn't really meet Julia then because she was one of the fat ass bitches who was sitting at that one table and wouldn't lift a bloated finger to pick up even one goddamn pencil. Thanks fat ass Julia, I hate you.

I met Courtney at Brooklyn Tech, when we went to school there after 9/11, when our school was closed. That school was the most bootleg shit ever. But, having a 1:30 to 5:30 schedule was pretty awesome. Me and CoCo had the same lunch period and chilled in the auditorium together with a bunch of other kids, and so the madness ensued.

Delta was maad chill, but it's time to move on to bigger and better things, like ruling Stuyvesant High School. It's crazy how many kids from Delta go to Stuy, it's like we never left our Upper West Side haven, on the other hand, Stuy is completely different. Now that I've completely and totally contradicted myself, I think it's time for me to go.

The whole reminiscence thing was good while it lasted, but I guess it just made me realize why I hate you bitches so goddamn much.

P.S. I love you.

~ Linds

Hey! I'm back! Just to state for the record: NO ONE (Sophie) should be listening to Paul about relationship advice. What do needy little boys know about these things? The sooner we all (and the world) forget about paul, the better. Since his whiny, neediness overwhelms his hotness, he holds no value anymore. I realized that Paul was put here by God to fool with us girls. The situation with Paul is like when you go to a deli to buy some chips and when you open the bag, there are only like 2 chips in there, the rest of the bag was filled with air, and on top of that, they taste like shit anyway. So you end up paying 50 cents for a bag that wasn't worth 3. Paul is not worth 50 cents or even a bag of nasty potato chips.

O.k., I'm done this time.

I'M OUT. peace,

Lindsey

omg my hair is straight -CT

sugar and oil I am so fat

Blah, Blah, Blah, Please piss on me, Blah, Blah. Sigh. Blah.

6/19/02

Yooo watup? Sorry it took so damn long for the notebook to circulate. I've been hoarding it for a while, not getting around to writing in it.

Oob#1: Ugh you guys. So I know he's my ex and it's completely taboo not to mention downright stupid to fall in love with your ex again but I saw Dave playing drums on Friday at his band practice with Tyler, Tom, and Wes, and I know he's all dirty and drugged-out now, but god do I still like him! Y'all know he plays drums and since at the studio I was sitting like RIGHT IN FRONT of the drums, I had the mad nice view. And oh, when he shakes his head and that oh-so-greasy jew-fro of his swings around, it just gets me so hot. Or ready to take a bath. OK, so the boy could use a haircut. _{to say the least - CT} But we were making the mad eye contact and he smiled at me and, well, Sophie, think back to the days when you liked Dave, is there anything quite like that smile? I think not. _{Not at all! -SPC} Lights up my day, man. Actually, if you think about any guy you've ever had a crush on, or who's just hot (Yes, I swear Dave's hot, he's just not your guys' type!) you know their smile just makes you feel all special…in your pants, and u know what I'm talking about. But lemme tell you, I am not feeling those vibes with Joe. No sir-ee. And by coincedence, me and Dave left the room at the same time and Tyler was all, (btw, this is second hand from Tyler, I didn't witness) "Yo, Dave, you make out with Julia?" and he's all, "Nah, dude, she has a bf" cuz he saw me hookin ↑ with Joe at GayDay! Fuck Joe! I'm done! Fuck the world! Joe can go to the crapper! I love Dave! Joe isn't half the guy Dave is, literally by height and, ahem, length of something else. Just joshin ya! I threw that one in for Coco, who still can't stand to hear about anything sexual-Dave related. But that's my dilemma. I think Dave may be interested. Maybe. I think I'm so into him that I'm interpreting meaningless things as signs just to convince myself. But hey! Whatever works! Just hooking ↑ is cool with me I guess. We shall see, mes amies.

yeah thanks that was so nasty -CT

↳D do whatever you gotta do, but just remember to wear deodorant. -SK   sophie would know -CT

Still freakishly in love with her ex, as always -CT
  ♪ Bizzle in the hizzle

Dave @ band practice:

← crazy greasy jew fro

ha, ha, his facial expression is so funny. -CT

♡♡♡
me (with ~~a strangely~~ my usual big head), being all stupid and smitten.

what are you holding? -LW

★ Oh, and I'm writing this whole thing on the toilet. haha.
EWWW! Get off the can.
                              —LN

← me
on the
can!

Thpbpthw!

forgot the
year
6/23/~~~~02 ←

Hey everyone,

Well, Wednesday is the last day of school this year and I'm going to ↗ pooping takes a lot out of you. Literally! —SPK

miss you all so much. Watch out this letter is gonna be maaad long! Let

Courtney is the masta of the novel-like letters! —JB

me speak about a few of the issues raised lately before anything moves

further: First I have a really funny story about the first time I met Sophie, seeing

as Lindsey brought up some similar stories. It's kind of a two part story, so

here's the first part. Sophie and I took the same prep-course class for the

Stuy Test and she sat in front of me with some other girl. Someone

pointed you out to me as "Sophie" and I was like who? Anyway, one time

during class your friend knocked over her bag and this whole giant

box of tampons spilled out of her bag all over the place and it was really

funny. You were helping her pick them all up and trying ^not to get

totally embarassed, so I figured I'd help. Then about a year later,

once we got to Stuy, you came to the Globe for Tom's birthday (Nov 20th)

and you started talking to me when he was there and we instantly

bonded. Then you came back to the Globe every day that week and

the friendship was born. Wow, how weird is it that I remember the exact day we met?

do you have a crush on me? —SPK ↓

    Also, speaking of Sophie, we really need to consider this situation with

Tyler as a major issue. A guy just doesn't turn over and start

fingering you for no reason. Obviously there is something going on there,

whether it be feelings, or just plain sluttiness on his part, but it's

something. More on that later. ★

Cartoon relating to aforementioned issue:

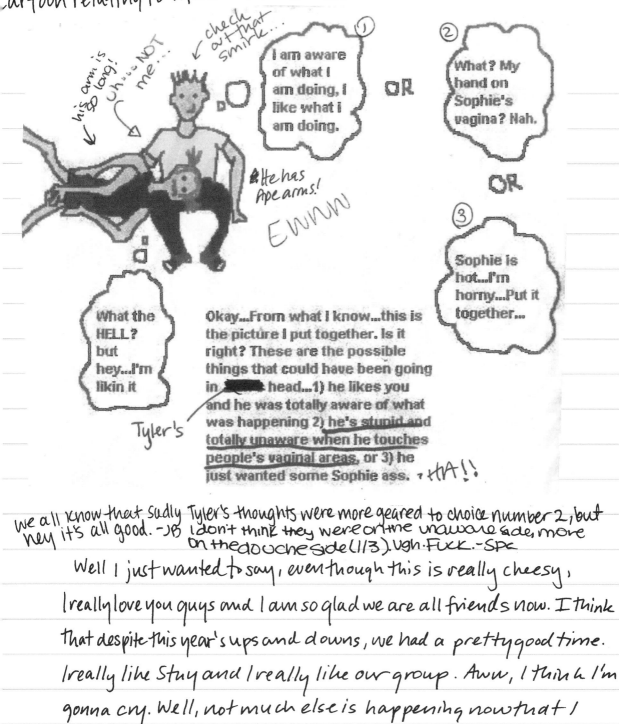

we all know that sadly Tyler's thoughts were more geared to choice number 2, but hey it's all good. —JB I don't think they were on the unaware side, more on the douche side (1/3). Ugh. Fuck. —SPc

Well I just wanted to say, even though this is really cheesy, I really love you guys and I am so glad we are all friends now. I think that despite this year's ups and downs, we had a pretty good time. I really like Stuy and I really like our group. Aww, I think I'm gonna cry. Well, not much else is happening now that I need to write about, so I'm gonna make a homage pages to each of y'all (in a non-sexual way). Each of you gets a page that says why you make me happy (again in a non-sexual way, →

except for Lindsey). Let's keep the "summer news" to the letters so we can keep tabs on each other. Ok, I'm off the toilet, here goes the pages, alphabetical order so no one feels bad.

♡ Courtney

Lindsey Newman

(oops, in the alphabet,
Julia should come first.
oh well!)

god I hate you
Courtney. -JO

Yo Linds, I know we haven't been friends for that long, but you are the woman. You can always make me laugh, even if you are making fun of me, which is most of the time. You always have a smile on your face and an insult up your sleeve. People think you are shy but that is the last word I would use to describe you.

You care about your family and friends, and there is so much you have to say, it's just that most people don't listen or don't understand. But I do. We can always talk about TV or movies or Marley if it comes down to it. Aww, our poor-ass ghetto Lindsey.

AWWW...
-LN

Love ya man, by the way: eat my shit.

SUPER PASSION

I hope my Jewish star is good!

My Jewbah,

Yo man, you are like the nicest person ever! I just have to say that. I would die if I had to be as unjudgemental and sweet as you are. You are never mean, or cranky, or anything, which is a nice change from Sophie. And we'll always share the bond of Dave (him being your ex-boyfriend, him my ex-best-friend). Thanks for being so real and special in that Julia way. You are always there for a good talk (esp. about masturbation) and a nice compliment. There isn't anything I can't talk to you about

and I love your silly humor and bright smile (even the fake tooth). Our little slut! Love the cock ♋! You always make everyone feel so special!!

aww, thx! i'm gonna cry!
-JB

Sophie Pollitt-Cohen

sophie's horse

Homeslice,

Ah the friendship that we've built. I didn't know you before, but now I can't live without you. Clash, Rancid, music, boys, → ah the things we share! We've had the MAD deep talks, and I know that we make each other better people (even if we are making fun of all the people that we mutually hate).
There isn't much more I can say except that we are the ultimate team; partners in crime.
     Keep it real homie!

I love you because we hate all the same people. SPC

COURTNEY TOOMBS

look at
that
magnificent
cleavage!
SPC
WOAH

Court, you're amazing! You're one of the most insightful people I've ever met, and all your theories about people and what they're thinking, who they like, what they do, everything u say is mad true. This summer I missed convos with you, I missed ur bright fun clothes (yea mighty mouse and rolling stones t-shirts!) and ur silly comments. Great for a laugh, a chat, a friend. I love you!

julz.

Hey guys—

oooah the end of the year + we's gonna be sophomores!

And now for something completely different (yeah monty python!)!

soph, take a deep breath...

I just wanted to clear up the Tyler/car/vagina thing. WHAT THE FUCK? I hate him, I hate myself, I hate the world! In the car coming home from his country house, he randomly started to engage in some inappropriate behavior w/ my Axl Rose (vagina!). I tried to talk to him about it the other day, + he was all like "Uh...I didn't realize what I was doing...?" What?? That sounds like a bunch of BULLSHIT + he's trying to get out of a sticky situation. I'm so mad + upset. Times like these get me so frustrated + angry b/c he seems like just a really close friend until these weird moments where I have no idea what he wants + I just feel used and cheap, like Courtney's mom.

All this Tyler drama is making me feel like I'm gonna grow up + have meaningless relationships w/ married men. Tyler doesn't have a girlfriend but to me it's similar

That's just because you wouldn't go out with him for longer than a week, so he's bitter. —CT

just in that I'm not really important in his life—I'm just a rest stop on the Tyler expressway, the place where fatty truck drivers take showers, eat hot dogs, and pop amphet-amines. I've also confessed this fear to some of my guy friends + they seriously agree w/ me, like especially Paul, who says I'm too scared of real relationships.

Speech Team is also hell b/c I haven't memorized my piece yet. I know I've talked about this before, but I thought I'd have grown up a little since Freshman year. It's like unless I have someone watching over my shoulder, I won't do any work. I try to be like "Soph, you have to do your chem HW," but my brain interprets this as "do whatever, I really don't care."

In other news, the WORST thing happened to me today. Court + I got on the train this morning @ 72nd St (gotta love that 2 train), + when the doors closed, Courtney said "man what is that smell?" I turned around + saw this BIG pile of human SHIT right there in the middle of the train car! And then I realized that... I HAD STEPPED IN IT!!! Damn you Jesus, you played a sick joke on me. It's not enough that I have

I remember that, it was so gross. —CT

Jesus' jokes are always sick ones —CT

to be on the train @ 7:30 in the goddamn morning, but I had to step in a big ol pile of human feces. And then the guy @ the deli by school wouldn't let me use the hose to clean off my shoes which I don't know if I can wear anymore, because after washing them numerous times with seriously hard-core soap, they're still pretty noisesome(yeah trying out some PSAT words. If you don't know what "noisome" means, break out that dictionary or you will fail the test and life in general!). Maybe if you stopped being a cracked out whore, you'd pay attention to where you're going and not get stuck in SHIT. -LN

Speaking of subways. I was on the train the other day and I was sitting between these two ghetto girls who were really pissed off about something. The 1st one was like "I'm so mad, I want to hit someone!" And the 2nd one was like "Yeah, I'm gonna hit this girl right here!"(meaning ME). I had my headphones on, though the CD was over, + I was like "oh lord...Sophie, pretend you didn't hear, pretend you didn't hear..." that's really funny -CT

I HATE MY LIFE.   HAHA........ha......sigh.
        -Sophie

LOVE IT. LOVE IT. LOVE IT.

7-1-02

BIG UPS TO BIG L! WOO WOO!

So here I am @ camp. Today was my first real day as a CIT - it sucks sometimes, but mostly it's more fun than anything.

Last night I had to help make dinner for the campers, so I was peeling apples for fruit salad. I dropped the peeled apples on the floor so many times! I was just like "er..."(and back in the bowl they go!) "who wants fruit salad? Yum!" Yeah, I skipped out on the fruit salad last night.

I found this book in the bathroom (so I like to read on the job... is there anything wrong w/ that?) called <u>Sex Smart</u> and I was all excited to have something to read until I saw the sub title: "Five hundred and one reasons NOT to have sex." God damn! one reason is that "a real man doesn't need to 'score'. He is self assured about his sexuality. Guys who need to 'score' are usually the guys who

Boopsie.

Summer time!

don't feel very good about them-selves." WORD.

The book also recommends "other ways to please your lover." I first was excited, thinking this could be some pretty juicy stuff, but their suggestions were : care for each-other if you get sick, play footsie, learn to play "chopsticks" on the piano-make beautiful music to-gether, make a model car.

Bunch of sick-caring-for, footsie-playing, chopstick-playing, car-building assholes, God I hate being poor.

Keep it real homie
-Sophie

A Letter from Courtney to Sophie at horse-camp:

July 6, 2002

Hey slice (as in home slice),

How's camp? Smoked any of that weed you bought yet? Well, on a lighter note, last weekend (like June 29th ish) I went to visit my cousin at college and it was really awesome. On Friday I took an eight hour train ~~ride~~ up there and then we had a BBQ at her friend's house. We had a lot of beer and chilled but my cousin got a migraine so we went back to her room. So the next day we went to lunch (but no dinner) and went straight to the parties on an empty stomach.

Wow did Courtney get drunk! I had a half bottle of wine, two huge cups of whiskey and coke, two white Russians, wierd vodka and soda out of a plastic tub, and then lots of beer. Thus I don't remember shit that happened after that. Oh and then her friend was being a jerk so I slapped him across the face. I also got a wierd cut on my hand from ~~God~~ knows what. Shit, I'm gonna get TB!

Then around 4am I sobered up a bit and felt like ~~shit~~ deadshit. I slept for about 3 hrs and then threw up all morning. God being hungover on an eight hour train ride is the worst thing ever. I hope you never get that horribly drunk. And just when I thought the soothing sounds of my headphones would save me from the pain, my batteries were dead. Kill me.

So how's life without Tyler? Liberating? (Good Times? Have fun + write me back.

Love Courtney

PAR AVION

SUMMER LETTER!!!

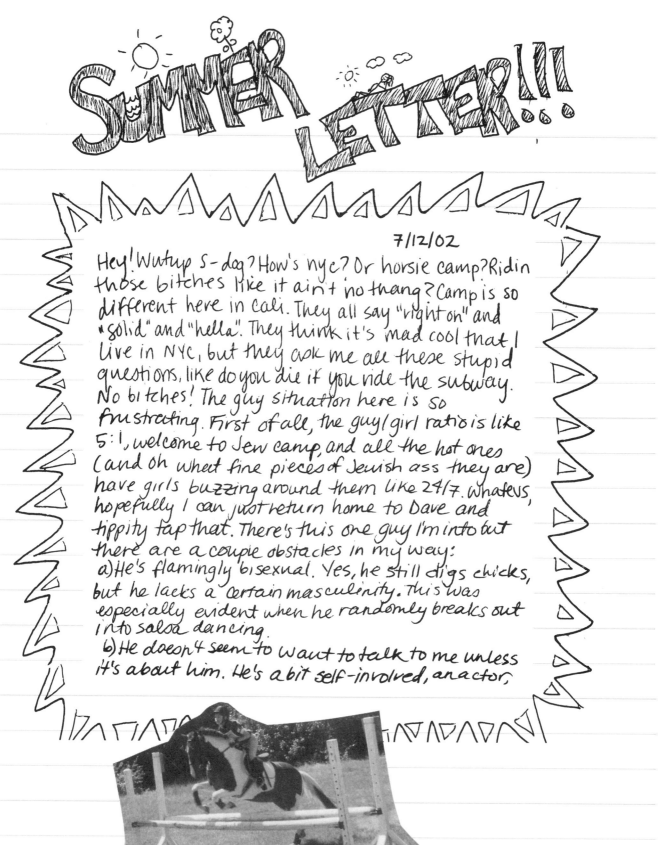

7/12/02

Hey! Wutup S-dog? How's NYC? Or horsie camp? Ridin those bitches like it ain't no thang? Camp is so different here in Cali. They all say "right on" and "solid" and "hella". They think it's mad cool that I live in NYC, but they ask me all these stupid questions, like do you die if you ride the subway. No bitches! The guy situation here is so frustrating. First of all, the guy/girl ratio is like 5:1, welcome to Jew camp, and all the hot ones (and oh what fine pieces of Jewish ass they are) have girls buzzing around them like 24/7. Whatevs, hopefully I can just return home to Dave and tippity tap that. There's this one guy I'm into but there are a couple obstacles in my way:

a) He's flamingly bisexual. Yes, he still digs chicks, but he lacks a certain masculinity. This was especially evident when he randomly breaks out into salsa dancing.

b) He doesn't seem to want to talk to me unless it's about him. He's a bit self-involved, an actor, you know the type. The only conversation we've ever had was when he noticed my shoulders were peeling (the punishment for pasty white girls trying to tan) and he wanted to peel me. NOW ISN'T THAT SENTIMENTAL? God, I'm a loser. Well, I hope at least I made you laugh. Well, I g2g strum some guitar—I'm the Jewish music masta now. Luv ya and see you soon! Oodles of noodles!

Julia Gulia Schmoolia

p.s. 5 days till my birthday!

Hello hello hello!

peace out Sophie!

7/14/02

Dear
~~To the loser~~ Sophie,

Oh my GOD! it's my
~~15~~ and 5 ~~month~~
B-day!

Wow, what a ~~piece of shit~~ nice letter you sent me. I'm sure if I had read it, it would have been very entertaining. ANYWAY... yesterday I hung out with CoCo, we had fun (gotta love those mcflurries.) We were talking and CoCo told me about some guy at the place she works. She was like "you know how some guys are Indian and Hot? yeah, This guy's ~~is~~ Just Indian." Ha, Ha. Well, I thought it was funny.

I saw the notebook and I heard about you and sex buddy ~~Tyler~~ at the Hamptons (you know, something about him lying in your lap and... well yeah) That computer drawing was disturbingly weird. That whole experience must have sucked.

OOB #... I lost count : Anyway, I'm having fun at my job as a camp counselor. So far I've kicked a kid in the face and they had so much blood coming out of their nose, it was like ~~tomato~~ ass bitch all over again. If anyone asks, it was by accident. And then another girl broke her toe. I wonder why they won't let me near ~~around~~ the kids anymore... hmmm. But it's fun 'cause ~~they won't let me do anything~~ I don't have to do much. I get to hang out with the other counselors.

I just got a letter from Julia too. She sent me yours also so its in this envelope. I'm trying to fill up this letter with a lot of crap to fill up the page... maybe I'll draw a nice picture on the back.

~~Please~~ I hope you shit yourself happy.

♡ Big L

god I hate ~~my life~~ you.

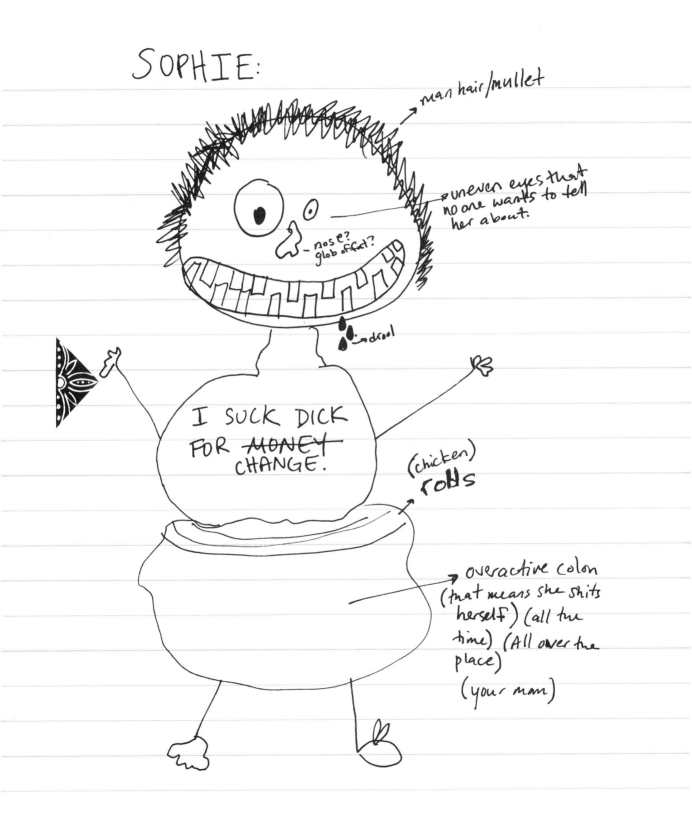

9/16/02

Hello, hello, hello!

OMG I missed this notebook so much, sophomore year is starting, let's hope it's a good one!

Having fun with oob #1: i have nothing real to say, but I just needed this oob to work with my rhyming scheme, you'll see.

Lighting a doobie with oobie #2bie: Yarr I need some tree in my system. I'm getting agitated. Maybe when I drop sculpture (what a bs class! "Today we're going to be sculpting with paper as a medium because clay is not yet available" Translation: we have a low budget and are never getting clay, so we're using paper maché like in 3rd grade) and I have two free periods, I'll get more opps to smoke. Hmmm, gets me mad relieved just thinking about it. Wooaa I gotta chill out, can't let the bud take over my system. But I sure am fiending.

Smokin some tree with oob #3: School. It's the same as it's always been, yet ~that was deep. -SPC~ so different. I feel like this place gives me different mood swings every day. Sometimes I'm really antisocial and bored by everything that's going on, sometimes I love ~everyone~ sucking dick -LN and get reeeally happy. Sometimes I look around at all our "friends" and feel like I have no friends at all.

The other day, I was thinking about how much it sucks that like the minute we got here, boundaries were made, social lines were drawn and everyone has their own little group, and now we're stuck. That's the end of it. There's no social mobility at all. It's like you'd be shunned as a social heretic if you even attempted to enter someone else's little bubble. Why are teenagers so arrogant?

The wall has also lost some of its grandeur too. Somehow, sitting around watching kids smoke just isn't cool anymore. WHAT IS THE WORLD COMING TO? (she says sarcastically). Maybe it's because those stupid volunteers painted it like Alice in Wonder "I'm-a-volunteer-and-I-work-for-free-and-I-can't-paint-for-shit" land. And OMG who else wants to shoot the next person who whips out a TV camera and starts talking about 9/11? Stop exploiting us. Yes we were there, yes we're still here, yes it was horrible and never again do I want to relive that day but no I do not want to tell you about it and pretend I'm damaged for life just so your undergrad film studies class can ooh and ahh at your wonderful dramatic masterpiece. Get out of my face!

[margin note: WORD.. -LN]

But enough said, I'm out to whore myself on the streets
[margin note: -LN]
Luv J to the ulia
P.S. # Lindsey got the mad cool pipe yo!
[margin notes: crack? -SPK -CT   probably yeah -LN]

COOL DESIGN:

The Girls

Hey,   9/18/02

 1st oob: Last week was the first anniversary of 9/11. It felt really
creepy because I know it's only been a year but I feel like it
happened a century ago. That day is like a movie that I can play in
my head whenever I want because it is so vivid. Getting up, going to
the third day of high school, absolutely beautiful day, plane hits
the building 8:45am English class, fire smoke outside my
French class window, thought it couldn't have been real, tv
new on in the classroom, it's war, lights flicker, tv goes
out, everyone running on the streets, people bleeding, back
to homeroom, evacuation of the whole school, 3,200 people
running down the stairs, first tower falls, whole school shakes,
kids screaming, running, dust rushing towards the windows,
someone grabs my hand and we're running outside,
smoke, coughing, dust in my eyes, running, crying, police
screaming, are we running in the wrong direction, made it
to Canal street before I stopped running, calves burning, call my
dad crying, scared and pained, burnt business papers littering
the ground 80 blocks away, get home after many hours, can't stop
watching the tv, who's dead who isn't, friend's dad's picture on the tv,
he's missing, she's destroyed, candlelight vigil two days later,
waiting for him to come home, he's found, funeral, days in bedroom

smoking ciggarettes in the ~~bathtub~~ empty bathtub, his picture still in my bottom drawer and I haven't moved it in a year. I guess there's a lot more than that but I can't really stand to write anymore.

Last week on 9/11 Julia, Tyler, Sophie and I decided to cut classes in the morning because we all felt a little numb and didn't want to be stuck in school with everyone asking us if "we're ok yet." We went and sat in the Irish Potato Famine Memorial in Battery Park. I guess it's the closest to a memorial we have. Just sitting there a few blocks away from the site being silent was right. It was our way of remembering because every ~~thing~~ time I thought about that day last year I got a wrenching sickness in my stomach, but since the day at the Potato Memorial if I think about, the memories are there but the feelings are gone. I don't know what I'll tell my kids when I grow up, how will I explain to them what I experienced? Maybe by that time the memories will fade too and I won't have to think about ~~it~~ it again. <u>yeah, being senile will be fucking awesome!</u> -SPC

<u>2nd ookie</u>: So with the weed stuff. It's cool, but I feel like it's too much of a thing now. I hate how shit like that feels like something to keep us occupied because we can't find anything else to do. It's like we need to have something to plan for or look foward to. I mean I'm obviously not against drugs, but I just feel like we've tired out

with that. -SPC ;

weed and it's going to get so boring, so fast. I just really liked hanging out with Linds, Jules, and Tali and just TALKING about stuff! It just felt really nice and relaxing. It's just that sometimes the weed situation more stresses me than mellows me out. I guess I get sick of the whole cycle of getting high in the park, watching for popos, smoking that shit really fast, walking around for a while and chilling, then going to McDonald's once we've got the munchies and losing our high. I'm excited for Friday, but not smoking everyday anymore. If you look back at last year, my calendar has about 4 to 5 days a week that we smoked. That's a lot. But I doubt I will change anyone's lives too much.

3rd oobie: I totally understand Julia's thing that "Stuy feels the same but different." Let me explain. Last year was freshman year so you spend the whole time pretending that you like everyone because you want to make as many friends as possible and have everyone like you. Then we all finally met eachother out of the 3,200 kids at our school and made a good thing with this notebook. But now that we are back from the summer and it's Sophmore year, everyone's groups are defined and we can feel like we totally fit in. But I understand Julia, it's just hard right now because everyone has changed a lot over the summer and they need to figure out if they still want to be your friend. In the end they will probably decide they hate you, but at ~~maybe~~ least now you know the reason why. For me I'm not exactly feeling every single moment of this school. I just feel like I'm crawling in the dark sometimes. Like I'm searching for something I can't even see, and I can't see back to where this all began. *what the fuck does that mean? —LN*

4th and final oob: Sophie's B-day is ~~soon~~ soon! We'll probably do something, maybe give her a bag of shit. Yeah, by the way, ~~no~~ no one knows when my birthday is! It's **DEC 3!** Thanks for not knowing. But back to Sophie's birthday. What are we doing? I'm sure since this is the first birthday we are going to celebrate as all real best friends, we'll do it right.
*you better.
—SPC*

COURT

I found this sticker on a telephone pole. hobo.

TWINKY

magnafrying glass (looking @ the cream filling)

HOHO

Sophie's nasty armpit hair - JB

-Hey boys, I'm ~~Julia~~ Sophie. wanna play?

9/29/02

'Sup, Twinkies and HoHos?

It's a half day today! You know what that means... actually, lemme lay that beat down in equation form: (Got Blunt) + (Got weed) = light that shit, smoke that shit, pass that shit. Yay, I love math! Court and Julia wrote about weed in our lives, so check this out:

NO FUCKING WAY! -CT

Someone referred to me as "smoker sophie." What the fuck? I haven't even smoked in a while! OK...3 days. But still! I don't want to be "smoker sophie." I know I blaze kind of a lot, but WAY less than I was ~~doing~~ @ the end of Freshman year (definitely needed to tone that down a bit), and I really don't want to have weed define me.

Oh, GUYS: my lunch group and I have discovered a hidden treasure of the Tribeca food circuit. It's this tiny little hole in the wall (not to be confused by The Hole In The Wall, the little store near Stuy where everyone buys candy, Snapple, and cheap cigarettes) that serves BBQ. You can get ribs, fried chicken, BBQ chicken, baked potato, fries, all that jazz. Plus, it's pretty cheap-you can buy a BBQ chicken breast for like $3 or $4. Top that off w/ a bottle of your finest H₂O, Poland Spring of course, and you're ready to go. The food reminds me of all the AWESOME BBQ places my dad + I ate at on our trip to memphis. You don't understand. I LOVE ribs. So juicy. So succulent. So good.

On a more serious note: weed again. Even though I smoke a lot, during the day @ school, I'm thinking "why do I smoke?" and then I think I don't really care about it, and wouldn't mind never smoking again. But then I go do it like ~~&~~ 3 or 4 out of 5 school days a week plus weekends, and I like it. When I'm not doing it, I don't really care about it. But then the minute I ~~do it~~ smoke, I'm like "oh right, this is why I smoke weed -'cause it's awesome!" Oh lord, I'm very confused.

PSATS soon!
Love,
Sophie

he has a mohawk -CT

Guys I did really well @ my horse show last weekend. Me + my horse rocked out!

I made him a gangster horse -CT
He looks like he's in the Rat Pack. More like the Horse Pack. haha -CT

He needs a bowler hat -JB

2 months and a day to my birthday (Dec 3)!
Sweet Sixteen Bitches!

Dear Everyone, (well not **everyone** but you know what I mean)
Straight to the oobs!

oob # 1 : So, went to Tyler's yesterday for an hour. That was fun. He's cool to spend time with when you don't have to work to get his attention. He told me all about how Lou Pearlman might sign their band to his label, which would totally go against ~~my~~ everything I believe in about music, but it's still pretty hott. If they were famous that would be really cool. When he told me about it, I was like "oh yeah, we'll show up at all of your concerts." And he was, " Yeah, I'll open the door and it'll be you and the other girls, ~~them~~ and I'll be like oh, it's just my best friends from high school, so let em in." He actually called us his best friends, which ~~is~~ coming from someone like him is a one in a million sincerity. God how what Tyler thinks makes me happy? NOT! But it's cool when your friends let you know how much you mean to them. Sometimes he can be a pretty nice boy. Sometimes. Especially when he isn't wearing his shirt. Oh the small nipples and the MAD happy trail too.

happy free way! -JB

What, were you taking notes? -LN

So that Lazer Tag birthday thing is a good idea. Karyn had a birthday party there in 6th grade, back at Delta, and it was really fun. Her older sister (you guys know her) came and all I remember about her then, before we were friends, was that her cake-makeup glowed in the black light! Even ugliness can shine in the dark. That was a good one. Well we should go some weekend and have tons of good times. Or just take a big crap.

hahaha!!! -JB

Courtney

VS

Lazer tag vs. taking a shit: only one can win the battle! -SP

A TESTIMONY TO NOTEBOOK LOVE:

HOW JULIA SEES LINDSEY:

She looks like Tom Sawyer if he had Down Syndrome!

Side view →

← saggy boobs

↑ fat ass droopy bitch belly

asshole butt!!!...

also a Jew

although nobody knows

why is this funny? because she's always like "HA!"

"You guys I'm Jewish"

three Check it out, TRIPLE CHIN SPLIFF!!! nice...

Saggy ass boobs →

CAMEL TOE!

TOMATO ASS BITCH

← nappy ass hair

eyes all slit "cuz she's stoned" or she thinks she is...

freckles

"popcorn joints"

Big fuckin feet in clown ass basketball shoes

How the World Sees Julia:
by Lindsey

freaky ass, toe jammy, plaque covered, demented little fang tooth

- hair

uneven eye syndrome (that no one wants to tell her about) like Sophie

→ ugly smile (that everyone tells her about)

deformed hand

I'm A Jew!!

→ Flat ass ~~Boobs~~ Pecks   ohh that's harsh -ct

→ back view

→ fart machine!

hair (she's got more hair on her ass than her head except for that MUSTACHE)

— her self described "cooch" hahaha hehe he -ct

— little legs that are smothered by fat ass Julia suck a lot cock a lot forever.

Hi guys,   10/15/02

<u>Why don't you shoot me with a gun with oob#1</u>: Last Saturday night was mad fun. We have to do stuff like that more often. This was the first time I've ever hung out with the infoumas "guys" all together. You know, Dave, Tom, Wes, Tyler and Brody, a.k.a the band plus one. They were really chill.

<u>Drunkie #2bie</u>: Saturday was the first time I've ever had the pleasure (or pain) of drinking alcohol (a.k.a. Downing that shit) Damn. Jack Daniels is NASTY, especially when it is mixed with orange juice. Orange juice is only supposed to go with pancakes and waffles and buttery morning goodness. Not nasty DEATH (a.k.a J.D.). By the way, Sophie, nice job on spilling the whole cup of orange juice with J.D. in it all over Tyler's carpet. Tyler broke out that cleaning fluid and we saw you clean that shit on your hands and knees to the break of dawn, or something like that. Here's a nice tidbit of information for everyone; according to all the guys, J.D. + orange juice + cleaning fluid=smells like cum.

After we chilled at Tyler's house, we went out for pizza. Sophie, "the guys," and I went to the park to smoke a joint. ████████████████████████████ ██ ██ ███████████████████████ Damn. Dave gets mad crazy when he's high, but he's mad funny. After everyone got sufficiently fucked up, we went back to Tyler's house ████████ and Wes, Tom and Dave, how do you say... jammed. That was cool. I know they're in a band, but I'd never heard them play before. While we were all

↑ dumbass cracker can't hold her arsenic—ct

J.D. a.k.a.
DEATH in a
cup.

Good song
-SJC

just relaxed, not really ~~saying~~ saying anything "Knockin On Heaven's Door " by Bob Dylan was on the stereo, I was on the bed and I could just imagine each of us in like 25 years. You know those times when you just pause, and you realize it's a moment that you're gonna remember when you're older, and be like, "man I remember when I was fifteen...mad good times." It was weird and cool at the same time. Plus, Brody is mad hot. <u>aww Linds, write shit like this more often</u>-cT

<u>oobie #three...bie</u>: What's up with Wes? He was freakin' me out. That night when we came back from the park, he was really freaky. He just sat in a corner, all bunched up and looked like he was gonna have an emotional breakdown. Isn't it weird when guys show a sensitive side like that. I mean, they spend so much time trying to be all tough and macho, that to see a different side is weird, but good. (At least they're human)

<u>OOB# 4</u>: Mood swings. Yeah, smoph, I kinda know what you're talkin about. Mood swings suck, and it sucks to be at an age where you're so goddamn emotional. Sometimes I get upset about stuff, and I think "why am I so upset, this is such a stupid thing to get worked up about" but I can't help the way I feel. Other times I look back at stuff I was sad or emotional about and I'll just think how stupid I was.

Anyway, cool to the shul and keep it real,

Big L

Wow mood swings suck. mostly because I don't get them -cT

shut UP. -SD.

Prozac poster child.

cool crazy waves!

10/18/02

Shalom Chaverim! (That means hello friends in Hebrew, the language of the o.g.s, original gangsters that is, wandering the desert like it ain't no thang. God I'm stupid.)

→ They kept it reAL for 40 years yo! -SPC

A random thought: I was singing that Aerosmith song yesterday, Walk This Way, and I realized I'm it's the dirtiest ~~Bitch song~~ ever.

Oob#1: I'm in history right now and I want to crucify my teacher. He'd probably just keep talking cuz he never shuts up. And he's so stupid. I want to laugh in his face.

Oob#2: So. Mark. The new boy. The interest of the month. I cannot figure this boy out! He's just so chilled out that it makes me neurotic. Ha-w. Maybe I'm over thinking it. But oh my lord it was so hard to finally get to hook up with him, I feel like I have to do all the work while he sits back and watches me struggle, and I don't know if I have the energy to do it again. But then again, I really wanna hit that shit so I guess I'll just work hard. I hate boys, but oh how I love them.

damn! can't keep track of all your lovers. -SPC

Oob# ~~Smu~~ tree, get it? Like three?: OMG smoked with Tyler yesterday. It could easily have been the worst day of my life, or at least the worst smoke. Right after I smoked I began to feel really socially out of place, which then went on to affect my depth perception, and all of a sudden, the whole world was flashy and dark and all I could do was sit down, hope not to puke, and wait for it to end. I always think I'm so cool whenever I go smoke but I always end up around a group of guys that I don't know, certainly don't care about, and who I definitely have no

trust in. i always end up wishing to god I had just gone home and watched some TV.

(I'm too good)

That's all for now Peace out sistas!

Julz

At least I have my girls to make me feel better. Some entertaining pictures:

(Sophie) Calling her agent. There's actually no one on the other end of the line. Oh so literary...

Gambling her life away. A sad tale...

courtney has uneven eyes!!

SIGH

Shiny can, $10 bill in hand, ready to hit the town. or sophie

What's up ladies!   10/21/02

<u>oobie #one-bie</u>: So Linds, those entries you wrote were really cool, seriously. You opened up and stuff and it was really sweet. It was very cool. Also everyone should look back on the entries to write on them and read stuff, like me, right now. Speaking of my immense love for Lindsey, a few days ago we were in the theater at school and let's just say that we had a "little incident." So I get up to get out of my seat and step over Lindsey. Of course she had her arm at a right angle on the armrest and when I stepped over her she jerked or something and fisted me in the crotch. I have never felt so violated. Even though *This is NOT how it happened. —LN* Lindsey and I have become very close friends, a fist is a large thing, and thankfully my vagina is not. Well if anything, I now know what it will feel like to give birth. *▷that'll be a pretty small baby. —SPC*   *No, she got it in the bag. Almost. —JB*

<u>Ooob #twoob</u>: ~~Julia~~ Julia is still trying to get that Marc-ass in the bag. But just wait, he'll come back for some more. I can't believe that you guys hooked up at Tali's loft when we were all right in the room, seeing as most of the rooms are merely divided by a curtain. That was nasty when we heard "Ohhhhh!" and we all <u>freaked</u>. I said if he's eating her out, I'm gonna kill myself (I mean that's awesome, but not when your friends are in the next room.

But I hope we all get some loving soon because we are gonna rip each other's heads off other wise. That leads to the next oob: →

<u>oob#smoke weed (3)</u>: Last week was everyone's hell week of the year. I just had <u>so</u> much work, a fierce amount of Speech, a hellish self doubt, and you guys were <u>crazy</u> too! Also, <u>Sophie and I</u> had our periods! Damn that ain't cool! I'm the last person to use that as an excuse b/c it's really not, but when more than one of us have it, that's just bad news for planet earth. <u>We</u> can say that having our periods makes us crazy, but when other people (like guys) say that, it's so fucking obnoxious. It's like those times when you are crying and upset and screaming at someone (parents) about your problems and they just look at eachother and say, oh she's just tired. Ahhhhh!!! It's like ~~everything~~ everything you feel and all your emotions and beliefs are discredited as being some physical or hormonal problem. God that sucks.

Back to my life specifically, it was really cool on Saturday going to Speech. It was nice to make new friends on the team and have new experiences. And it felt nice to win a trophy, (Sophie and I took yeah! we ~~kicked ass~~ SPC kicked Second Place in our category – Duo Interpretation) cuz you know that hasn't happened in a while.

      Love Always,

          Courtney

i never win anything! Except a fine bunch o' hoes. –JB

10/21/02

I need to comment on the aforementioned "incident" that Courtney was talking about. Ok, that is totally not how it went down. This is what happened - Me and Courtney were sitting in the theater, talking, blah, blah, blah. Then, Courtney gets up and tries to climb over me (obviously not very successfully). So, Courtney kicks my leg, the one on which my arm had been leaning, and I hit my elbow on the side of the armrest. Now, you know what it's like to hit my your funny bone, when that happened, my NATURAL reflexes acted up and it made my elbow jerk. Now, At The Same Time the ever so graceful Courtney tripped over me and when she came down, she fell right on my fist. **THIS IS EXACTLY HOW IT HAPPENED** I should know, it was my fist. Courtney, I'm sorry, but I felt just as violated as you did, and now I hope that we have a mutual understanding that we will never speak of this matter again...
Unless, of course, you liked it.
        ~Lindsey

Whatever you loved it - CT

I mean Hi.   10/22

    Oh my god. I'm in homeroom right now, awaiting my report card.
Why Lord, WHY! Why do I totally SUCK at Science?

SORRY this was a very hectic time in my life.

10/23/02

Hey guys, this is going to be a pissed off entry about my life (like that's
a change of pace). Specifically, I want to write about the piece o'shit
basketball team, man I love those guys. It just sucks that basketball takes
up so much of my time and I don't get to see you guys as much as I'd
like to. But it's a good thing that we have the notebook to keep in
touch, because as much as I'm out of the loop now, I'd probably be
TOTALLY out of it without this piece o' crap, I mean the beautiful
notebook.

    I totally love playing basketball, but I also love hanging out with my
friends. Basketball is a lot of work, practices six days a week, and it's one of the
longest seasons in high school sports. But, it's definitely worth it to be able to
be on a team and improve throughout the season, plus if my bitch ass coach
doesn't make me captain of the team when I'm a senior, I might have to beat

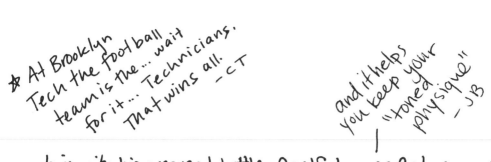

him with his overused bottle of self tanner. And as much as I love chillin with you guys, it's cool to make friends with people I never would have met otherwise. The basketball team is way cool. GO PHOENIX. I don't know why we're called the Phoenix, but at least we're not the Peglegs, like the football team.

The Peglegs, what a great name. Everyone watch out, the one legged football team is coming to kick your ass... Nah, I don't think it works. Plus, the football team totally sucks. I don't understand why they get so much goddamn attention in the school. It's just cause they're boys and football is supposed to be a "school spirit sport." It's the same thing with basketball. The boys team gets so much more attention than we do just because they're boys. The girls team actually does better than them, we got to the playoffs and what happened to them? Oh, that's right, they got SMACKED by every team they played. I can relate to what Sophie said about not being taken seriously about things labeled "guy stuff," basketball being one of them. Whenever I play on the court outside of school, the guys there don't want to play me because I'm a girl, but I can totally keep up with the competition. Either, they don't really play you seriously, 'cause you're a girl, or they any just use the excuse "I can't guard her 'cause she's a girl," like they have to have pity on me or something, when in reality, I hit that shot in their face, regardless of them guarding me or not. DAMN, guys have such big egos, but its fun to get on the court and kick their ass. That's right, I throw like a girl, a girl who can kick your ass. But that's the end of my rant for now.

PEACE OUT
~LINDSEY

Lindsey, you're an empowered woman with pent-up rage. Just let it out.
-JB

yeah, do it for us all (women that is) -CT

Yeah. (I just didn't want to be out of the comment loop. But I do agree).
-SPC

11/1/02

OH my god.....

I am so fucking pissed off right now. My Friday night was officially ruined AGAIN by having to go to synagogue. I only really get to chill once a week anyway, I need this Friday time, but according to my mom, we "do" synagogue at least once a month and dinner EVERY Friday night so I'll just have to deal. Not that I don't like it, when it comes down to it, I actually am really happy that my family's observant, but sometimes I really can't deal with it. Reality: Yes I'm Jewish, yes I love my religion and most aspects of it with a passion, but I can't bear to spend 2 hours in the midst of a community that I don't really have a connection to, being led by someone who (I believe) doesn't really have a connection to god anyway. I'm so sick of looking around my synagogue and wondering if half of the people there really find any meaning in it, or if they just find comfort in the tradition of it all. Tradition is all good, but there should be more to prayer than that _totally-CT_. Also, there's always organ music that is THE BIGGEST downer I have ever heard. I swear, if someone was in a happy mood, all they would need was this organ to change their tune (ha! Get it?). When a group of people gather together to rejoice in their common beliefs, shouldn't there be a little joy? My rabbi certainly doesn't augment that aspect of the service, and besides what makes him qualified anyway? _Just was that a question?..._ because he went to school and has a certificate? Fuck that! I believe for myself and because I was shown that true religion is a loose interpretation with tradition as a backbone that all goes into this big mold that is your personality and your consciousness and it comes out as an outlet for you to vent and a guide for you to worship.

WORP.   Honestly, I believe that religion is one of the most beautiful things in the world, but it is also optional and flexible, and I don't appreciate being forced into it on nights when I just want to chill with my friends! Uggh sorry for the bitchin I just had to get it out. Peace. Power to the people! —SPC
          Julz (who else?)   ~~WWWWq~~ I totally get you Julia—CT

Later that night.....
   12:18 Am
      OH MY GOD YOU WILL NOT BELIEVE WHAT JUST HAPPENED. i'll give you
                                          you finally waxed down there?—LW
two hints: i've been wanting it forever, and it has a massive jew fro. That's right
                                          YAY!!!!—SPC
ladies and gentlemen, I hooked up with Dave!!! I know it's a hooooorrible idea to
hook up with your ex, but honestly, would you resist? Oh my lord I am so happy right
now.
   I need one of you, all of you, to talk to!! I'm all smiles and tingles. Ahhh! Best
night ever! So lemme start from the beginning. i was hanging out with Tyler and Dave
and their crew and they walked me home, seeing as it was late and the upper west
side is oh so dangerous at night. So suddenly Dave and I were alone and he pulled
                       make up your mind you freak! —spc
me in and.... YEA! Ok Mark is awesome but out with the new and in with the old!
Dave is still the best kisser I've ever met in my life. You know when two people just

I love that Julia canbe hooking up
with 2 guys at once and it's not cheating
because she's never really "dating"
either of them. - you are like a guy - CT
So true. - LN

seem to fit together? But wait, the best part is yet to come. We had sex in the
bushes.... just kidding. No really, so I said I had to go and he said "This just
awwwl! spc
feels so right" (!) And I (being bold) said, "I miss you" and he said "I know"!
He was all holding me and touching my face and hair and I AM IN LOVE.
Heavenly heaven I'm in love. Awwww... Barf - LN

Ahhh

I'm so horny right now! *ew. - spc*

Julz

And yet another entry on Sunday....
    Yo so much shit went down this weekend, fucking craziest most dramatic thing ever!
    OOb#1: Sophie's surprise party, frikin amazing! Most fun in my life, and Sophie
didn't have a clue! (that was the funniest part). From singing bad 80's pop on the
karaoke machine to Sophie yelling "Who's got the vodka?" while Tali was on the
w/ her mom - spc
phone, to me stepping on the cake (sorry, coco, I know you worked hard on it, and
oh, that makes it better, not! - CT
if it's any consolation I ate some first), it was too savory a time. Memories fo eva.
    OOb#2: I know, I know, I'm in for a slapping if I say one more thing about Dave
but I just have to get it all out and then I'm done, I promise. I think I made a really
bad decision. I liked him for so many months, and I knew he was uncomfortable
around me because I liked him. So I tried really hard to get over him and surprise!
It actually worked, but after this past couple weeks, especially Friday night,

it all came back and I'm at square one. And he never called me after that night. I'm so sick of my emotions being toyed with and never knowing whether to give up or not. I just can't keep hoping for something that's never gonna happen, it's a little pathetic. I guess there's a reason you're not supposed to hook up with ex's? Good Riddance.   whwe's the L♥VE?
-LN

Julia

FUNNY FACES PHOTOS!! -CT

11-6-02

Good morning sunshines!

Here I go. Oob #1: So we had the <u>mad</u> religious debate on the subway this morning, aka Court, Tyler, and Julia yelling at me, but I'm a survivor. Actually it was really interesting. Even tho. Court says I'm a "closed minded atheist," I ~~still~~ liked hearing all your opinions. Even if they were wrong. Just kidding. No you're not.
‒LN

And Julia, don't think I was attacking <u>you</u> when I said
I think
that ~~there~~ are some sexist Jewish customs, like circum~~cision~~ scision
separating men + women ~~during prayer~~ in the synagogue, not letting women lead services, etc. I know these are features of orthodox Judaism, not reform, but they're still a part of Judaism and its history. True, there are aspects of Judaism I disagree w/, but there are also parts I do agree with, and more importantly, your religious beliefs don't change how I see <u>you</u>. Just because we disagree on some points doesn't change what good friends we are. Awww how sweet. BARF. BAARRGGHFHGFFF.

Tampon. And by that I mean oob #2: My surprise birthday party! It was amazing, thank you so much a million times! Hana, I can't believe I ~~bought~~ brought that BIG bottle of vodka to my own surprise party. You have no idea how much it (and you all) meant to me. And we rocked on Karaoke! When you guys yelled "Surprise," I burst in to tears. Lame, I know, but it just made me so happy that you all would do that for me. Awww I love you guys! As Julia says, we're like the back bone (whatever that means). *Yeah, what does that mean? -LN*

   Ooh so far it's #3: Yeah. so... shit happened w/ Tyler on Sat. night. This is what happened: When we went to Tyler's house for more partying, I was pretty drunk from the surprise party. We were in Tyler's small-ass bedroom, and being there w/ all the weed smoke and cigarette smoke and people and noise was making me feel kinda sick, so I went to the living room to lie on the couch, drink some water, watch TV, and be by myself. I wanted some fresher air and to just chill until I felt better. Tyler came out of his room + sat down next to me on the couch, so I was resting my head on his leg, and then... *He touched my Axl Rose!* the stuff that happened *in the car right?* We talked about it, + basically he said he was *NO, the stuff that just happened (above paragraph)* "bored" (??!!), stuff w/ his girlfriend Maggie was fucked *sp* up, and I was "hitting on" him, so he just...went for it. But I wasn't hitting on him! He came + found me +

sat down next to me after I left to be BY MYSELF! I just
put my head on his knee, but that is NOT hitting on him
or code for "Please, Tyler, touch me!" ~~Tyler was~~ Tyler was
like "I got the feeling that last year you liked me, but
you don't anymore." I told him "I don't want you to
get the wrong impression, I thought we both made
that (our hookup) happen." I didn't sit down on the
couch w/ any intentions, like 'ok, the game plan is..!'" He
was like "I know, don't worry about it," but I feel so
immature (1M or 2?), b/c I'm thinking about this so
much + he doesn't seem to be. He seems to find it strange
that I think this is a big deal. I just want some closure,
you know? I want to understand what he thinks/feels about
it. I also want to understand why I feel so shitty about
the whole thing, b/c I'm really confused. Like our man
Jimi said - love or confusion? Or like Julia's lover, Avril
"I suck dick for money" Lavigne said "WHY'D YOU HAVE
TO GO AND MAKE THINGS SO COMPLICATED???"
God damn it!!! And then there's the issue of him
having a GIRLFRIEND. On the one hand, I feel like him
cheating on his gf isn't really my problem, but then I think

Well it
kinda is.
-CT

maybe I'm a total asshole to participate in his being a complete phsychotic.

adult#4: I'm stressed out, my friends. Not only about Tyler, but just life in general. I feel like I've basically given up on school, b/c I know all I want to do is play guitar, so once that seed was planted in my head it's so hard to take school seriously. Everything is just mounting up in my head + I feel like I'm going to have a nervous breakdown/midlife crisis. OK, I know it's annoying, but last thing about the Tyler issue: I feel so degraded, like he doesn't respect me at all. OK, enough about that. Life is just fuckin' fucked up.

Philots are red
Violets are red
Roses are red
Roses are blue
Roses are blue
Violets are blue

this heart beats fast in its place
faster and faster
jumping into my throat
and it chokes me and won't let me live
then it takes away and
leaves a burn and a fuzzy tip tongue
then its leaves are cold
and let's go
I am free of this grip

WOW. You are such an idiot. -SPC (who else?) 11/7/02

Ladies,
    So yeah, I wrote that poem while on mad haze last night. I
forgot it was in here. I know I am so lame! yeah. Sorry guys :: and that scribble
on the top of the page is when I couldn't figure out (roses are red,
violets are blue) in my head. It just kept coming out wrong. That shit
was crazy. Our hearing was so fucked up, like this person on the other end
of the block across the street was talking and Sophie and I could hear

everything they were saying really loudly like they were talking right in our ears. Then we huddled together in this ~~doorway~~ back doorway of a building on 79th street squatting and smoking cigarettes, staring at stars, tripping out about the sounds and the lights. So anyway... don't remember that much else about last night! Except <u>Jackass</u>! Fucking best movie EVER!

I LOVE Johnny Knoxville sooooo much!!!!

I wanted to like suck that cock the whole movie. And my new fetish is guys with their shirts off, in low slung pants, and big-ass hottie sunglasses! Omg! So hot I got like successive girl-boners for hours! And sometime during the movie Sophie gave me weed to eat, which just got stuck in my teeth and didn't get me high at all.

By the way, Sophie and I are gonna do mad stupid shit and film it! Like not the gross shit they do, but the other stuff. So fucking funny. I'm sorry, I have a weakness for boys that do shit like that. Man I loove boys so much! Now I'm <u>way</u> horny! Crap, and all I have is my own fucking hand right now! NO WAY! Not ~~today~~! (Julia knows what I'm talking about) YES! -JB

Oh, and I named the video Sophie + I will make: Stunts and Bluntz

<u>OOB#2</u>: Sat was Sophie's suprise party. It took me so ~~g~~ fucking long to make that cake. And then it got smooshed on the subway downtown to the karaoke place and Julia stepped in the rest! Idiot who was drunk

off like 1/2 a glass of vodka/sprite! So I was really happy that Sophie liked her party and that made it all worth it! Then Tyler's house was chill after (except for Sophie I guess). I was really happy I talked to Tom and he wasn't mad at all, and Wes looked really cute in his new style. And it was nice talking to Dave again. I really miss him sometimes, not in the way Julia does, thank God! There are just some people that slip away from you and you regret that. But it's cool to just think about how close we were in middle school, how every time someone dumped him (which was suprisingly a lot) he would call me crying and be like Courtney I need someone to talk to, or when I wrote in his year book that he was one of my closest friends and I would really miss him, and he wrote in mine, "ditto, best friends even." Just like guys to write the nicest things in less than five words.

Yeah and then Monday night (last night) was chill, which I recapped above. In case you missed it, the haze rocked and made our hearing so fucked up! But it was cool lying down and looking at the stars.

yeah we heard cars driving that were like 7 miles away!
—SPC

Chambers Street Station
1 2 3 9

auww... the place we call home/hell.
—SPC

Dave vs. Marc   "Who is cooler and why"

DAVE	MARC*
① has a cool nickname (the Captain)	① doesn't have a cool nickname
② is an awesome guy	② has no apparent life
③ loves all your friends	③ isn't too nice to your friends
④ lives in manhattan	④ lives in Bayside a.k.a other side of the WORLD -LN (cuz you know we don't like to commute)
⑤ has a cool band and nice friends	⑤ well other bad things I can't think of now
⑥ Has a Jewfro	⑥ has a big nose

* Gave ~~you orgasms~~ in Tali's attic NOT REALLY!

Clearly Dave is the better choice. But that decision was made days ago.
So Tali has Marc now. What's going on with that? Good thing we never let her
in the notebook. I mean Marc is a nice kid, but Dave is cooler and,
~~so true! -SPC~~
this is hard for me to say, but ~~Dave is~~..... hotter. Ugh, I had to
scribble that out. There, I said it, Dave is ..... hott. So anyway,
Julia, I think you'd go really well back together. And it would bring our
whole group back together. But this time you gotta call him back! A boy
calls you, you return that call! But I'm gonna do what I can to get you
two together.

I know b/c he didn't last night ☹ -JB

So this long-ass letter is almost done now, I think —

oob #5 (I think):

So Tyler. That shit is not cool. Not to hang on to it too much, but let me lay down my principles on this:

① he loves the power - knowing he's the shit and any girl wants it

② he gets horny and thinks that urge should get satisfied by whoever whenever

③ he likes thinking that he has someone wrapped
    ⌐ (the power trip again)

④ he doesn't have to pay, he never gets in trouble, because who's gonna jeopardize some Tyler-ass? Who's going to want to stop being able to say, "I've gotten fingered and it was by Tyler."

So do we agree with these principles? Hopefully I'm not the only freak that psycho-analyzed this situation right? The problem is that basically, he's a guy. This is what guys do, when they know they can have it, they use it, in the worst was being used can mean. So Sophie and I set down a plan for this. She needs to do one of these 3 things:

① get over Tyler. Stop wanting him and be able to push him away, and not need the ass from him anymore   I'm working on it. It WILL happen. -SPC

② go after him. Try to get him as yours. NO. -SPC

③ let things stay the same. Let him have this power and don't stand up. Stay friends but love him secretly. ← will only mean more pain -SPC

<u>the oob of #6:</u>

So my last oob, I think. And it's about Rob. Now I don't think I like him yet, but I'm just kinda interested right now. I saw him in his gym shorts and was like oooh, <u>no chicken-legs!</u> just nice boy legs! (nice legs on a guy are real important) ~who are you? -JB~ And he's so sweet to me now. It's really cool and I just think he's a really cool kid. Sophie and I were talking about how he's kinda socially inept, and she thinks it's a turnoff. I see that, and it's kinda endearing I don't really like boys who are so "oooh me!" Center of attention! Like some boys we know... He's just happy where he is. He's just kind of innocent and I dig that because I want to mess him up. I guess I have a ~virgin~ (slut) complex. And he's really passionate about music, and I like that. Claire is making me a cool classic metal mix so he and I can talk about it.

<u>Ok one more oob, I swear:</u>

So last week Julia was like, "Courtney, are you, oh, ya know, with yourself," and I was like oh yeah. But I want to lay something down to y'all cuz you guys are my girls. I don't really feel good about myself. I'm by no means fishing for compliments, I just want to say that I love my personality and my talents, but it's hard feeling fat in a thin world. And that makes me ~~████████████~~ second-guess everything I do. It changes who you are when you feel your outer appearance is shit. And you feel like maybe some day, when this all drips away, there will be someone to love here, someone beautiful. Now I'm not depressed, but I had to tell you guys that, so you can understand me a little more. It's not easy to write stuff like that, so please try₂ to understand that it was difficult for me. For more reference to my life see Paul Simon song: "I am a rock." That's kinda me in a way, and I hope you all understand that but don't think I'm a freak.

Love Always,
Court♡

NO way, man. we understand. I mean,
we do think you're a freak, but
not b/c of this.
       -SPC

I thought that said laundry.
                    -LN

P.S. You know when you are feeling sad/angry and all the words of all songs suddenly seem to be about you?
Love Court (I'm gone.)

11/8/02

Ladies in Waiting—

Uh, I mean, hey guys! I'm here in chemistry. Mrs. Rhada...don't even get me started. Well well well, my ~~stomach~~ is grumbling like a dying baboon. Or whatever. The point is I'm damn HUNGRY, but of course, the Third Reich, aka the Programming Office of Stuyvesant H.S., gave me 8th period lunch, which means I basically don't get to eat until... never. But I already know what I'm getting. That's right, my PERFECT CHICKEN SANDWITCH. For those ignorant people who don't know of the beauty and the perfection, allow me to explain: Breaded chicken, warmed to a steamy, juicy delight. Lettuce, both cool and crunchy, so pleasing to the tongue. A roll, sweet, bready. And a SHITLOAD OF MAYO. Sex, drugs, and chicken roll, that's me.

Sophie's not homo-sexual, or hetero-sexual, she's chicken-sexual! —CT

Ewwwww I HATE mayo! —LN

Yo, I told you about that sandwich. I invented that shit —CT

Guys, I've come to the conclusion that gym class is the biggest joke of the NY Educational system. Do any of you actually do anything? That's right, NO. All we do is sit around and try to avoid doing any physical activity ~~also~~ and laugh at the dumb kids who are playing basketball. Also, the 3rd floor gym is an awful, awful place, b/c besides having those really bright lights and those

Hey :. —LN

Funny. I hear people say the same thing about you. -LN

More like Ms. REEMing! haha -CT

Way to be the ONLY one laughing at your own joke -LN

tiny little prison windows at the tippy top of the wall, the ~~entire~~ ~~smell~~ entire place smells like feet. And then there's Ms. Remming, what a joke. OK we all know that gym class is not the time of looking especially cute. But this lady comes into class everyday wearing super-tight shorts, her hair perfectly blown out, her nails all done, and then she does these dainty little on-your-knees push ups, and it's so clear that she does NOT want to be a gym teacher. Which is good, because I think she got fired. Except for Ms. Knight's kickboxing class, which is the best thing in my life right now, gym class is completely ridiculous. Kickboxing is awesome, b/c even though we have to listen to ~~the~~ god-awful techno music, we all get really buff. The class is all girls, so no-one cares about getting sweaty and gross, so we all just ROCK OUT and KICK a whole lot of ass. Some days we do Yoga, which is a pretty cool change of pace. We listen to this "calming" ~~song~~ song about "think of the children, they are the future" and also we must "call the dolphins!" The funniest thing about Yoga is how Ms.Knight, who in kick-boxing is like "YOU GUYS ARE CRAP! KEEP GOING! YOU'RE ALL CRAP!", suddenly transforms into the little Buddha.

Sophie bursting out... looking like an alien. Sorry bout that. -JB

She speaks in a calm, melodious voice, all "now we're moving into the prayer stance...now reach for the sun...now become the mountain...now a fetus." I LOVE fetal position!

Responding to Courtney: You're right, I def. think this is a power trip for Tyler. We talked about it on the phone last night, and he was saying how he was having girlfriend problems, so he was sad. So I guess he took refuge in me... and my vagina. Ah kill me!

For shits and giggles

Sophie

Also if you (Tyler) are feeling inadequate about someone you care about (Maggie) who is being cold to you, you run to someone who loves you (Sophie) — like when germs are at war in your body they take refuge in the stomach or the warm, soft vagina — CT

Courtney never runs out of vagina factoids!
— LN

(NOTE: For this entry I was speaking in a British accent.)

Well hello there. Nice to see you again, gov'nah. Pip pip.   11/13/02
Tally ho and away we go. Aye-Aye! Shine ya shoes for a
bob and a ~~who~~ crumpet? 8c

is this in a British accent too? —CT

OOB#1: Now I'm in Chemistry. Damn, I hate my life, but you
already knew that. I wonder if I look back in 15 years, actually
next year even, will I remember the shit I'm learning in chemistry?
Probably not.

*we're?
we're —CT*

OOB# ~~lost Count~~: Last week, coming home from school was a
lot of fun. We were just walking down the street (rappin,) ~~ahaving~~

—JB

fun, and it was just a moment of pure friendship, it was really nice. We
were having so much fun just being ourselves and we forgot about
everything else, like drama and things that affect our relationships and
then eating dinner at City Diner was really fun. Plus, I fucking
love mozzarella sticks.

OOB# Your Mom: Friday night concert at (CBGBs) - that was
pretty disappointing how we couldn't get in, cause some of us aren't
sixteen yet. (You young ass bitches keepin us down) I was kind
you'll be singing a different tune come ~~minute~~ time
of excited about hearing ska in concert, 'cause I've never really —JB
actively listened to ska. Outside the concert, seeing old punks was kind
of weird, but also kind of cool. Doesn't it kind of bother you that
there's no real original culture for our generation? Like, the punks that
were into ska back ~~there~~ in the day invented it, now our generation is using it.

OOB# Tyler (Again): I think we can all agree that this notebook is

↑ we have La Bouche and the Spice Girls... —JB

Totally! —CT

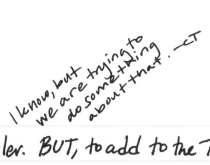
I know, but trying to we are trying to do something about that. —CT

practically a novel about Tyler. BUT, to add to the Tyler business, Sophie, I feel for you on this fucked up situation with Tyler. He's ~~come~~ definitely on a power trip. Even though he's a cool guy, we all have to admit that he has one HELL of an ego. He's the kind of guy that fucks over so many girls for no reason, but in the end he's the one who's the most fucked up and lonely. The situation you guys are in right now has more to do with his shortcomings than with you. It's not fair that he's fucked up, and now you're the one who feels bad about it. Why can Tyler get away with EVERYTHING?! (b/c he's cute —CT)

OOB# <u>whatever</u>: I'm thinking of telling my parents about weed, no, not educating them, *haha —CT* letting them know that I've smoked before. Not the whole truth, just a little. Cause if they find out that I've been doing it for a while, or that I have a pipe, they'd seriously kick my ass. My life with you guys and my life at home is completely different. My parents have no clue about anything we've done, and a few days ago my mom asked me for my friend's phone numbers and I was like ALERT... ALERT... I know this is gonna cause trouble later. Having our parents in communication is a bad thing because then they can compare notes. *your parents take notes? —JB*   *I know exactly what you mean! —CT*   *Yeah, my dad rocks the legal pad. —SC*

OOB# <u>Courtney is a freak ass bitch</u>: Courtney's always like "I don't have to be home till... next year. My parents don't care when I come home." But THEN I get home and Courtney's momma's on the phone, all like "Oh my god! Where's Courtney, she said she was comin home... blah, blah, blah." And I'm like "Uhhh... I just got home, she's on her way... she said she was... going to Starbucks... yeah." And then my parents are all concerned and shit and they make me call the next day to make sure Courtney's alright. DAMN. I try to set the record straight, and say "Mom, I'm not gonna call. I'm sure Courtney's alright, and if she's not, we'll probably hear about her death in the paper or on the news or something." hey! -cT

OOB #5: Off topic, just a smidge: Why do teachers always say stuff like "you guys are in Stuyvesant, you should be better than that. (more mature)." Why do they think that just cause these kids are smart, that they're mature and shit? It's actually sad to see how immature these kids in this school can be. so true! -SPC

YES -cT Another thing that bothers me about our school is the racial divisions Has anyone else noticed this yet? Our school is mad divided by race, I mean each floor is a designated hang out area for a certain racial group. Example: fourth floor Indian Bar, the sixth floor sophomore Asian bar. I think that it's stupid that kids only associate

check out in the back of the book — ct

my chart in the

☆ yeah, one of my teachers showed us a Stuy yearbook from 1973 and it was so racially equal, each page had at least 3 kids from every group. now... not so much. what happened? — ct

with kids that are the same race, or came from the same country. I have some teachers who went to Stuyvesant when they were younger, and they have said that they think it's worse now than it ever was when they were here. This may have some bit of truth to it, but I doubt that it's totally true. I feel like back then the school was mostly white, instead of now when it's like 60% Asian.

☆ And the divisions were still there, but since the majority of kids were white and hung out with white kids, it was considered more normal. For example, in schools that are mostly white and have tiny minority groups, no one complains about the racism and racial division. I think this whole thing about race is a problem at our school and is really fucked up.

The non-diversity of our school is especially apparent to me because when you're one of like ten black kids in the school, you notice these things. Try being in a class, the only black kid, and whenever something about black people comes up, everyone turns around and looks at you. It's like they look at you and expect you to represent every single black person. I can't speak for everyone, just myself. Sometimes when I meet new kids, I can tell they're a little shocked when they talk to me because they expect me to live in the ghetto or something and talk in ebonics and shit like that. They think all black people live in the ghetto or some shit like that. Sometimes these kids who live in these tiny little bubbles make me want to scream. They don't understand that there are places and things beyond what they grew up with and there are lots of things out there that they had no idea existed. Like when I tell people I'm Jewish, they ask me like ‡ ten thousand times if I'm telling the truth, and I'm like YES fuck off. A black jew, who knew? ← and also a poet (you rhymed) SPC

too cool for shul,
Lindsey

by Lindsey Rachel Newman

A challah! Yo, that's my favorite food!
— JB

Challah Ladies, (even though I'm not a jew)   11/16/02

Wassup homies? God it's so fucking rainy outside, but it's really blue and beautiful.
Ahh the ~~coolness~~ coolness...

<u>Ooooooob to the ~~boob~~</u>: So about the Sophie thing on a "string of meaningless
relationships with married men," it seems kinda accurate. Soph and I talked
about it and my mom has a friend who is really similar to Soph. She has the
same exact family situation(divorced parents, really close with both of them,
only child) and she's gone after attached men her whole life. She even spent
the past 4yrs going after a priest. She wanted it to be this whole romantic
thing where he left the church, and he did, but for another woman.

I just see the correlation btw Sophie and her in that they want to get
<u>that</u> guy that can't be had. But you don't want to be that woman who is
58yrs. old and alone, and you don't have to be. Also this has been somewhat
of a pattern for you:
  ① Jason (middle school love) [Heather]
  ② Hunter [Annie]
  ③ Paul   [Zoe]
  ④ Tyler   [Maggie] [~~any~~ other girl he's dated)
Ahh the boys. So many, so strange. Wierdness. But this doesn't have to be forever.
You can strive for guys who want <u>only</u> you, not their girlfriend too.

<u>ooob # tube</u>: Yeah, so Zoe, Sophie and I hung out last night, which was
cool. I know you guys have spoken/unspoken issues and all, but I thought

you guys really bonded and had fun. It was cool eating penis gummies, watching TV, and ~~toying~~ playing with our hair. It was a chill night and I got a dime of hash from Sophie instead of a dime of weed. Nice trade! It's all concentrated and shit. Sweet Sophie, we should smoke it at that big sleepover Speech Tournament; Villiger. I'm excited for that trip.

<u>oob #3:</u> I was thinking how when you guys aren't around, like even when one of you is absent, I feel like a little piece of me is missing. It's mega-cheesy but true. I just like h.s. more than I thought I would, esp. Stuy. It's really fun and social and I like being around people who are seemingly smart. Seemingly. haha

<u>oob #4:</u> So the thing with my mom calling you guys. She randomly freaks out when I don't call and then tries to "punish" me by embarassing me by calling you guys. I'm just gonna find her Palm Pilot and change like one digit in every phone number she has of my ~~friends~~ friends. Haha then she won't call you guys, she'll call someone else. Haha. I'm a bitch.

<u>oob #5:</u> So is anyone walking out on Wednesday? I'm kind of feeling more political lately and I was talking to Jen and Tori about stuff like that. But I don't want to miss school and have to make up all those tests and the work I have this week. I know the war is shit so I want to do my part. In history class we had this debate for/against the PATRIOT Act. Fuck that bullshit—LW Tori and I were against.

of course Stuart Wordsworth and some tool were pro. And we won the debate (the class votes) and afterwards this girl came up to me and said her uncle was detained before coming into the US and her family was worried about him for a long time. It was really cool for someone to tell me that what I said made a difference to them. If we can do that for one person, that's an accomplishment if you ask me. And that really hot senior who used to have a mohawk named Ryan is mad protest-ie and I respect him for that. So enough of my hipster-liberal babbling.

oo6 # 6 : On to the issue of why I "don't like ghetto guys." I only said that because I'm <u>totally</u> intimidated by them. It's a completely different part of society (in terms of interests) and I feel like they look at me and say NERD! I totally think they are hot, and they love women, but I know they would never find someone like me attractive. That's the only reason why I rule it out so quickly. Maybe you can see what I said as not an insult to Lindsey, or them, but as an insecurity.

On the issue of my love for black people (which Lindsey also brought up in her last entry) and politics, last week we were watching this video in class about the civil rights movement and we watched the footage of Martin Luther King Jr.'s speech "I have a dream." Alright now guys, brace yourself because this is going to get really lame soon but I feel like saying this: That moment gives me the chills, the best possible →

chills in the world. If I could pick one moment in history that I wish I could have been there for, I think right now that would have to be^ it. All those people at the monument, everyone together, everyone feeling the same thing at the same moment I don't really know if I believe in God or anything but I feel like at that moment there was a part of some sort of ~~god~~ god in him, and he gave that to the rest of the world. Just thinking about it now makes me feel something really good. I just won't ever understand racism and I won't ever understand how truly important his words were. Now that the whitey that I am has written about all the shit I wanted to write about, I will leave you because you guys are sick of my babble.

Thank god.
—LN

♡ COURT

my cheeks are like teeking over the word. —SB   WHITEYS! ♪

11-19-02

Sup ladie lovaaans? It's like 10:20 @ la notte and I'm coughing up a lung here.

OOB #1: Yeah court, I know what you mean about hottie ghetto guys. I think they're hot too, but it's kinda intimidating b/c I know they wouldn't want to go out w/ me. Gin Boners! YES.

OK, now to something more serious. I was talking to Tyler on the phone like an hour ago, + he said Court + Julia told him that I used to like him, last year. And that you weren't that reserved about saying it... you just blurted it out. I'm sorry, but that is so disgusting I don't even know what to do. The fact that you would tell him the one thing I didn't want him to know is repulsive to me. You guys are supposed to be loyal to me. By choosing him over me so that you could feel special knowing something he didn't, you're saying maybe your loyalties aren't w/ me. And that is why you told him, don't even try to say it isn't. When you tell someone a secret, you're the cool kid who has the inside ~~scoop~~ and can offer advice and feel special. The fact that you chose him + feeling special + needed by him ~~you~~ is wrong. What was

Tyler gonna do w/ the information? What did you intend
for him to get out of the experience? Or was it "hmm...
sophie feels to comfortable around Tyler. Let's shake things
up"?

whatever. I'm just really confused about what's going on.
— Sophie

✷ Maybe by choosing his word over ours you're hurting us too.
Remind us Sophie: who's spilled more of your secrets, who's been
more honest? Him or us? —JB

I agree, also I don't need to talk about you with tyler to have
an interesting conversation. And Tyler knows that we
never told him. Also, who treats you more like shit and
has caused you more pain, him or us? —ct
Yeah....
—LN

11/22/02

Wooa it's been a while. Damn I'm hungry.

Take some ritalin! -spc

God I think I'm developing ADD. Like, I can't just do one thing at a time anymore. I have to doodle while taking notes, eat while studying *(that's not ADD, you just a fatty -spc)* (that one's gonna come back come shopping season), listen to music all the time, call my hos on my cellie while I'm fucking Courtney's mom ..... God it's ridiculous!

OOb#1: So I have to tell you guys about my awesome NFTY weekend (shushup, NFTY = North American Federation of Temple Youth = me being Jewish and hippie with lots of other cool teens from around nyc and suburbs). It was amazing. The people I meet are just so intelligent and accepting and refreshing. You become close friends with people in a matter of hours and everyone's just so, well, different than what I'm used to. It's wonderful to be able to find people who are actually interested in who you are and not your plans for Saturday night. There aren't many places like that left. Plus it's JEWISH ✡ *I hope we're like that for you too - cT*

OOb#2: Soph, we would never betray you to Tyler! I mean why would we? To be cool with him? In terms of that, I'm done. I've wasted too much of my life trying to impress him. Chillin with him is mad fun, but I feel like he's not really dedicated to our friendship. In conclusion, you rule, he sucks, I would never chose him over you. Girl power! -LW

OOb#3: So this anti-Iraqi war walkout that's happening at school today. It's

pretty intense. i feel bad that there are so few people walking though.
→ LATER, AFTER THE WALKOUT... I represented too!
~LN

Wow, what an experience. Even though Stuy was pretty poorly represented, there was such a variety of people there. 400 students from NYU! We marched down Broadway cheering and yelling ("hey hey, ho ho, this racist war has got to go!" "What do we want? Peace! When do we want it? Now!") and so on. I saw lots of Globies, not that any of them recognized me... when did they decide they were too cool? It was just awesome to be united with a group of people who wanted to take a stand like me. This one woman was dancing around with no shirt and it said "No shirts for peace" on her chest. A little over-the top maybe but 5 points for not being self conscious I guess. We got to Washington Square Park (by the way this Stuy freshman got arrested for using sidewalk chalk... WACK!) And people from all different schools got up on the podium and spoke about the war and how wrong it was. It was informative, but a little too radical for me. Everyone was so one-sided, they didn't even stop to consider the pros and cons of the situation, they just went with popular opinion and never really bothered to say exactly what we should be doing instead. If you're holding political protests, you have to have more to say than "The man's putting us
WORD-LN
down." Also, some guy started talking about some Latino Studies program in NYU which was awesome, but TOTALLY unrelated. He started talking about how this country was built on the backs of minorities (this is where the white girl

*Guys, time for a huge apology from Sophie: about the Tyler situation, I am SO SO sorry I got upset @ Julia + Courtney. I know you wouldn't betray me. It was just easier to think you wronged me than to admit to myself that Tyler is a horrible person and our friendship is unhealthy and totally down the drain. Please forgive me ladies.

♡ Sophie

That's the problem, you chose Tyler over us.
We forgive you. And Tyler is a horrible person — CT

hides in the crowd) and, well, maybe true but Latino studies and Iraq? Am I missing
whitey. - LN
the connection? People also brought up anti-Zionism, and I started to get a little agitated. NO one messes with the Holy Land. If there's ever been a touchy subject with me, it's Israel, y'all know that.

Either way, it was inspiring to hear youth speak up and empower me with the ability to rise up and make my opinion heard. I'm kind of more of a social activist than a political activist, like I rather would have been getting something done than bitching about it. I'm not so much into protesting as much as working at homeless shelters and physically making a difference. Argh writers cramp. Time to lay this entry to rest.

Peace in the Middle East!

Julz

Awesome sign someone was holding

her hands are mittens because I can't draw fingers.

→ The hippie-dippie semi-naked protesting woman

FIGHTING FOR PEACE IS LIKE FUCKING FOR VIRGINITY

oh how time flies...

THE NOTEBOOK GIRLS IN 15 YEARS... BY SOPHIE

<u>Courtney</u> – Kind of like the next Charlie (Charlie's Angels), but for 3 hot, gay, beautiful men. The voice behind the intercom. <u>STILL</u> won't let us in her house.

<u>Julia</u> – Really rich, but not by her own accord - tripped on her own foot + landed on a million dollar bill.

<u>Lindsey</u> – Liquered up in some random Caribbean island, not knowing <u>what</u> she's doing. Wears lots of jewelry. Deemed "eccentric but harmless" by the locals. Owns a crappy cabana.

<u>Sophie</u> – Plays guitar at loser yuppie coffee bars for chump change. Still calls Tyler EVERY DAY. –JB

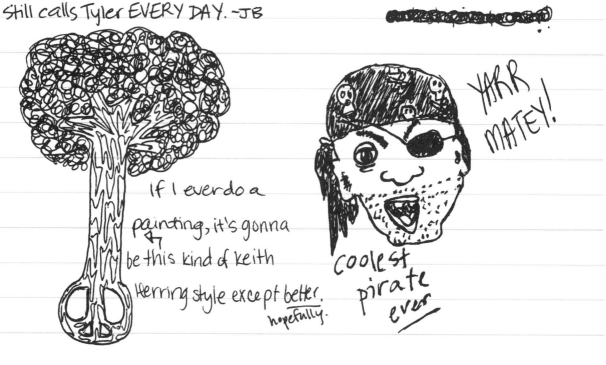

If I ever do a painting, it's gonna be this kind of Keith Herring style except better. hopefully.

YARR MATEY!

coolest pirate ever

11/23/02

Yeah, I'm back on the bus on the way home from the Speech Tournament. It's dark again and I'm writing this by the light ~~on~~ of the Lion King on the TV screens. This weekend was just so chill. The team is ~~$~~ like this new family I love and ~~who~~ that takes care of me. Even though Somph (haha) and I didn't make it to finals, we were so

You mean Smoph? As in Sophie? You and your dyslexi a....—JB

happy to go in and watch our teamates reign supreme. Also after the insane awards happiness, we got on the bus and sang WE ARE THE CHAMPIONS, which was kind of ^arrogant^

That was ill, and so was everything else. I'm really excited to get better and polish my craft and maybe get a big ass TROPHY! (cuz I already got a big ass SO-PHIE) holla holla. It was also nice being with people who are not so hung up on Tyler ~~■~~ holla x3. Also there were ~~so~~ mad hott Catholic school boys, which y'all know I'm nuts for! Ties and button down shirts. Automatic Girl Boners! I get so many at these tournaments that the girl boner goes on autopilot! It's funny how guys go nuts for catholic school girls but they don't even know that it goes both ways. I was reading one of those women's magazines while I was getting my hair cut and they had a list of the four hottest outfits that guys can wear, b/c you know us girls are usually more attracted to guys when they have at least one piece of clothing on. The four, which I can agree about three on, were: — a guy in boxer-briefs with no shirt and a gold chain around his neck (the chain is a little gay-guido)

EW. I hate boxer-briefs!
—SPC

   — a t-shirt and basketball shorts (bc you know you can see up those^ shorts)

   — no shirt and low slung pants with a studded belt ← yeah!
—SPC

AND THE GRAND FINALE:

A button down shirt with a loosened tie. God that is hot. By the way the guys were cool and always approach you to talk. One of them stepped on my shoes in Wendy's and I freaked out (they were new shoes) and he was like sorry "Cinderella." Sophie was like "oh diss" but later he came up to me and said he didn't mean it as a diss and asked if he could call me Cinderella from then on. What a line.

And there was this cute punkish kid who was macking on Sophie. And then another kid from one of my competitions was making smiles/eye contact with me at the awards ceremony and he was cute. So to sum this all up, Sophie and I are so in need of COCK that smiles + small talk make us horny. Or at least it does for me. Wait, did I say that out loud? Ok, gotta go now and sing Akuna Matatta.

                                                    LION KING!
                                         I ♡ SIMBA!!
                                          -LN

   Peace,

      Courtney

MORE words, huh? -JB how about you capitalize and underline some

I was there, I saw it. She had bulging muscles! It looked something like this. -SPC   11/25/02

(hand) Portia

Hey Ballers! Shot Callers!

Just came back from a basketball game → I scored 9 points - yay!! We lost though. But we knew we were going to lose because we were playing MLK Jr. High School. They're really ~~get~~ good, but not as good as the top competition we've faced. Even though we lost, I still felt okay because, damn, those girls were UUUgggllllyy! One of them had her name~~s~~ TATOOED on her arm! That's right, her __NAME__ __TATOOED__ on her __ARM__! What, does she plan to forget it or something? Guys, if I ever come up to you in the future and say something, like "hey, I was thinking of tatooing my name to my body," please slit my throat right away, promise? of course! -CT   don't worry. -SPC

aww -CT

Whenever we go to their school, they have lots of kids who go to the games. We never get the same kind of crowds at our school because the kids at stuy are all involved in after school activities in order to fill up their college applications and no one cares about the sports teams at Stuy unless you have a friend on the team or something like that. But hey! you guys ~~are~~ have a friend on the team (ME!!) so I expect to see you at my next game... Please? I beg. Sometimes the kids at schools like MLK jr. try to say shit to us when we walk in the gym, like "ooohhh Stuyvesant is here" and they

mmm... Thanksgiving

gobble gobble gob

+ a replica of those "hand turkeys" we all drew in Preschool.

my Turkey

mmm... cranberry sauce

PIG!

-JB

try to intimidate us. But they're just mad cause we know how to read.

I gotta go do work now. I have to make up like **500** Chem Homeworks.

Oh my god! It's Tuesday!   11/26/02

Tomorrow is Wednesday! Now, normally, that would <u>suck</u> but it's Thanksgiving on Thursday. I can't WAIT. This is such a fun holiday for me because I get to go and visit my mom's family all together at my cousin's house. It's just nice to be able to chill with family sometimes, especially when you never get to see them, it gives you a nice, homey feeling. I just hope no one gets shot in the car on the way down to Maryland, cause you know, my mom, dad, sister and me all in an over stuffed car for hours can get a little stressful sometimes.

And now, for some random spazes:

By the way, what classes are you guys signing up for next term? Precalc, Classical Lit, French, Chorus, Chem, Gym, Global History – CT

↳ I don't think Lindsey ~~actually cared~~. - SPC

Oh my gawd! Hannukah is so early this year, way too early. And on to oob #10: I feel like I haven't seen you guys in like forever. I haven't been on the train because I'm always late, and I can't hang at the wall because of b-ball.

lazy as shit - JB

O.k. I have to go do work because tomorrow's the end of the marking period. I hope I don't fail. Don't worry, I'll be back.

you already indicated that yesterday —CT

Thanksgiving is tomorrow! Why does 4th period 11/27/02 chemistry always seem to go the slowest on the Wednesday before Thanksgiving? you really hate chemistry don't you? —CT

OOB# La Guardia: You guys have to come up to my basketball game on the 2nd. That's a Monday, right? We have a home game against La Guardia. There's a good chance we'll beat them, so it should be fun.

Quick: Chemistry SAT II question:

If Sophie passes 2.004 mol of $FaRt(g)$ at 79°k and constant pressure, how many friends will she still have left?

Answer: Still? Let's get real here. SOPHIE SUCKS

this is Sophie's + your friendship in a nutshell —CT

THE BIG ONE.

— joke from Sophie: What's brown and sticky?
Lindsey: Your underwear
Sophie: Hey!... well... yeah.   gross! —JB

Peace in the Middle East!

Big L

Hey ladies,
Oh my lord, it's

SNOWING

12/5/02

→those are snowballs!
It looks like the anarchy symbol.
—SPC

Yeah so I ♡SNOW! I just love New York when it snows. There is nothing
~~what about black Christmas? —JB~~
better than a White Christmas. I'll just go to my (b)oobs. ~~no, that would be would be Dave —JB~~
~~the only time of the week Julia takes showers →—SPC~~
I ♡watching Julia in the shower, at night, on Sundays: So I guess this
has been another ~~hell~~ ~~week~~. We obviously don't need to talk about
hell weeks. They are like that kind of noise you can't here. But I gotta
say something about my birthday. I know Sophie already heard all
of this crap from me in front of the lockers, but I was kind of disappointed.
I know it's really selfish, but I just felt like no one cared, but I know that's
really not true. I was too concerned with the material things, like signs,
balloons and flowers. I know that birthdays always suck b/c they are
never what you expect them to be, so I try to make others' better,
but I can't expect everyone to fall all over themselves for me.

000b #paper cup: So I was talking to Julia (wow my whole entry is about
Julia, I gotta love the pussy) and she was like oh, so Courtney psycho-analyzes
people and says all this mean stuff about them but ends with, "But I
→

really love him/her!" Now, this may be true, but I only psycho-analyzes people so that I can understand who ^they are, so thus I can love them more. Example: I was watching Scrubs and the Hispanic girl said, "I know I tell people how to live their lives, but it's only because I'm insecure." Maybe that has something to do with it. But I hope that I've never told you guys how to live your lives, b/c I'm sure as hell not one to judge how people handle themselves.

Speaking of couples, Julia and Cole? What's going on with that? You want to kiss him, you want to date him... you know the bit. So give us the 411 before I call 911 on your ass!

oob# this letter is over soon... I think: Well I was talking to Cindy (little Asian that bitched-out Sophie) and she said, "Oh my friend Malika (who's black) said that you (Courtney) are the only white person she's ever ^really talked to at ^Stuy." And I was like, now that is not a good thing. I'm not ^an idiot, I can tell Stuy is divided racially, but we were barely aquaintances in Freshman Bio. That just weirded me out. And that fucking Russian exchange student won't stop touching me in gym class. Also she hugs you (full on) and won't let go for literally 10mins. Then she starts tickling me and it creeps me out. I am obviously not homophobic, but I just feel like a boy when a girl touches me a little too much. And it's just fucking creepy!

DAMN! The Pinko Commie Bastards

Peace I'm out: C-love ♥ and Special Sauce

12-6-02

challa ladies!

Speaking of shit weeks, this has DEFINITELY been one. I got a note saying I gotta go to the guidance counselor today, and I'm FLIPPING OUT, b/c I think they're gonna tell me I failed chem. Holy shit. I told my parents, and they weren't too pissed b/c I'm doing above 90 in everything else, and they know chem has been really hard for me. But then I didn't do my chem HW til this morning b/c I knew it would only take like 2 seconds, WHICH IT DID (it was just copying like 2 numbers out of the book), and my dad FLIPPED OUT + was yelling and shit. But OF COURSE when I yelled back he got even more pissed + told me to "shut the fuck up." UGH. Recently my parents are just driving me CRAZY. Even tho I know they're doing everything for my own good (bet they never thought I'd say that), and they go out of their way a lot to help me (like reviewing history w/me when I have a test coming up), it's also hard to not wish they were dead sometimes. Like, when I get home from school + sit down to eat a snack, my dad brings over his legal pad where he wrote down a list

of things he has to talk to me about. I get that he's the
kind of person who likes to write things down so he
won't forget (I'm like that too), but that fucking legal-
pad-penutbutter-jelly bullshit is SO IRRITATING!
Also, all he talks about—seriously, the only things he talks
about—are his job and whatever book he's reading/movie
or play he just saw. And he doesn't seem to understand
that we don't need to watch TV together. If I'm watching
something he doesn't like, like Real World or something, he'll be like "sorry, I can't watch this," and stomp
off in a huff. But if he was watching the knicks
game, he would never change the channel—but I
would never ask him to, b/c I get that different
people like different things, so he can watch the game
+ I'll watch TV some other time. SOLUTION: we need
another TV. That would solve all my problems
in life.

we made   On another note... Lindsey's Basketball game
it on the street
with sharpie   was awesome! We surprised the shit out of that girl,
and
looseleaf   showing up w/ the huge "GO LINDSEY" sign we made.
aped together
       -T   Lindsey, we were so proud of you—you ruled the court!

It's annoying how that girl Agnes gets all the fame, just because she's so fucking huge that she can just clomp around + put the ball in the net. You score more points than her and are fast + quick-like a lemur!

→ Woah. I'm giant. I'm a GIANT Lemur. Cool.
 -LN

Lindsey the Lemur.

Alright dolls, I'm out for a tea and a crumpet.
 Sophie

HAPPY BIRTHDAY COURTNEY!

COCO'S Bday was a few days ago!

Mysteriously gross spots on the toilet seat...
 -JB

Hey,   12/17/02

OOb#check out my ass: So Julia + Cole knocked boots? Did the nasty?
no we didn't - JB
Put a bun in the oven? OK they 'just fucked! Ha fooled ya, they just
kissed, but that's ok Julia. So he's a sweetie and all, but he and I don't
really connect well. He has a habit of making everything I say sound really
dumb. But I'm glad you guys finally Sed↑ Like his hook up your giant
↖what the fuck? → it's a hook bitch - CT
-LN
pussy! gross but
funny... bad
visual - JB   H's called PMS honey.

OOb#12: So lately every TV show makes me cry. It's like I've been getting so much
more emotional lately. Maybe I'm stressed, well I know I'm stressed, but
usually I'm not so fucking vulnerable. And along with the uncontrollable crying,
I've been having these awful dreams. Lesson in Courtney's life, I dream EVERY
Yeah, and you never
hear your phone ringing - spc
time I go to sleep. I can't even take a cat nap without falling into deep sleep and
having these intense dreams and they feel so real that when I wake up I freak out for
about 10 mins before I take a deep breath + realize they are not real. I guess that's
why I'm always tired, because my sleep is not sleep, it's like this other life I'm
living and it's every fucking night. In the dreams I'm usually having sex with
Eh... - SPC
someone + it's really fucked up. But I guess the good dreams mostly
balance the bad ones, so I don't go nuts, but lately all I can dream about is
my impending doom. And fuck Tyler! Now he uses that dumb girl
Emily's house as a "safe place" to hang out b/c her dad smokes pot
too. Now he hangs out with them all the time b/c they smoke so much
fucking weed. Ahh a-holes! On a lighter note, CHRISTMAS IS COMING!
                                            XoXoXo Court

12/18/02

Hi guys,

OOb# almost got my balls burnt off: So do I have a story for you guys! Y'all *Woah there.*
know I'm not a regular cigarette smoker, but today after some jewish guitar
lessons (i'm going to marry my teacher, but more on that later), I just felt like
one. So I bummed one off this guy, quality Marlboro Light, smoked that shit like
it ain't no thang, and went home. However, being buzzed and cold and then
transitioning to hot and uncomfortable leads to unpleasant nauseousness. I drink
some water and lie down ready to just puke. Then, my mom hugs me, inquires
about the strong smell of smoke, and I tell her (quick, on-my-feet thinking) that
good one! Tyler decided it would be funny to blow smoke in my hair today. which is true,
not! but totally irrelevant. And then she says, "you're telling the truth, right? You don't
smoke do you?" And I got all confused and was like, "yes... I mean no, I mean
what?" Wonderfully done, I know, but I'm off the hook for now.

So all goes well until my dad has to go and compliment me on my hair (great
timing, dad) and my mom's like "oh but honey, smell it!" Bitch! He smells it and
then asks to smell my breath, which means I'm TOTALLY screwed. So I run out of
the room, screaming, I can't believe you don't trust me! And shove a handful of
popcorn in my mouth and rinse my mouth (no mint, that's suspicious). The
whole thing blows over, they write me off as a drama queen (no one takes me
true seriously) and life is normal. Halle-fucking-luyah *oh lord, the saga continues-SPC*

OOb# Julia and Cole: Yes, there's a new boy in town. We became friends during our lunch period and, well, I'm just really comfortable around him. I can be totally stupid around him and we're similar in really insignificant but cool ways like we both attempt to snowboard, move our hands a lot when we talk, get hooked on expressions and keep saying them, and pinkie swear people when we want them to keep a promise. I know, match made in heaven. Right. I know he's liked me for a while because a) Courtney said so and she knows everything b) I sensed it c) I'm hot stuff and everyone wants to tap my ass (no). So we ended up hooking up when that big group of people went to see the play that Maggie and Tori were in at the hardcore boho lesbian theater in the village. He's surprisingly not as bad as I thought he would be, not that I thought he'd be bad...err. He called the day after (ehhh, clingy? Not good...) But there's no ensuing relationship. Yet. He always leaves his classes to come find me and while that's cute, I'm a bit smothered. There is such thing as too much Cole!

It's fate -jw

Julia you are SO complicated! -spc WORD -lw

OOb# 4ever more, from sea to shore, oily pores, hardcore: Damn. I've peed like 8 times today. That's not my oob. My real oob is about how I'm going to marry my jewish guitar teacher (I told you I'd get back to this). Why, you ask?

a) He's Jewish. God save me from the Jews, I love 'em
b) He plays guitar. Insanely well.
c) He's a hottie (physical appearances are always a factor) and he's awesome
d) Can this man sing! He's training to be a cantor (cantor= jewish singing prayer leader in services) and his voice makes me melt and then cream my

they're cooler than this. pants.

I thought that was going to be the creme in your pants. ewww. —LN

me "literally" melting.
The other mentioned is a little too NC-17 to draw right now. Maybe later.

e) He has cool Shoes.

As you can deduce from the following evidence, the conclusion of Lab #julia, titled **CHEMISTRY IN THE ☆SHUL☆**, is that Julia has found her soul mate. Or at least one of them. Now she just has to be 25. We'll work on that.

Good luck with that. —LN

H to the izzo!
JULIA

O O O

The ladies, thinking and working ↘

Dear Everyone,   1/1/03 → It's the new year!
     DAMN gotta love blunts.
I hate hate h to the ▓ a-t-e HATE coming back to school.
The only good thing about going back to school is seeing my
friends which I don't see much of anyway.
     Oh yeah! Happy 2003!! I hope this year sucks slightly less
than last year. me too! -CT

OOB # twinkies and Hohos: New Years party! That shit was really
fun. It's nice to laugh. When I went out with Sophie and
                    ...yes...it is -CT
Heather, I bought cigarettes for them. They told me they wanted
Marlboro lights, but when I went up to the guy in the magazine
stand I got all flustered and asked for Malr/lallbolo Lights or
some shit like that. Why would you put THREE hard
consonants all next to each other?! It always takes me
like four minutes of prep time in my head before I can say
Marlboro. I thought for sure he wasn't gonna sell to me if
I couldn't say the fucking name, but he thought about
it, realized he was poor and sold them to me. nice -CT
     The party at Zoe's house was cool, it was nice to chill
with everyone. But damn, how much ash did Sophie and
Courtney leave on Zoe's porch? It must have been like
two packs worth. it was, but we were stressing so we needed
           -our fabulous lives are stressful.   them all
                                    -SPC   -CT

OOB# <u>Homie Ass Suckas:</u> PARANOIA: My mom got so paranoid on New Years Eve. She wanted to know where I was at EVERY MOMENT. Other than that, my parents are just stressin' me out. Everything my mom tells me just sounds so critical, and it just gets to me so much. They also don't seem to think I get enough pressure from myself and from school about grades, so they feel they have to double the pressure. Damn, I hate my life.

I know your pain! –CT

OOB# Why is Julia always getting Ass? *Because I'm hot. Deal with it. (kidding) –JB*

It's really cool that Julia and Cole finally got together, but I feel like I don't really know him that well. And I would think that if he really cares about you, he'd want to get to know ~~your~~ your friends also. I wanna know what's up with this kid, and serious mental illness he has that made him think that Julia was cool (just kidding... but seriously).

Eat some sno' with oob# fo': Get it? Snow = sno', and Four = fo'? God, I'm a genius. Anyway, Courtney's favorite season is underway and that means that snow is here! I love snowball fights, they're so much fun. After it snowed this week, during school me and my friend Haylie from the basketball team decided to have a snowball fight with two of our gym teachers, Mr. O'Brien (one day I shall have his babies) and Mr. Napoli. I know you're all jealous cause this was pretty much the best day I've had in the past year, thanks to the undeniable hotness of Mr. O'Brien. So, Haylie and I spent so much time preparing snowballs outside of school to get ready to ambush them. I was making beautiful, perfect snowballs and I had a mountain of them too. When we saw them coming out of school, I grabbed as many snowballs as I could and cradled like 50 of them in my arms. When they were

close enough so that we could hit them, we threw some at them and they started running. Me and Haylie start chasing them with our snowballs and as we're crossing Chambers Street after them, I Slip On The Ice And My Feet Slip Out In Front Of Me and I Land Right On My Ass! Now, normally, this

wouldn't be that bad, but I was in the MIDDLE of the street, like at the yellow line, and I basically fall right on top of all the beautiful snowballs in my arms that I had just spent so much time preparing and perfecting. And, it was

right in front of the wall, so everyone could totally see me fall on my ass. It was really funny, but since it happened to me, it was mostly just embarrasing. But I guess god loves

me, because after I got up and chased Mr. O'Brien, we had a little moment that I will cherish forever. He looked me in the eyes with those big blues, and asked me if I was o.k., and I said yes. It was MAGIC! that's awesome!
                                                        — CT

H to the IZZO
C to the HEEZY

I'm a Jew!

Blah, blah, stupid shit, blah

Julia

Julia talking

Potato

Me

I'm dead from boredom (and seeing an ugly face)

blood

hey! what did I ever do to you? And be born is not an acceptable answer. — JB

why are you bleeding from your pits? Your super-acidic B.O. is eating away at your skin I think.
                    — SPC

★ You know those times when you are mad, but not mad at anyone, and you aren't going to get mad at anyone, you just feel like crap? Well that's this year of my life. But maybe it's ok because this year's only been three days so far. CoCo

You always need medication, bc you're always studying sidr -spc

The black doom that is Coco's life ~~~~~~~~~~ —JB
1/3/03

Greetings,

Oob# 1: Life officially sucks! I'm basically like an insomniac who needs serious medication! Life is sucking sooo much ass right now that the oobs in my entry are going to depress you all so watch out! And I didn't even have the heart to make up bad oob titles! La vie n'est pas belle.

Oob#2: I am perpetually asleep. My life is like a fucking walking nightmare. I can't wait until finals are over so this hell will END. Then there is the break in February. Peace at last. So I just have to grit my teeth until finals are over and then non-stop FUN. Oh, and that foreign exchange student gave me a Christmas ornament before she left for Russia. What a douche. I couldn't hate people more right now.

The only times he's read it w/ me is when he read it over my shoulder. So I never show it to him, in the way you're saying. But I see what you're saying. I'll be more careful about putting the notebook stuff out. -spc
screenshot of the traveling notebook

Oob #3: Tyler told me about how Julia + Sophie have been so showing him entries in the notebook, and he wasn't lying because he quoted exact things like Sophie saying, "I was just so excited when Paul asked me out, wow he likes me." So I don't appreciate people fucking showing him shit because then nothing can be personal and the point of the notebook is defeated. If you want to show him shit, then I can show other people shit, and I don't think you'd like that! Also he was bragging to Paul, "Oh I know everything they write in there, they show it to me!" I don't like that.
(my mom, not Lindsey's - CT)

Oob #4: I know what you mean Linds about your mom being so critical! She fucking yells at me + my sister all the time about shit. Like don't wear that, I don't like your hair like that blah blah fucking blah. Like I don't get that shit from myself already. Why doesn't she just die + leave me alone? Courtney
Haha, my mom yelled you. -LN
★ (hating life all the time)
Just keep on keepin' on. -LN

1/5/03

Hello, yo

Well see I was planning to write an upbeat entry, but since Coco decided to bring us all down (with her very heartfelt, but slightly melancholy issues) I'll just go bum some Prozac from papa Dr. Baskin. To respond:
↳Drug addict.

1) Yes yes yes we're all tired and stressed about finals, and the prospect of studying for them is less than thrilling, but Coco you are like the most brilliant and coscienscious (sp?) person I know, you'll ace them! Of course you will, you're a Stuy kid, best of the best! Ugh. Seriously, don't fret, Mama Julz got yo back. aww thanks -CT

2) Moms are always critical, it's their job to make their daughters feel like there is some impossible image that they have to live up to. That's why female comedians always make fun of the moms, cuz they finally found a way to have a happy life and they know it's worked out better than momma's plan. You just gotta love them anyway, and get them to make you yummy food (not that dads can't make good food too ... don't get me started on mine) holla stay-at home dads who also cook! -CT
My dad def got cooking skillz -LN

MORAL OF THE STORY:

EVERYONE L♥VES COURTNEY UNCONDITIONALLY BECAUSE SHE'S HOT. true. so ~~hot~~ true -CT uhhh... ok. LOVE YOU COCO! -LN having ~~grammatical~~ vaginal issues

OK Court, now that I've addressed your concerns, ~~need~~ on to ~~dish~~ dishing the gossip.
Boob# ~~entry~~ smear: Cole! I am so content with him right now. We've developed

uh oh. Never ends up good, esp. if you're the girl. You are a girl, right? —LN

into a very successful friends with benefits type couple, which is awesome. And we get to kiss in the hallways, which is like the hottest thing ever. It just puts a smile on your face for the next class. It's really liberating to not be bound to Cole, because I don't have to feel like his *that's a good thing —CT* actions reflect on me. He gets a little strange sometimes. But, it's refreshing, and I like that I don't have to think he's perfect for me. Also, it's nice to have someone around that wants you.

oob#2 (just kidding about that oob# only business before): where oh where has Lindsey gone? Seriously, where are you? Hiding? *I'm right here! —LN* This sports team is eating your spare time like Sophie eats Popeye's *oh my god I fucking Popeye's fried chicken! —SPC* fried chicken. Man alive (to use yet another Coco phrase), I never see you. Miss you! We need some serious weekend plans.

I'm exhausted, feeling the burn of math homework.
   Julia Gulia

P.S. I almost lost the notebook today in a magazine store. Can you imagine the hell that would ensue? OH. MY. GOD. *—SPC*
      Yeah I had to go back and look with her. Thank god it was
                                  still there —CT

1-8-03

Hey Ladies—

I'm so dumb. ^(yep.) The guidance counselor didn't want to tell me
I failed chem, they wanted to talk about college recommenda-
tions. How bizarre is it that we have to think about college now?
☆Anyway, as COCO says, straight to the oobs!

[OOB #1]: SO this morning I got off the train @ chambers st
and was walking towards school, when I heard this big HONK
from a truck. I looked over + the stupid guy driving the truck was
waving @ me. This stuff makes me so mad! There is no guy "I think you're
not" move as dumb as the honkhonk. Like I'm supposed ~~to give him an impro-~~ ^(to give him an impro-)
-mptu striptease
or something? The other one I hate is when I'm walking down
the street + a guy says "smile!" Maybe I'm not smiling for a reason,
you DOUCHE! OR maybe im thinking about something, + I'm not
putting on a show for YOU.

my mom told me this story today about when she went to
live in Paris w/ her best friend their senior year in college. Moms
was walking down the street + this creepy guy was following her
for blocks. Finally he caught up to her + asked her to have sex w/
him… in exchange for a stick of butter, which he held in his hand.
^(Butter? Sweet!)
WHAT???!!! I swear to God, men have completely lost their minds.

[OOB #2]: So speaking of guys being complete idiot assholes: Tyler.

What the fuck is going on?! He's officially not speaking to me, for NO REASON! He basically woke up ~~the~~ one day + decided I suck. I don't get it — we go from being good friends, spending lots of time together, to him hating me. The other day, Rosa went up to him (he was w/ one of his guy friends, Alex I think). And now, Rosa/Tyler conversation: a drama in one act.

I know! What a fuck!

Rosa — Hey Tyler, can you do me a favor?

Tyler — Sure.

Rosa — Can you tell Sophie [Tyler cracks up laughing] that I can't meet her after school today?

Tyler — [laughing so hard he can't talk]

Alex — Uh... he's not talking to her.

Tyler is just laughing + repeating "no, you don't understand, I'm not talking to her."

FIN.

What is going on? I have absolutely NO IDEA what's happening. And blurgh. This shit w/ Tyler and Tali hardly talking to me anymore, I'm feeling really alone right now + like a BIG LOSER who can't keep friends. It really makes me appreciate what amazing friends you are, and how much you all look out for me. Because you know what — Tyler is <u>no one</u>. And you guys are everything. I got yo back!

FO sheezy.

I am so fucking white. True.

-Sophie

PS-Julia, I'm going to marry my guitar teacher too! He played w/ Joan Jett, The Clash, The Ramones, had a band w/ David Johanssen, and is the _man_. But he also played w/ The Bangles...I'll let that one slide.

yeahh...mine has cool shoes.
losers   -JB

What up homie g's?   1/16/03

Going to concerts is the ill shit! We should definitely try to go to more (or any at all). It sucks that we couldn't get into CBGB's last weekend cause we weren't "of age." Why do you have to be 16 to get into those shows anyway, that's just stupid, it's not like there's such a big difference between 16 year olds and 15 year olds.

After attempting to get in, that group of kids we were with, like Tyler, his girlfriend Maggie, Dave, Lauren and others disappeared. But that's okay because all the cool kids were still with us and they were only dead weight anyway. I saw this girl I know from summer camp at CBGBs and she was talking to Gracie and Maggie and told me that they said something like "Yeah, we don't really like anyone in that group we were with except Tyler because he's my boyfriend." God, what a lame biotch. I mean, what the hell, we didn't want to hang out with her either, the only reason she was there with us is 'cause Tyler gets pussy from her. After we lost all the dead weight, lame bitches, it was fun to just hang around St. Marks Place and chill. There's such a cool atmosphere down there and cool people.

<u>OOB # HAHA:</u> My teacher just drew something on the board and it looks like a PENIS! Why is no one else in my class laughing?

<u>OOB #2:</u> Sophie don't feel ~~XXXX~~ too badly about your "break up" with Tyler. You don't need him! Especially if he is going to make you feel like shit. You have soo many other people who think you're cool and have always been there for you. TRUE-CT   aww!thanks
                                                                    -SPL

<u>OOB # PARTAY:</u> The party on Friday was so cool. Thanks Sophie for letting everyone in your house. I would be too paranoid to let anyone in my house if my parents went away. I have too much stuff that could get broken or destroyed. I would never be able to relax, 'cause I'd be so tense, praying that everything worked out okay. But Sophie, you were pretty chill about everything. Plus, my parents would never let me stay home by myself. I think they have some ridiculous idea that I might have kids up to the apartment and have a party or something. Who would ever do a thing like that? Big Ups to CoCo for getting the booze! hey hey! Most of the kids who came to the partay were cool, but what the fuck was up with Rob's friend? At first he seemed alright, then

word! Lindsey is God! -CT

he was all freaky and messed up. I kept watching him, waiting for him to pass out and have a seizure from too many fucking drugs (tranquilizers?). But catch me up with what happened after I left. Did you guys ever go to sleep? ? yeah, at like 4am -CT

<u>OOB# Cat Calls:</u> Sophie, I totally know what you're talking about with pick up lines and guys honking at girls. When guys whistle or say shit to girls on the street, what are ~~they~~ they really trying to do? Do they expect that when you hear them whistle at you or honk their car horns you'll drop everything and run over and have sex with them? When guys say something to me on the street, on one hand it makes me feel good that someone thinks I'm pretty or hot, but on the other hand it also just makes me feel embarrassed, like how am I supposed to respond? It can also make me feel degraded and disgusting. Whistling at a woman like you're calling your dog isn't gonna make her wanna strip off all her clothes on the spot and have sex with you douche bag. But, then again, when you walk down the street and pass a group of guys, and no one says something to you, you think "Am I not looking hot anymore?" Well, that's it. I totally agree → -CT

Fo Skeezy, BigL — THE CONSTRUCTION WORKER PARADOX. A mystery of city life. -JB

Whatup lovahs!   1/22/03

So man alive I am hungry! I just took my French Final (oral section - just like sucking dick, which should have quenched my appetite) and the whole class cheated so much! I think I got almost everything right. YAY!

oob#1: So basically life is better now. My last entry was depressing, but the school term is almost over (finals this past week) and that is brightening my life! Once finals are over we have the whole Thursday Friday Saturday AND Sunday before school starts again for fun!

And that's the kind of fun that means everything to me because there is no possible work you could/should be doing! And then we get awesome new classes and all new lives for next term. So speaking of fun...

oob#2: SOPHIE'S PARTAY! Oh man that was the party of the century! Yeah so alcohol rocks my world. That night was fun off at first when we girls just sat around drinking, laughing, listening to Queen, and humping the Christmas tree. And then I dropped and wanted to die! And then Rob and his freaky friend Tranquilizer Kid arrived and really scared me. So then I hid in Sophie's room b/c I did not want Rob to see me at that moment all drunk and coming down. I don't really want him, I just want to chill with him and be his friend, and I know he thinks the shit we do is stupid. Especially drinking, but later he was all concerned + glad that I was feeling better. Then after Sophie got sick we went outside for the second time to have a cigarette on her stoop. Then freaky people on the street were staring at us and I was like ahh let's go inside. yeah! -SPC

It was also cool that Tom and Dave came b/c they are the boys. They are still the same guys when they are drunk, which is cool. We've lost some connection with them since Delta, but that's because we are going through this experimental stage in our lives where both us and the guys are sometimes embarassed to do stuff together because we turn into different people. WORD. And my God Mother Fuching Alex! He like felt up everyone! He basically tried to have sex with everyone while we were all on Sophie's mom's bed watching TV, which is nasty. And we'd only known him for a day! Where did he come from and how did he get into our party? (P.S. I think Alex is a sexual harasser, but I don't want to go there) he is + he made out w/ a drunk girl who puked on him! -SPC

Enough about Alex, let's talk about me. It was really sweet that when I went to lie down in Sophie's bed to be alone, Dave came and played quitar while I was chilling. Then Andre got there and was like, "OMG is she naked? What's going on?" And I'm like, "uh I'm not naked I'm just wasted." The he was like, "oh can I come give her a hug?" and Sophie's like, "Everyone leave!" And I was like, "nooo, I'm fine now." It's just cool that he and I are better friends. We really bonded at the chorus Concert and he was being really sweet. It was nice to get a kiss on when I said goodbye

the cheek from him^ b/c it ~~told~~ made me feel like his really good ~~friends~~ friend.

I felt really bad when we were at his mom's because he was yelling at her in Hungarian and he looked really upset + I felt really bad. Well, in the end, I was dead on Friday and ready to go home. And then Dave + Julia got their freak on! YAY! So you need to ditch Cole, by the way. He is not the (aptain (Dave), no man is.

So much love for Friday ^and Sophie (house) + CoCo (drinks) = fun!

<u>Oob #3</u>: Tyler. Oh Tyler. Well he's officially a dich and sucks cock. I'm really mad that he decided he hates Sophie and plans to ignore her and doesn't want to speak to her again. Whatever, fuck him! It creates too much division between us and him, which makes things shitty. But at the same time it's good because you NEEDED to get OVER him dude! Also, I think you ~~guys~~ treated your relationship with him like you guys were boyfriend and girlfriend, which could have fucked things up. That's why it hurts so much now that he's "dumping" you. But now life will be more simple. And he'll show up much less in this book. Speaking of this book, Andre is throwing paper at me in chorus so I gotta go ☺.

CoCo
Fake Party Photos

me in the corner of the room →

ahh the pain!

lala uhh...

Julia

LaLa dancing!

Lindsey

b/c I messed up! -SPC
↳ why is there something up your butt? -LN

me (Sophie) projectile vomiting

1/23/03

I'm back! God this notebook is like my long-lost kidnapped friend that I just finally found. Poetic I know. More like Crap. -LN

OOb# gluttony: I know this has been covered but SOPHIE YOUR PARTY WORD! -SPC WAS FUCKING AWESOME!!! I've always had this philosophy about abusing certain lovely substances: it's all about the people. If the people are good, the times are a-rockin. And lemme tell you that party was kicking like a horse with a hernia. There were some horny boys who needed to put the mouse back into the house, WORD but it was mad chill. Sorry i didn't help clean up.

OOb# morbidly obese: les garçons (da boys): So I got it on with Dave (again) Julia, you never learn! -SPC behind Cole's back. I feel bad, but it's not like we are exclusive or anything. It did seem a bit ho-ish though. Even though there's no written rule that says Cole and I were "together" sometimes things are assumed even though they are not said. I wonder what he thinks our status is. The one thing that's horrible about casual hooking up is that the terms are so fuzzy. Oy, I remember ever since middle school I've been looking forward to being able to "date" more than one guy at a time and not be in a relationship. Now it's all going haywire. Sigh. Those things never do quite work out do they? Anyway, I said I was going to stay away from Dave because he a) doesn't like me and b) is bad for my self-esteem. But he's so frikin hot! This is not good -LN quite the problem. Well whatever, it's not like anything is gonna come out of it and I don't like him anyway. Gotta Bounce.
Julia, Julia, Julia, sigh. -LN

Jibbles   don't you mean jibblets? -CT

1-24-03

{Hey guys–} Yes, yes, we know: my party was OFF THE HOOK! First I gotta say THANK YOU COURTNEY. YOU RULE! (For bringing the ba-ba-bacardi and etc.) I had tons of fun and I'm glad you guys did too. I'm also glad Dave + Tom had a good time. It was so insane! I'm really glad we had it. But Julia, calling my dad's house + asking for me when i'm supposed to be sleeping @ your house but we're having a party @ my mom's house is a BAD IDEA! *Sorry about that –ss* Bad parts of the party – throwing up (like 20 other people threw up too), dad calling me a million times, court feeling like shit. Good parts: hours + hours of everything else!! I was glad Andre could make it, b/c he + I have become pretty close friends. He's probably my best guy friend right now. Even tho he smokes way too much weed, he's a really chill kid and fucking hilarious. He's also just a genuinely nice guy.

Speaking of Andre, I was reading that entry I wrote a while ago when I blazed w/ him, Sam, + Jimmy @ their band practice + thought I was high ". GOD what an idiot I was! I wasn't high @ all. I was just dumb and a Freshman. YEP. –ct

Julia – I know technically (sp.? Sorry, I suck @ spelling – that's what NYC public school "inventive spelling" will do to you) *Yeah spelling is not your forte! –CT* you're not obliged to be faithful to Gale, I still think he would feel bad if he knew. It's a hard situation and I can see it from both sides. But also consider that if you're wanting to be hooking up w/ other Johnny Cochrens then maybe you don't like Cole as much as you thought.

Peace Ladies
Sophie

Photo time!

wow, what a fridge full o' fun! ↘

mmm, psoriasis! (sp.?)
—JB

LINDSEY IS WASTED ↗

Julia sucks it down ←

I can drink anyone under the table! (if it's a 22 of Corona)
—JB

Hello Lovahnns,   2/10/03

Ugghh. I am so sick right now. I want to die. The only
good thing about being sick is that I got a three day
weekend! But again it also means I'll just have twice the
work to make up on Monday. For the record I did not have this
notebook for two weeks (courtney). The only reason why I
used it for an extended period is because I was sick and
didn't see anyone since Thursday. riiight-ct

OOB#1: The LOOP. Not that I'm ever let in on what's
going on, but I'm sure the time that I was sick has knocked
me out of the loop even further now. But what's new?
Julia, you have to keep me up to date with what's going on
with you and Cole ... or Dave ... or that random guy on the
street. Who is it this week and what's the deal? I bet
on Dave. No Cole ... no, wait, Dave.

Also, can someone tell me what the fuck is up with
Andre? The only times I've had conversations with him, somehow
the only thing he can talk about is weed. "Dude, I was so
high ... yo, this one time when I was high ..." Is that kid ever
NOT high? I have to agree that he's a genuinely nice
person and can be sweet, but maybe he should lay off
the magic herb a little. My dad told me this story about

SHUTUP. -JB

when he was in the Army reserves during Vietnam, he worked as a social worker with soldiers who were in the stockade and some of them had some real psychological difficulties with being in war and whatnot. He told me that some of them would ask for weird ordinary items that they thought they could get high off of, like toothpaste and shit like that. I could totally see Andre rolling a toothpaste blunt if he ~~thought~~ thought it could get him high. It would make his breath minty fresh. —spc

OOB#ewww: I'm sitting here in history, trying to learn, and Courtney's coughing up her ~~fuckin~~ asshole next to me. ew- Why is this girl always sick? Courtney, you're compromised immune system is really annoying me. oh, I'm soo~~oo~~ sorry, is it bothering you? —CT

OOB #Countdown: On a lighter note: **4** freakin days till my birthday. I'm really excited, finally I'm gonna be 16. Let's think of all the things you can do when you turn 16. Get into CBGB's, get arrested... hmmm that's all I got so far. Now for list of stuff I'm not old enough for yet; cigarettes, alcohol, driving, clubs, R rated movies, EVERYTHING. I guess 16 isn't all it's cracked up to be. So I guess my choices are: either we can celebrate my birthday by getting arrested or by going to CBGB's. I say we go and party at CBGB's

get a drivers permit - yea right -JB

Only a week left (maybe) of basketball. Then I'm FREE and we'll get to hang out again!

For Sheezy,
Lindsey

JULIA'S BIRTHDAY NOTE TO LINDSEY! ↴

YAY!

Lindsey's HAPPY BIRTHDAY Page!!!

2/14/03
(the day of looove)

Dear Linds:

Happy Fucking Birthday Man!

You rock the house!!! (well, actually, with the weight you just put on, I'm sure you really do rock your house... wait this is supposed to be nice) You're so awesome and a hilarious person and being bestest friends with you is such a blast. You make me smile when I feel like shit, and that takes talent. Everything is fun when you're around. It's been awesome getting closer to you this year, and watching you change from an introverted, smelly, ugly caterpillar to a beautiful, outgoing party girl (ok, ok you were always a party girl... but you still smell!) Big ups to the big L. I love you fo eva!

2-15-03

Hey guys, check out my drawing, THE MANY PHASES AND FACES

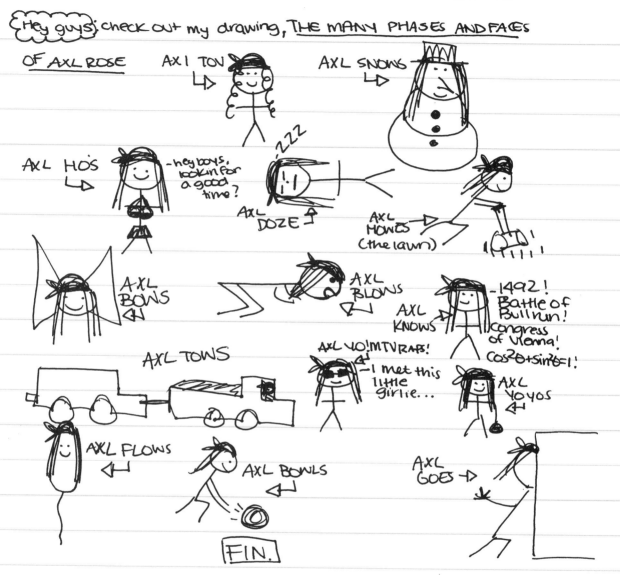

So the FBI's issued a warning saying everyone should be on alert and have extra food, h₂O, flashlight, radio, etc. They also said to seal up your windows in the event of chemical warfare (yeah, rockin the CNN jargon!). While ½ of me isn't worried—they've issued like 6 warnings since 9/11 and nothing has happened,—and the gov is always doing stuff like this (50's "duck and cover"), the other part of me is kinda scared. I mean, imagine if we woke up to WWIII, bombs going off and stuff. I know that's really morbid, but think about London in WWII - it was bombed daily. And that was just how people lived. Either way, I feel like something big is gonna break out.

    000# Protest - so speaking of the war, my dad's job won't let him go to the anti-war ~~demonstration~~ demonstration on Saturday! How messed up is that? If he goes & they find out, they could fire him. God, stuff in our country now is so strange. Well, it was always strange, but right now it's <u>really</u> strange. that sucks.
so much for free thought

XOXO
Sophie

2/16/03

Well hello people...

My English teacher always says "hello people" in this shrill voice and it pisses me off like no other. Plus she looks like the Kool Aid man. But enough about her. Let's talk about me. Straight to the oobs. *Ha! -LN*

oob#1 nation, under god, indivisible: Sophie, I hear you babe! The world is in such a strange phase right now! First of all, it's really messed up that your dad can't go to protests. I mean, it makes sense, seeing as he does write for a newspaper, so I guess he shouldn't affiliate himself with certain sides of certain causes because he's supposed to be neutral. But going back to issues like the duct tape on the windows ... you're right it is really scary. But also, you have to think, how much is true and how much is the current administration playing on our fears. The really scary thing about being in such a precarious international situation like we are right now is that I feel like our government and media can totally fuck with our emotions. When you think about it, they have the power to make us panic, and that makes me want to panic. Or move to Canada.

oob#2: So we all know about this already but for the notebook's sake, I have to mention that me and Cole are officially kaput (that's "over" in Jewish). Now I think he hates me because I broke his heart (or so I've heard). I feel bad, but frustrated at the same time cuz this kind of thing ALWAYS happens to me. Things start out all nice and chill with a hook up and some sexin' (not literally, of course). *Then stop breaking guys' hearts! -LN* Then all of a sudden it's way too attached and pseudo relationship-y. And I never want that cuz I don't have really strong feelings for the person so something bad happens and someone ends up breaking it off (by the way, this situation is often vice versa too) and then it's awkward for a while. Story of my life. My problem is that I feel unwhole without a bf or boy toy. Sad but true. It's such a security issue. Guys, I need you to help me get over this. Don't let me hook up with boys or have pointless flings if I don't like them. ~~~~ Unless they're really really ridiculously good looking.

OOB#SAME SEX : So I actually think I've found a way to solve the above problem, and that is my new progression from the world of dicks to the world of chicks. One word: Tori. OMG I wanna get with this girl so badly! She's just so cool and so not afraid to be herself and she's always funny and so interesting...OK bottom line is that I'm really attracted to her. Maybe it's because she has a mohawk, ooh sexy. But anyway, it is so frikin difficult to even begin to think about how to try and flirt with her or hook up with her. I mean, obviously I'm not a lesbian cuz this isn't natural to me. It all feels kinda new and different but hey, whatever, a crush is a crush, right? But I mean, she's a girl. She knows all the tactics. She's not a dumb horny guy who just wants ass. This takes strategizing. I'm considering asking Jessica for help cuz she's gone out with mad girls. I talked to her about it a little bit, and she said she used to like Tori too but Tori totally wasn't interested in her and probably hates her. I told Jessica that she sucks at giving advice. God this is so hard. You guys got any advice?

maybe he does just want ass. lesbians aren't that different from us. —CT

it's gonna be a new set of skills to work on —CT

OOB# SUPER EXCITING:

LINDSEY IS OFFICIALLY OLD ENOUGH TO ATTEND A CONCERT AT CBGBs!!!
(OMFUG)

(aka she's 16 !!!)

WOOOORD! -LN

*I Forgive you -LN

I'm so sorry I couldn't be there but you had my signs at school and my bday present to remember me by. And of course, the words of wisdom, most of which are just me being stupid.

But yay Happy 16th!!!

☮ peace

♡ love

✡ and jewishness

oh yea baby.

♪ Julia

my cool tag style:

i know. it's beautiful. vvmmm... -LN

P.S. Aren't you proud of me? I took less than 24 hrs to pass this fatty blunt. I mean nbk. Ahh weed.

yum -CT

Hello Lavahs,   2/22/03

Sorry if my writing's a little off, I'm balancing on bottle caps. On to OOB#first: My freakin Birthday. So, instead of going to the concert at CBGB's, me and my girls (plus Heather and minus Julia) hung out around St. Marks Place and had a wonderful time anyway. It's really cool to hang around a cool place with cool people and shop for novelty gifts like a gyrating blue ~~lol~~ balding freaky clown, that looks like it's jerking off. It kind of sucked that we couldn't go to the concert but we had fun anyway, right? We would have ~~m~~ had more fun without you young ass bitches holdin' me down (Sophie). It was sooo cold that night that I nearly froze my ass off. Literally, it almost fell of my tail bone. We *a 2nd f? where? -JB* were wandering around outside for awhile, looking for a place to smoke up, but even if we had found a place that wasn't covered in snow or ice, we never would have gotten the bowl to light anyway. I felt like we were four sad characters from a Charles Dickens novel, you know when there is always some sad little orphan left out in the cold in a ~~snow~~ snow storm. The only thing missing was the english accent. "Please sir, could I 'ave some more, pip pip, tally ho?" *Buns in the crumpet! -SPC*

But, then we finally sat in a Subway sandwich joint and

chilled, or should I say, thawed. Heather had a bottle of Bacardi 151 (the hard stuff, not the sugary stuff) in her bag, and of course, like the genius she is, ~~I~~ Dropped Everything On the floor of Subway. As soon as it ~~hit~~ hit the ground the bottle crashed and broke, drowning her whole bag in moonshine, including everything in it, like her cellphone and weed. It was sad. very sad, and dumb as well—cr

OOB# Vay to the cay hay: Vacation. Man I love that word. February break is the best break we get because none of the private schools get time off now and it's the ONE time we get to hold something over their pampered, spoiled heads. Basically, I didn't do anything for the first half of the week. BUT on Thursday I went to visit my sister at college upstate. It was soooo much fun. The train ride there wasn't that bad, it was two and half hours, but I kept getting paranoid that I wasn't gonna get off at the right station. I thought I was gonna get stranded in some hick town in upstate New York and never be heard from again.

So, I got to College on Thursday night, hung out, got acquainted with my sister's room. Her roommate moved out this semester, so she has the whole room to herself, which just means more room for ME! Friday: went to two classes with the sis. It was pretty boring, but it wasn't too bad because class started at 11:30. College schedules are definitely something I could get used to. Friday night: I had to go to Shabbat services (you know what I'm talking about Julia) so that I would have something constructive to tell my mom about. But services weren't that long, so after we ate and I met some people, we went back to my sister's dorm and got ready for the party. My sister's boyfriend got so much freakin alcohol, it was just BEAUTIFUL. Lots of people came over and we started the boozin. The goal of the night was: Get the 16 year old sister SMASHED!! I got so drunk, it was awesome. All of my sister's friends like me because I was the young drunk girl, it was great. AND... I didn't throw up, so mission accomplished. On Saturday I just recovered and downloaded music, hung out and then returned to the homestead.

OOB# Realization: I can't wait for college. It seems like so much fun. Doesn't it seem like high school is getting kind of old? I was thinking, how much fun would we have together in college? Actually, I can't decide if we all roomed together,

I think it would be scenario #2. I love you girls, but come on, who are we kidding? —JB

whether or not we would get sick of each other, and someone would get <u>murdered</u> (Sophie) -CT or we could have fun partaying ~~and~~ and be able to keep our distances from each other during the day.

Oh yeah. I forgot to document: we met a new drug dealer, Roe a.k.a Dave's biotch. He was cool, except when we were waiting outside, every black guy Courtney saw, she'd be like: "hey, is that him?" and we'd be like, "that guy's 50 years old and is wrinkly and walking with a cane!" or "that's a Chinese guy on a moped delivering food."

Yes Indeed. Ya just gotta keep praying it'll get better.

FIGHT THE POWER

I AM NOT A STEREOTYPER —CT

Lindsey

YEA BOOO!!! FLAVA FLAV! —SPC

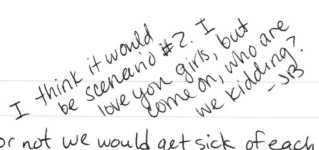

~~Roe~~ a really fucked up **FIST** used to fight the man with. maybe that's why people who try to fight the man always lose. Cuz they have fucked up fists. —JB

Lindsey's scrapbook from her weekend at College...

Little Lindsey says:

College is off the Hook...

DAMN cookies are good. shit.

Some College Math to try:

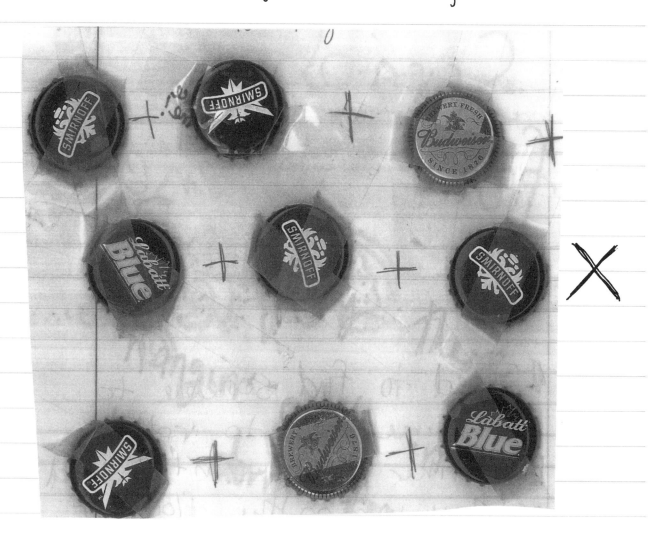

I tried to find someone to teach me how to roll, but either they weren't around, or they were on the floor of potheads and cokeheads that my sister wouldn't let me go and visit alone...

*OMG TORI JUST WALKED BY AS I WROTE THAT

Tokers! Smokers!   2/24/03

OOB#1: Today was a mizz-other fuckin suprise half day! YAY. I loved all of

us just chilling + arguing in A$ (Starbucks) It was just a good connection

I get it! —LN

and stuff. Why don't I jizzump to the next oob...

OOB# OMG Julia sucked cock (for the first time): He jizzumped

in her mouth! Zach-so that's hot and give us all the details in your

But please don't be like Courtney + draw really

entry.   gross (yet surprisingly anatomically correct) genitalea -BPC

OOB#Cole: Julia and him are ooold news. Today in the hall I saw him and

he was about to wave to me, and even though I saw him coming I looked right

past him (by accident) and I think he thought I snubbed him. But I didn't,

I was just spazzing. Oh man, all my friggin entries are always about

Julia... Julia's just my ho. And that goes to my next oob →

OOB# gay: So I disagree with what Julia said in her entry about Tori,*

"She's not a dumb horny guy who wants ass," and bottom line: LESBIANS

LIKE ASS TOO, THEY'RE HUMAN. Just because they don't get to

jizzump doesn't mean they don't get horny like men OR women do.

I mean, it is different, but they still have the same policies about

relationships that men and women do. If we treat them like some other

species then they'll never be accepted. Word. And with Tori, just be

yourself. No games and tactics.

OH... MY... GOD......

And guess what I just found out about lesbians today: some

women can get their clit so hard and big they can have sex with it →

like a penis. Now that might indicate another species.

oob#war: Fuck this world! I hate all the BS we get ourselves into. Fucking BASTARDS! -SpC
war and trying to take away abortion. Suck my dead baby! I do feel that
eww, NO! -LN
retribution should be paid for 9/11, but not an eye for an eye... And
Sophie said, "I'm so sick of 9/11," and I see how that's possible,
everyday
but at the same time you didn't lose someone you love and have
to think about how their body burned to death because some people
didn't like our country. That's not freedom, or God, or anything
right and just, and to forget those people who died is fucked up.
That doesn't mean you start unjust words but you have to respect.
Just because it didn't affect you doesn't mean it's not important. It's
like that quote, when they came for the Jews I did nothing, when
they came for the homosexuals I did nothing,.... and when they
came for me, there was no one left to fight. You can't just let people
vanish because it wasn't part of your bubble.
That's my piece.
Courtney
well said. -JB

→ wonder what
Julia's looking at....
Penis. Probably. haha, esp. w/ the
-JB expression on her face
-SpC

3-1-03

sup ladies? straight (or not, in Julia's case) to the oobs! →

[000#1]: So Julia ♡'s the chicken (cock)!!! Congrats, that's very exciting. I can't explain it, but it's like you're on this whole other level from me. While I'm buying makeup + stressing out, you don't worry, you are who you are, and you get more ass than anyone I know. It's very ironic, I think (in the actual meaning of "ironic," not the Alanis meaning). I know there's a lesson in that somewhere - it's like just the way you ~~feel about~~ feel like you always gotta be w/ a boy, I stress about my looks + shit, which is a lot more superficial. What I mean is, maybe stressing about looks inhibits hookups. But then *totally'.-cT* again, if I was getting mad ass like Julia, I wouldn't be stressing about image. OH the viscious cycle! Ok, enough of that...

[000#2]: Tyler so out of the blue, he called me. We talked + I guess I'm glad. He was like "oh don't tell anyone about what happened @ your sur- *you never did -cT* prise party" (b/c now I wouldn't have any loyalties to him/reason to protect him + not tell anyone about him cheating on his gf). I get why he doesn't want me to say anything, but basically I told him <u>too fucking bad</u>! once he decides he doesn't want to be friends, I have no obligations to him anymore. I don't need to protect him it's my story too + he understands that. It was so weird, b/c even tho we literally hadn't spoken one word to each other in a month, and a half, we still fell right back into talking comfortably, even joking a little. *uhh oh, don't fall into his trap -cT*

000#911: count, i'm sick of 9/11, but not b/c i'm not sad. I am sad, and I'm also sad for people killed in Bosnia, Rwanda, Afghanistan, Palestine, Israel, just to name ~~words~~ a few. It's not that I don't appreciate how awful it was, I just hate the way so many people in this country acted like the fucking world ended on 9-11, but don't even bat an eyelash when thousands are dying everywhere else. Our gov. is gonna kill a shitload of people if we bomb Iraq. And what about last October when we bombed Afghanistan? And it's not like they're getting a multi-million dollar monument erected for the people we killed, nor is Iraq or Nicaragua, or ANYWHERE! Like Julia said, I'm also sick of those stupid reporters asking us questions about 9-11. that is annoying! -CT

Julia, don't worry about Toni. There's only 3 things you gotta remember in this situation: ① Be you   True.

② Do what you do   True -LN

③ The clit. Shit thanks -J☺

i'm out!

-Sophie

3/2/03

Hidey ho Winslow!

I'm in French, ready to fall over. So tired I can't even form coherent sentences. Oy.

Later that evening....

Ok girlies, let's get this entry started. Brace yourselves, this is a biggie. Let's start with MY VACATION.

OOb#1: Julia goes NFTY-ing. —is that slang for something? -LN So I went to NFTY Convention, which is this huuuge event that happens every other year. It's a North American Event, which means that every reform Jewish high school kid in all of NFTY, is invited. Imagine: 2000 kids in a Grand Hyatt with laid back security, friendly people, and hot Jewish boys, my favorite type. You make like 12 new friends every day, some more than just friends, which leads me to my next point...

OOb#2: Julia becomes an official COCK SUCKER. I knew it would happen. -SPC That's right girlies, I sucked the big one. WOW. Julia just made all the jokes about this, I feel so cheated, that goddamn'cocksucker. -LN Actually it was pretty average sized. Ah! It's so exciting! I don't know why this makes me so happy, I'm just really glad to have the first time over with. Here's the full story...

So I met this really hot junior named Zak (spell it right bitches) from Arizona at one of our programs. We clicked and flirted a bit and he ended up being this awesome and hilarious dude, and he likes ska. Always a plus. We decided to exchange room numbers, and after that day I called him (empowered woman!) and I asked if it was cool if I could come chill in his room (which, by the way, was sooo against the rules and I was mad afraid of getting caught with him). Well, one thing led to another and I don't really need to get into the nitty gritty of it all. My only advice: don't leave the lights on, it's weird.

Actually, I will say one thing about the whole experience, which is that while I was in the act, I just couldn't stop thinking, "Jesus Christ, I can't believe I'm doing this, I've always wondered what this would be like, and finally this is it." Well, now it's over and I feel so... cool I guess. It's weird, I always envisioned the act of giving head as really demeaning, a kind of "get on your knees and suck it bitch" masculine power trip. But after it was over, I didn't feel that way at all. I felt so empowered. I was walking down the hall back to my room, and when I passed some guys, all I was thinking was, "Yea, I could suck your dick, and you, and you, and you..." Don't worry, I won't go on a cock spree, ~God I hope not -SPC~ I think we can all agree that I need to chill out for a while. But I just thought it was interesting how you can assume one thing and then experience it and have a totally different reaction. And he told me I was good ~for my first time.~ *How kind of him. -LN* Yes, you can all say it, I'm a natural cocksucker. It's not funny. *yeah it is -CT*

don't get too excited -SPC

Jew to the woohoo,
    Julia

PS- I know I said in my last entry that I'd moved from dicks to chicks, but I revisited my old favorite this weekend and sucked it.

Julia, you are such a fucking flip-flopper! —SPC

sorry, I spilled water on this while I was reading cocksucker. oh wait, that's Julia. -LN

this. -CT

Hello Twinkies! (and HoHos)!!   3/3/03

   Well, well, well, Julia finally realized what she was put on this earth to do: suck the big one. Congrats cocksucker, I ~~knew~~ knew you could do it. Thanks? -JB

   <u>OOB#1</u>: Heather, CoCo, Smoph and me went to "dinner," a.k.a smoked that shit. That was my first time smokin in like a week or two, and it was actually fun, unlike most times when I've ~~freaked out~~ freaked out and it's like a bad dream. I've had a couple of bad highs before and they can be really scary. One time we smoked up next to the huge building complex across from school and I freaked out soon after blazing went down. All I remember was being so high that I just felt like ^I wasn't myself anymore. It was like ~~being~~ I wasn't myself anymore. ^{were you not like yourself} It was like I was watching everything happening, trapped in my own body and everything was fucked up, like a second dimension. It felt like the fucking Matrix, you know how Neo finds out that the world he thought he lived in was actually fake and there were like two different worlds/dimensions? When we walked down the street I felt everything slow down, and then it was like those special movie effects when they stop the action mid-sequence and rotate the camera angle 180 degrees. It felt like the fucking Matrix, no joke. But back to smoking with Heather, CoCo, and Sophie: After finishing

the bowl, we went to the only place you can go after you blaze: Mickey D's. When we were standing in line to order I realized just how high we actually were:

Heather: "Courtney, I'll pay you back the money I owe you after I break my twenty."

Lindsey: "Hun, that's a metrocard in your hand."

Heather: "Thanks."

oh the joys of the student metro card... —JB

MTA MetroCard Student Pass

<<< ← Insert this way / This side facing you

into Sophie's ass —CT

Man, what would we do without McDonalds? Where else can high ass teenagers spend their time and get deliciously greasy food to fill their munchy needs? Where else would all those greasy-ass old guys who have their "McDonalds after dark" parties go? The world would be a much sadder place without you, my beloved Mickey D's. And after every night spent in your loving embrace, while I wash my pores to get all the French fry grease out, I'll say a little prayer for you. (Break out in song right.... here.)

Speaking of songs, SING! is about to start. The annual celebration of senior dominance in our school. Nowhere else can you find such a spectacular display of mediocre adolescent talent in all forms on ONE stage. All year, kids look forward to this event that supposedly prompts unrivaled school spirit and an excited embrace of the school that we usually love to hate. No doubt, the only reason the administration still allows this, ~~enough~~ one of the last events at Stuy left that gives us even a shred of cheer, is so that they can have something to hold over our heads, another privilege that they can "take away." But, I guess I'm a sucker for nostalgic shit that doesn't really mean anything.

So, GO SOPH FROSH SING! 2003! Holler.

Big L

Holler! I'm the Art Director so you guys better show up to help paint the set! -CT

Eat it suckers!   3/3/03 ^{awesome date}

Uhhh I mean, I love you guys! So this weekend was a bust. Friday night we went to the diner Gee Whiz and had slices of cake. ^{mmmm... cake:¬)} On the train ride home Sophie was sitting next to me and this kid was leaning against the door and Sophie looked at him and he looked at her and was like, "I know you from somewhere, but I have no idea where." Sophie was like, "Yeah me too." Then he realized that she was a friend of Andre's and we resolved to only remember that. How small and weird the world of New York is. Then Julia and I came home and had one of our maaad Masturbation Talks on the benches in front of our buildings even though it was mad cold. Since Julia's my homegirl, we share all the secret tricks and shizits. Also how to make guys jizzump!   ^{man, you gave away our cool code. —SPC} ✓

On Sat I didn't do crap until I spent some dollars (smoked some weed) with Linds, Soph, and Heather. That was really fun, but what ~~happens~~ ^{always happens} is people (Sophie) crash really early and then the night is over. When we were huddled together in the park smoking weed in the snow, some guy walking his dog was like, "I hope your smoking something good so I could join you." Cracker, we ain't givin away none of that shit. I just wished we'd been messed up longer. I think we ate too quickly at McDonald's so it all went away. Which sucks a lot.

Sometimes it's kinda fun to be at home and be high, but mostly it really sucks. Except there was this one time when I came home high and I →

Courtney staring at the toothpaste:
—JB

ooch.. red eyes, cuz she's hiiiigh!

TOOTHPASTE!!!

wanted to go home to go to sleep because you know how tired you always get after being high and running around and doing shit. So I went into the bathroom and I was gonna brush my teeth and then I grabbed the toothpaste tube and just like held it in my hand. I just stared at it and couldn't stop looking at it, and then I just read everything on the toothpaste tube. Has that ever happened to you guys? Has anyone ever actually read everything that it says on a toothpaste tube because it's a lot of information. I guess when you're high it's just really easy to obsess over things that are so intricate like that. Then I looked at the toothpaste tube today and what a fucking bore. It was much better the first time I read it.

Excluding present circumstances, everyone takes a million yrs. to ~~xxxx~~ pass the notebook, at which point I've already told you guys most of the shit that's going on in my life. I feel like THE NOTEBOOK IS DYING! b/c ~~xxxx~~ nobody cares enough to pass it along quickly. If you wanna stop writing in it, it's cool with me.

White so I gotta be right, and a horrible Oppressive Privileged Whitey. But I love you anyway.
—LN

Courtney

Hey Lady Lovers

So it seems like lately, I'm having a lot of intense and exciting things to write about. Which is better, I guess, than just wasting trees to insult Lindsey all the time, which is what I'd do instead. There might be some hardcore juicy shit goin down up in here, so just keep your pants on. But first:

whatever, cocksucker -LA

:Ob#1 WEEKEND FUN: So on Friday I hung out with the Jewish friends (woot woot to the clan!), went to Shabbat Services had a little dinner, the whole production. It was a great time, but while I was there, I couldn't stop thinking about you guys and how much I've ditched you in the past two weeks. I really need some girl chill time. From now on, the gals are A-number one on my list.

Drot to be confused w/ Klan -SPC

good, we should be -CT

006# PEACE IN THE MIDDLE EAST, AND ON WEST END AVENUE: So speaking of Jewish, Tyler, Coco, and I had this huuuge heated religious discussion. Linds, I know you were there for some of it, but I wish you hadn't gotten off the train early so that you could have helped me defend myself. I think it started out talking about Israel, probably Tyler attacking my intense pro-Israelism. The conversation basically turned into an argument where Coco and Tyler attacked the fact that I have such strong faith and that my faith is exclusive and discriminatory because it doesn't involve them. Apparently, that notion, especially concerning NFTY and Jewish youth, is like Nazism b/c it categorizes people and separates them and it's like communism in that it's a good idea that

that wasn't really what we said -CT

didn't really work out. And it's also not fair that I don't learn about all
religions in Hebrew school and because I don't know every fact about every religion,
I can't legitimately say Judaism is my religion of choice, it was just the one
shoved down my throat by my parents. Intense, I know.

By the end, I was walking home crying w/ Court b/c I felt like both she and Tyler
respected me less because I believe strongly in my religion, and that's just so
upsetting. Courtney helped me out by making it clear that she's just trying to see
what I see, which is awesome, but there are ways of doing that without having
to put me on the defense. What I realized is that yea, it sucks that not everyone can be
involved in NFTY and experience the amazing things that I do there, but NFTY is
based on a celebration of faith, and if you don't put in the effort to have that faith, then
you can't reap the benefits of it. Also, the people who are involved in NFTY care
about Reform Judaism, and it's a really big part of their lives. Talking about how
exclusive NFTY can be is the same as talking about a sports club that doesn't
admit people who aren't interested in sports. It just doesn't make sense. Even if
you were involved with NFTY, you wouldn't have the same experience because you
don't believe in the reason the organization was created in the first place. My religion
is a huge spiritual commitment to me (i.e. I'm not going on the school Italy trip spring
break because of Passover and that whole not being able to eat bread and pasta
thing). I DO NOT jump in half-heartedly: I am involved all the way, but that
doesn't mean I lose my judgement and my sense of inclusiveness and morality.

It's a part of me and it dictates how I live my life, and though it should be questioned, it should ~~also~~ also be respected.
And I'm spent, a-thank you.
Luv Julia

A visual depiction of oob #1:

Jewish

us!

3/4/03

CT,JB,LN → DAMN, I haven't seen this thing in awhile! OK, OOBs.

OOB Julia & her Jewish strife: OK, we know there was some hostility, but I think there's a larger issue here. Maybe CT said stuff that hurt your feelings, but JB, you gotta start telling us how you feel. This has happened so many times before, when you get upset but just don't say anything. It's not fair to just wait ~~around~~ for whoever you're mad @ to figure out that you're hurt when you don't even act upset. You gotta be upfront + honest. Be the big empowered woman! Have my babies! OK, maybe that was just a scootch off topic. maybe?

I know your religion is important. Your faith/NFTY isn't discriminating — not everyone can be in every group (sorry CouA, I have to disagree w/ you here). But @ the same time, I disagree w/ some parts of NFTY. I could be wrong, cuz I don't know a lot about it, but the "celebrating your faith" ~~xxxxxxxxxxxxxx~~ I hear about seems to consist of a lot of hanging out and a lot of dick sucking. I feel like NFTY wants to have kids associate Judaism w/ fun good times, but that doesn't seem right — it's not a good representation of Judaism as a whole, and what it means b/c sometimes it doesn't have much to do w/ the religion. I realize that from the inside it's like "hey, we all get together, chill, keep the faith, do a little dance, make a little love, share our bond in Juda-ism," but from the outside it seems a little Sons of the Wolf/"have some pizza, isn't Judaism great?" I don't mean their politics or beliefs are alike, just that they both attracted people using methods that sometimes

Fascist comparisons are kind of offensive. — JB

had little to do w/ their message. Also like the Salvation Army being like "you get a meal, but stay for the sermon."

But I'm also factoring in a point that CT brought up – it all starts w/ your parents. Not necessarily "shoving it down your throat," but it's all you know (as in "A Jewish child is all we know," what Jerry Seinfeld said when asked what he'd name his baby). I realize this may sound offensive, but I don't mean it to be. I just have a lot of problems w/ religion. Anyway, moving on to a topic where Julia + Lindsey won't beat me up.

Wait, actually I'm not done. I want to talk about Israel. Julia's bracelets commemorating Israelis killed by Palestinian terrorists got me thinking. I'm all for remembering and paying tribute to those killed in such a tragic way as those in Israel, but I think paying tribute just b/c they're Israeli is like saying the Palestinian deaths don't matter. Why do certain deaths count and others don't? This is like what I was saying about people's reaction to 9/11. Peeps gotta recognize that death <s>is</s> in general is sad, not just <s>if</s> it's on "your side." I mean, <s>we can agree that</s> we don't agree w/ Saddam <s>~~~~~~~~~~~~</s> Hussein, but we can't be like "well Iraqis suck + I don't care if they die." Remember logic proofs w/ Mr. Puerta, esp. DeMorgan's rule (~[P∧Q]→~P∨~Q] and Modus Tollens (P→Q; ~Q, ∴~P). Ok, those don't really back up my argument, but I still think my point is true. Too bad I'm so ignorant.
                                              –Sophie

Shalom! Salaam! What up!   3/10/03

OOB #1: Let me just start off with this whole Judaism/NFTY thing. Court: it's not that NFTY wants to be like "sorry, if you're not Jewish, you're not good enough to be in our group," and be all exclusive. I understand completely what Julia is saying, partly because I'm Jewish too, and <u>that's</u> the thing. I can understand and relate to Julia and other Jewish kids on a certain level, a certain bond we have <u>because</u> we're Jewish, and that's what NFTY's for, it's supposed to promote a Jewish community atmosphere for kids our age. And it's not like everyone is Jewish just 'cause "their parents shoved it down their throats!" That's partly what your Bar/Bat Mitzvah is for, to gain a certain understanding of your faith in an adult way so that you can start to make your own decisions about how you practice it. Because, when you don't live with your parents anymore, it's up to <u>you</u> to be Jewish. Dun. Dun. Dun.

<u>Oob# one more thing about oob#1</u>: Comparing NFTY to Nazism is kind of offense. because the Nazis are a discriminating hate group that is NOTHING like NFTY. And also, groups like Hitler Youth and Sons of the Wolf were meant to spread propaganda and brainwash kids into believing something. NFTY and ~~an~~ other youth groups don't brainwash you and tell you

That was Tyler, not me →

* I understand why it's offensive, but get the history right, ladies—Sons of the Wolf is Mussolini, not Hitler. I only compare them b/c I feel like both of these things got kids to be really into something by having them associate it w/ things that aren't necessarily related to the real issue. —SPC ● What "real issue"? The real issue is learning about spirituality, community and tradition, so NFTY and other Jewish youth groups are one way that Jewish community kids can learn about themselves and build their understanding of Judaism and what it means to them. Maybe your problem is with organized religion in general, not NFTY. —LN

that Jews are a superior race and you should kill everyone else, now do they? They are meant to promote a Jewish community and help kids understand one aspect of who they are, and I don't think there is anything wrong with that.*

OOB# September 11th: Sophie talked about people overdoing September 11th in one of her entries, but I don't think that's true of the average person here in New York. I think that 9/11 was no doubt a national tragedy, but people who don't live in New York or weren't here just can't understand some aspects of this tragedy. I mean, for people in Montana, they saw this go down on T.V. and when they turned it off they could go back to their life like normal. In New York EVERYONE was affected so profoundly and it's something that so drastically changed us that nothing will ever be the same. I feel like some people living in other places around the country see Sept. 11th as a reason to go crazy with patriotism and all that and go and bomb everywhere to show the world how dominant the US is. But, if we did that, who do you think would suffer from the possible backlash and retaliation attacks? Hello, NEW YORK CITY, not Nowheresville, Ohio. After going through something like September 11th, and seeing all the destruction, pain and death that war and violence causes, I wouldn't want anyone in the world to have to experience that again. Why do people think it's ok when a building in Iraq gets bombed and 3,000 innocent people get killed, but it's a vicious, inhumane act when it happens in America. September 11th was a terrible tragedy but it doesn't justify more senseless killing.

I do think that President Bush takes advantage of 9/11 for political reasons, and I think it's ridiculous what he's trying to do in Iraq. If he wants to spread war and more death and destruction, then he ~~much~~ has yet to learn anything from ~~this~~ this unfortunate and heartbreaking event. I wouldn't want anyone, anywhere to have to feel like people in this city felt when we were attacked. It's really horrible ~~how~~ how President Bush uses September 11th to justify the war in Iraq and manipulate the American public. 9/11 and Iraq are two <u>separate</u> issues.

But now, onto our little corner of the world:

<u>OOB# Weekend</u>: This weekend, the party that Jessica had definitely turned out to be a total bust. I <u>knew</u> Friday was going to suck. I <u>knew</u> that party would get busted. But before the party, smoking with Julia, Heather, and CoCo was <u>mad</u> fun yo. not as fun-tho we missed you Sophie-x Smokin at Joan of Arc! After, we went allll the way down to the party in TriBeCa and found out that it was broken up, so we went to Heather's mom's ~~dinner~~ dinner Party which was CRrrrazy. I hope that when I get older I have fun dinner parties like that. You know, even though you get old, you gotta keep things SPICY.

<u>OOb# Heather's freaky English party animal</u>: That English guy at Heather's mom's party was freakin ~~awesome~~ fucked up. He was a creepy middle aged guy who kept trying to molest us. He followed us around that party the whole time! First, we all crowded into her mom's room and tried to shut the door, but he followed us, and then we all ran to the kitchen to help make the whipped creme and he followed us there too! He was so dirty and stalker-ish.

<u>OOB# weird guy</u>: Just now (I'm on the wall) there was this guy in his car telling us (me + Sophie) about how Jesus loves us. He's going to hell.

~~Sincerely~~ Bizziza Bizzye,
Lindsey

* Maybe sometimes its good to be able to recognize characteristics that bond people. And maybe people need religious organizations in the same way that they need women's organizations or cultural organizations -LN

G's ---   3/10/03

So I guess because you all responded to the Argument that Tyler, Julia, and I had, I will once again need to discuss it. My point really had __NOTHING__ to do with NFTY. It's about organized religion in general, just using Judaism as an example. I don't judge what people believe __spiritually__, but in terms of other parts of organized religion, I don't always agree. There are three things I want to say about this and then I want to put this topic to rest.

__#1__: I __never__ said that Nazism was the __same__ as NFTY. It has nothing to do with the principles behind either one, it's just that I find both (like the Christian youth groups as well) to be exclusive. As a Jew in Nazi Germany all the other kids were part of Hitler's ~~~~ Youth and as my history teacher said, Jews wanted to be in it too. _I'm sure they didn't_ -LN None of the teens, Jewish or not, actually knew what ~~~~ was being preached, they just want to chill with their friends. But they couldn't and that caused this bond among the "Aryans" who turned against all the _Hitler Youth didn't CAUSE the whole Aryan nation/let's kill Jews thing, it was used as a tool to promote it. -LN_ others. Now obviously NFTY is not a Nazi organization and you guys are not going to bond together and kill everyone else, but it's the big organizations that separate people by religious beliefs that just don't settle with me. Using the _YES! -SPC_ Nazi example was __clearly__ __not__ a good idea b/c it made everyone misunderstand me, but hopefully I clarified the logic behind me using that in the first place. It had __NOTHING__ to do with NFTY's purpose or Judaism as a belief system.

For me, if I was in a Christian youth group I would __not__ be spending time with any of you because you were Jewish. I would go to a Catholic school and date only Catholic boys. That sounds like the most boring fucking experience to me _ever_! That's me, that doesn't mean that everyone else should care. I would never have met any of you if I had done that and to me, that's sad. Also, my world would be limited to upper-middle class whites.

^(That's a little extreme isn't it now -JB)

#2: In reference to my comment about "your parents shoving it down your throat," that is not something I said only about religion. I just see so many religious people who don't really believe in their religion, they just let their parents force them into it and that doesn't seem fair to me. It's about freedom of thought and I did not say that Julia's parents _made_ her do anything. I know you're a big girl. You believe in your religion with your heart and that's really good and I respect that more than anything.

Damn straight. I wipe my own ass ... sometimes. -JB

#3: I think NFTY sounds fun, and I know you "reap the benefits" of your religion's institutions, so don't fucking (not you Julia b/c you don't do this) put up a Christmas tree and ~~buy people presents~~ if you are so religious. You guys ^(that part's ok but trees are stupid if you're ✡) get cool bat/bar mitzvahs, we got Christmas. And don't give me that crap about how it's all commercialized. That doesn't make it right. I don't put up a ~~menora~~ menorah (sorry, sp?) because it's pretty. That's a joke. It means something to someone and I would devalue it if I did that.

At the same time you guys are criticizing me for not liking that Judaism is so exclusive, then don't complain when Christian groups hand →

out flyers and pamphlets on the streets. If one group wants to stay a tight-knit community it's ok, but if another wants to spread their community to others that's wrong? That makes zero sense. Yeah there are crazy Christians that yell at you and tell you that you are going to hell, but there are also Jews who are so ~~into~~ hardcore they won't (this is a true story) let a half Jewish girl's father read at her bat mitzvah. Either way, don't let the extremes dictates the purpose of the practice.

#4: <u>Whatever!</u> Some of us like religion, some of us don't, but to me that's not really important. It doesn't change how <u>I</u> see my friends, but it also makes me a little sad that there is a "spiritual level" that I can't reach with certain people because we don't have faith in the same things. But I guess that's why atheists and Bible beaters don't get along.

Now on to happy issues:

FRIDAY NIGHT!

So Friday night was chiz-ill. Rushed home to call the Roe-man to get some weed and went with homies Heather, Linds and Julia to 86th and Riverside. Smoked soo much. Went on the weed-odyssey with Julia (snow heaven) and headed down to Chambers Street on the train to the party at the hotel, blazing up the Sublime album all the way down. Then we saw Audrey and she was like, "uh Jessica's party got busted up by the cops," and

we were like "crap!" So we found Sophie + Andre who were with Wes and
Dave (who is hilarious when he's stoned). When you guys sat down in
McDonald's Dave came back to say hi and he was being so funny. He lit
up a cigarette right inside McDonald's. I was explaining this whole situation
to Sophie and I realized it's really weird for me too see the guys (esp. him)
on drugs because our friendship didn't start out like that, and now since drugs
are such a huge part of his life it makes it harder for us to understand eachother.
But the phone is the best way for us to bond lately and our talks are not
about drugs, so that's chill. I guess I just sometimes feel like they think
that it's lame to hang out with us because we've their friends from middle
school, and also probably because they want to hang out with girls that
they think will hook up with him.

Well after we ate and came off of our first (but not the last of the
night) high, we headed uptown to Heather's house and smoked up before
we got there. Lit up a bowl at Joan of Arc. Then we went to Heather's
mom's house, which is a whole crazy story! Basically we get there
STONED and EVERYONE is looking at us like, "hello!" We're foreigners!
Because, suprise! her mom's having a dinner party. Her mom was
drunk and kept talking like crazy and introduced us to Scary-
Statutory-Rape-Guy! He's like 30 yrs. old and works for her mom
and puts the moves on h.s. girls. He was so drunk and GAVE us wine.

Walk it, walk it....
—JB
Lindsey not at
Heather's, but on the
road to nowhere...

I guess he was bored from hanging out with all the stuffy adults so he started following us around. Then he would come in really close and whisper questions and stare at our tits. He kept asking about "the one hiding" aka Lindsey — by the way what was that, where were you?

Then after like a half hour of laughing and being stoned Heather's mom asked *us* to serve dessert! Ahh! Then he started taking pictures of us and zooming in on Heather and Sophie's asses when they turned around. EW-size. Eww. So gross. Loser. Eww I was gonna cry. No that's a lie. But it was still scary. I wonder where those pics are now! —JB When he asked Heather and me to pose for a picture and I took a lick of whip cream and he was like, "oooh la la, none of that in the work place!" EWW! He was drooling all over us as we ate the whipped cream with our fingers while we proceeded to plop it onto the plates of all the other wasted guests. Then I dropped my fork (worst possible thing to do) and I was like omg how am I going to pick this up without making it look sexual? So I crouched down and tried to grab it really quickly, but I could still feel his eyes bearing down on my ass. Then he tried to get Julia alone in the family room. I thought we'd escaped him when we all went into her mom's room to watch TV but he just came in and lit a cigarette. And then he leans in and asks for some cake,

. To Julia – I have the utmost respect for you and your beliefs.
's just a matter of preference of activities. Let's not let this become
uch a big deal ok? This doesn't change how I see you, I hope it's the
same for you. :•

left, but not before we got some more of that wine and his brother,
who was also there, intently watched me bend over to pick up another
utensil. Heather got freaked, but I don't think he'd ever tell her mom that
were were stoned.

We went outside to have a cigarette in our pajamas and winter
coats (which got some stares). Heather, Sophie and I fell asleep to
talk radio and then smoked up the next morning on her roof. Sophie
and I trekked home in the snow and went to eat bagels because we had
the munchies. LONG night, but chill. Still got a liter of vodka in my bureau
for that day. I felt like a true wanderer ~~First and foremost spc~~ that night. I had everything
necessary for life in my back-pack; I felt like a real adult, on my
own. I had a liter of vodka, some weed, a lighter, gloves, and a ~~scarf~~ scarf,
clean underwear, socks and a shirt, my favorite book, my cd player, the
notebook, and about $20. That's just all you need for a few nights in New York.

Ah the times! We had fun. Maybe this weekend again? Finish that vodka?
Today was a good day. Painting in art class started.

Last word on the whole religion thing. Watch how you guys who are
jewish took one side and those who aren't took the other. Again my
                    That was just cause you were wrong. –LN
point is proven. Separation. Not cool.

Courtney

umm, i was feeling spacey?

3/12/03 darkside of the moon! -SPc

SHOOBY DOOBIE DOO!

Julia here, back in, uhh, white, ready to rock the heezy! Damn there's so much to

more like whoreding -SPc

respond to! Sorry for ~~hoard~~ hoarding the notebook, I'll admit it, I was a nbk whore.

I was just sick for a while. And by sick, I mean I had an English paper and a

French test the next day so I BSed my cough/cold into a sickness. Score.

OOb#Friday night: I had so much fun with my girls! God I needed to smoke. I

forgot what the whole experience felt like. Groovy baby. Even if it means getting

molested by a 30-year-old English dude. Ewww linds, when you left me in that room

SORRY -LN

alone with him I wanted to shoot myself. And by myself I mean you. And court,

he wanted to feed you cake! We should've slapped the bastard. The British are

supposed to be refined. I know! -CT

OOb#disappointment on the girl front: Aah! The penis, the hardships of trying

to convert from straight to heteroflexible! I like Tori sooo much, but I'm getting

nowhere. I feel like she thinks I'm so naive! I know you guys are probably tired of

rHell yeah -SPc

hearing me talk about her but I haven't liked anyone like this in a long time, and it

gets to me when I can't act on my feelings. Also, I've finally gotten completely over

Dave (remember how he never called me back? Again? Yea he's definitely done

word! Be an empowered woman! -SPc

with me as well I think. Well, fuck the bastard.) and being with a girl I think

would be a really nice change for me. i always try to talk to her, picture what

I'll say but somehow it gets fucked up and I'm left with that wow-I-really-

want-to-say-something-but-my-mind-is-totally-blank-right-now phase.

And then I don't see her for the rest of the day. We never hang out after school (except for maybe that girl Jessica's party, but we all know it got busted early). I just really want to be able to get through to her, give her a hint about how I feel, but I can't. I hate lesbians! (But oh, how I love them)

Yarr!

Gotta go! Yahoo!

    J-dog

J-DOG—If Julia were a dog, she might look like this
                -spc

← is she rudolph or something?

← Is that a dog, or a penis with really long pubic hair and a big nose?
                -LN

If you ever get sick of other girls, you always have us Jules!
                -CT

Peepers my name
you are really lame
you should be ashame — d

Lindsey's career as
a rapper... just ended — CT

3/25/03

<u>1st order of oobi</u>: So, last week I went to this youth leadership conference, which was pretty inspiring, but once I left I had pretty much forgotten all the shit they tried to tell us and ~~totally lost~~ totally lost all momentary motivation. But at least I got to ~~miss~~ miss a day of school and I got to talk to some hotties that were there. I was talking to this ~~guy~~ one guy, and somehow we got on the subject of the popos, and we got on the subject of racial profiling and he told me this story about getting hassled by the police in the train station. He had been walking through the turnstile, when these two cops grabbed him and told him to step up to the wall. They slapped cuffs on him, searched him and started asking him all these questions, like where are you going, where are you coming from, asked to see id. and other random stuff. He told them he was going to school, but they didn't believe him and so kept harassing him. It turns out that they had gotten a description of someone who just robbed someone or same shit like that, and all that was in the description was a young black male, wearing a dark shirt and jeans. After harassing him, they let him go, but that shit was so messed up. It's so fucked up that this happens in OUR city, I mean, no wonder we're all so jaded and disenfranchised. This

wow, that's not totally general — CT

kind of stuff gives us youth zero reason to be hopeful for the future.

But on a slightly lighter note: when I was talking to some woman at this conference (a young adult, out of grad school, I think) I told her that I went to Stuyvesant and I got a strange reaction that I have gotten before. After mentioning where I go to school, she looked at me and said "I wanted to go there... I didn't get in." Now, what the hell am I supposed to say to that? I mean what's the point of telling me that? Am I supposed to offer some condolences to this heartbroken young woman for the excruciating pain of not reaching her 8th grade dream? Gloat over the fact that I am currently living the dream that she has replayed in her head so many times and obviously still thinks about now, in young adulthood, some eight to ten years later? Sometimes saying that you go to Stuyvesant can be a good thing, but other times it can back fire in your face. Why should I feel guilty for all the people in this world who have something against our school.

<u>2nd order of oob</u>: DRIVING! It's a car! Oh my holy highway! I got my learners permit on Friday! I went driving with my dad down by the South Street Seaport on Sunday which was crazy fun. First

I started out in the parking lot, starting out slowly and what not, but then I took that baby out on the streets of downtown Manhattan, and it was AMAZING. After about a half ½ hour of cruising, I drove on the FDR drive. At first it was really scary because it was my first time driving on a highway, and the cars go really fast and you have to keep track of like 10 gazillion things at once, you know, gas pedal, side view mirrors, rear view mirror, speedometer, radio, keeping in your own lane. Sometimes I drift into other lanes, but *haha -CT* when I almost hit other cars my dad makes a loud gasping noise like he's having a mild stroke and I know that's my cue to straighten out the car. *ahaha -SPC* I can't wait to get my license and then we can cruise around town in my hot VW station wagon!

OOB# Party: So the plan this Friday is to party at Sophie's house. If it follows previous formulas of craziness, it should be off the hook. I need to get my party on and blow off some steam.

Liquor = as much as possible

Hmmmm... who's coming? Gotta diversify the peeps for once and see if we can expand our social horizons. WORDUP! -CT

I need more smokey... chokey *hmm, nice diverse vocabularly there -CT*
  —Lindsey

WORD UP -JB

will you drive me somewhere? -JB

Yo it's CoCo,   4/2/03

I don't have all that much to say so I guess I'll address some common issues

amongst the group:

Someone mentioned how lately it's been the same old routine every fucking

day and eventually you don't really think you have any purpose but to

get through the routine. It's like how everyday I'm at some point in the day

and it's been exactly the same as yesterday and the same as it was for

the whole year. That's what makes kids want to get fucked up, b/c we're

bored and need change. So that leads to the two oobs I just thought of.

oob#1:

PARTY

HEY HO LETS GO

← confetti

OK so it won't be as exciting as my doodle, but hopefully it'll be off tho fo'sheezie,

and not cheezie. And I really need to get fucked up. Seriously, I can't take another

moment of sitting around and being bored. And whatever, maybe it'll be cool.

Johnny! Cock-ren!

oob #penis: Well my conclusion about everything we ever write is that all we

                    I want vagina - JB

want is penis. Our lives would be so much better if we had someone to snuggle with

and lean on. The fucking cock is nowhere to be found (except in Julia's mouth)

and that's just making us all crazy. So that's the point of our lives, not to die

jeez! - SPC

lonely. So much for intellectual advancement or creative expression, we

don't want to die alone. I hope we all don't cuz that's sad.

—— Courtney   WOW. Depressing.
                          THANKS FOR THAT.
                                        -JB

4/3/03

Grossest, yet funniest pick up line ever: How do you like your eggs in the morning, scrambled, or fertilized? 🍳

So. OOb#1: Speaking of crackwhores, where are y'all chillin Friday night? That's right poppin caps chez Sophie! It won't be as fun seeing as I'm there every night anyway doing her mom, but I guess it will suffice. Dave (the bane of my existence) and Tom are coming, and I'll call Wes too and ask if he wants to pop his head in there. Oh my god this weekend is so hectic! Friday = synagogue, then Sophie's, Sat = more synagogue..... Jews are so demanding!

OOb# everything: Ok, so I'm trying to be rational here and remember that last time I hooked up with Dave I got hurt, but I was talking to Tyler (who, btw Sophie, is very jealous that he can't go to your party because of the present lack of friendship situation) and he said that Dave said that even though we're weird around ~well FUCK HIM -SDC~ each other sometimes, it's cool when we hook up b/c it's just for fun. (!) I agree, it's ~I thought you were over him! -LN~ cool b/c there's none of that first-hook up awkwardness and we already physically know each other very well. By the way, speaking of sexualness, a word of advice to ~AAH, Julia! You will never learn! -SDC~ Smophums, you said that you thought Andre might like you but DO NOT get smashed and get with him, YOU WILL REGRET IT! It'll be one of those wake up in the morning and go "man I did WHAT last night?" type of things. Not that I'm the best giver of love advice.

I'm bouncing bitches!

J-money ca$h money

hops! Like what you use to make alcohol! —JB

Hippity hops, crazies! OK, let's start this rollercoaster ride.

OOB#party — Assuming I don't get in trouble (mama gets home late tomorrow night), that shit rocked the casbah! Things got a little shakey @ the end. Since Jules got sick, I kicked everyone out (looking back, I'm not really sure why). But mostly it was just really fun fun times! There were so many fucking people — I saw cats from all over my life.

Sub oob#Julia pukes a lot — Julia, I think you gotta be more careful when you drink: check this out → my surprise party — you puked. Party @ Tyler's — you threw up. Friday, my party you puked the big one. These are the only times I can remember drinking w/ you. I want you to have fun + be safe, so use a condom. Uh... I mean... be careful when you drink. maybe you should slow down. Because getting sick isn't fun for you... or me, which leads me to my next point: BITCH. PUKING IN MY ELEVATOR IS NOT COOL. ESPECIALLY WHEN YOU ATE FISH, WHICH STINKS FOR DAYS. I WAS ON MY KNEES IN YOUR VOMIT CLEANING THAT SHIT UP. YOU OWE ME. Buy me something pretty?

Sorry. I smoked some bad tree too. —JB

yeah that shit was SO nasty —CT

But all in all the party was good fun — glad the notebook girls made an appearance. It was just good our publicists were able to pencil that into our busy schedules.

Being @ the party made me realize something about girls when they drink. NOW OF COURSE guys can be dumb when they drink. But

@ least w/ the guys we hang out w/, they're kind of the same when drunk, just louder, sillier, more likely to destroy your furniture, etc. But w/ girls, there are a few distinct types of drunk I'd like to break down for you, incase anyone (read: Lindsey) is out of the loop, or their assistant forgot to tell them ~~on~~ in the stretch Hummer limo on the way to the party. Sadly, all these types relate to how girls act around boys. Why are girls such idiots sometimes?

① The Zoe: *Gets "drunk" so she can have an excuse to act ridiculously around guys w/out feeling embarassed. By "drunk" I mean she takes a
                          or something
sip of smirnoff iceand then pretends to be drunk. She takes off all her clothes, cries, falls all over guys, and is generally an embarassment to the gender.

② The Heather: Gets drunk b/c she wants guys to think she's cool and hardcore, and also so she can act ridiculously around them. She ends up hooking up w/ basically everyone, including your ex-boyfriend + your mom, though she has a boyfriend. Then she cries. She takes off her clothes, cries, falls all over guys, and is generally an embarassment to the gender.

③ The Michele - gets drunk so she can act ridiculously around guys w/out being embarassed. Wants to impress them + seem like all badass, so drinks 1/2 her weight in vodka, then ends up on someone's stoop feeling miserable sitting in her own vomit. she takes off her clothes, cries... you know the rest. oh yes we do - CT

how so many girls we know are really gross, and all their annoying drinking personalities stem from wanting guys' acceptance/approval. How lame + sad. look, I know even the best of us have fallen into the trap of doing stupid things to make a guy think we're cool + get his attention - everyone does it. But I hate doing it to the extent that the afore mentioned categories do, b/c it is sad. They need to realize that life is not all about impressing guys, and using alcohol as an excuse to act a certain way is really stupid. I love our friends, I'm not trying to say they suck all the time, I just hate to see them like this. Drinking is supposed to be a fun thing you do w/ your friends, when you act silly + have a crazy time. It's not supposed to be an excuse, ~~because you~~ a loophole that allows you to act in a really degrading way that shows little self respect. As I told Julia once before, because you looove me! aren't all entries about Julia? -CT be you, do what you do, the clit.

bob #something : Julia, (why is my whole entry to Julia?), I agree - hooking up w/ Andre probably would be a bad idea, b/c we're becoming such good friends + hooking up w/ him could lead to a weird situation. But then I keep finding myself being flirty w/ him, so @ first I'm like "what am I doing?!" but then I realize he's doing it too, and it's not any Madison avenue one way street bullshit, it's West End Avenue (2ways). Then I wonder what's going on, because I don't think I like him like that. Or maybe I do. No, I definitely don't. What the fuck?!

So... my life is fascinating. I went to the movies w/ my parents yesterday - even tho they're divorced they're still good friends. I realized I am so lucky to have that - b/c so many people I know have divorced parents that HATE eachother. It was fun, b/c as much as I rag on my parents + occasionally want to strangle them in their sleep, they're actually hilarious people. And it was fun to do something as a family. Til they started talking about the economy + I lost them completely.

-Lotta love on the upper west side!

Sophie

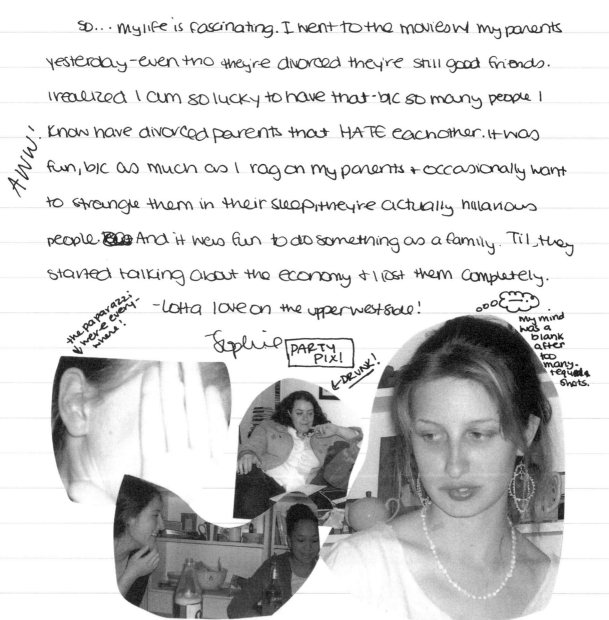

AWW!

the paparazzi were every-where!

PARTY PIX!

← DRUNK!

ooo

my mind was a blank after too many. tequila shots.

Yesterday was 4/20, and we had a real good celebration for this holiday, otherwise known as *National Weed Day*. Me, Sophie and peoples went to Heather's house and the guys came over. Later, Julia came too, but she missed the heart attack moment: Heather's mom came home!! We were all in the bathroom getting ready to hotbox that shit, and suddenly I hear some grown up voice and Heather jumps into the bathroom, turns off the lights and is like "MY MOM IS HERE!" At that point my heart is going like 50 beats a second. Now, trying to keep six boys who are already messed up and have lots of little things to play with in a very small enclosed space isn't easy. But then crisis averted and her mom left. So then we wasted no time in lighting that shit and I nearly coughed up my uterus. At one point I had to leave because it was actually too much. But after we finished smoking, it was cool just chillin with everyone in the dining room, listening to music ... eating cheese. There's nothing like apples and cheddar when you're blazed. ~~oru~~ yum! -CT

that w as the scariest time ever!

soap and toothbrushes right? -CT

-I enjoyed playing "hava nagila" on the piano. -SPC

4/27/03

Back... back again... HERE I AM! Tell a friend yo! Gots to record what happened for the rest of the week. I know you guys have heard this ~~am~~... but I gots to record it for the notebook.

On Wednesday I went over to meet Heather, Sophie and

throat. What was that? —CT
cotton mouth. SPC

*didn't you guys call Tyler + Andre to see if they knew what to do? yeah, but they were NO help as usual —spc

stuck in my throat

you guys tried to make me eat french fries — they kept getting

CoCo at Soph's house. I'm a walkin down the street and I see Heather meeting Roe on the corner. I go to blockbuster just ONE block away on Broadway to drop off a movie and then right to Sophie's. I get upstairs and they're just finishing up their bowl. They smoked that shit FAAAST. We go outside to Mickey D's and by about 89th street CoCo's feeling it. Then at about 86th street she starts to freak. We got to McDonald's and we're trying to figure out what to do. CoCo is crying one second and staring off into space the next. She didn't even let us finish our meals, so we left to go back to Sophie's so she can sleep it off. On the way we gots to call her momma.*(This is why you don't tell your parents you'll call them later when you plan to be fucked up.) We call to tell her Courtney's sick and when we call her back at Sophie's house she flips out and starts yelling about drugs and other such preposterous accusations. So CoCo gets even more freaked and we tell her mom to come get her. Coincidently, this was the first time I'd ever met Courtney's mom (what a nice way to introduce myself, "hi, I'm Lindsey, and you're daughter is fucking HIGH.") After that we didn't see CoCo for like 2 weeks!! How was rehab? We go back upstairs, crisis averted somewhat, and let our bloodpressures settle back down while we wait for Julia to come over and we play homemade Scattegories! It was mad fun yo. FREAKY SHIT: The

I didn't ACTUALLY go to rehab. ↓ Rehab = my room, grounded. —CT

Yeah, but Scattergories was a
crazy time
-SPC

next day I was at home and my mom walks into my room and small
talk, small talk and she says "show was Scattegories?" And I'm like
"how do you know?!" And she says "a mother never reveals her goddamn
mothafuckin sources." F to the R to the E-A-K-Y! Anyway...
Scattegories was maaad fun until it got worn out and old (like
Sophie's pussy.)

Saturday: Par-tay at Sophie's abode. That party lasted soo long.
Courtney, you were very missed. Oh yeah... Julia, you too were... missed.
It's a good thing that you're over Dave now because he brought his
new girlfriend with him. Of course she's not nearly as cool as you. ^not at all -CT
List of Playas (people who were there): Tom, Dave, Amy, Heather,
Patty, Gabby, Sophie, Tyler, me, Andre, Allie, Michelle in the
beginning, and that's it, pretty much the usual party crew. We
partied all night... literally. I smoked and drank so much I was
glazed aalll night... until about 5 in the morning. It was so
chill to be with good company and good substances. Oh yeah, I
blew up Allie's hands with some lighters and air freshner. She
was aight though.

I guess I shouldn't tell Sophie not to get involved with Andre...
cause she already did. I went on a beer run with Dave and when
I came back, I open the door (to the room where everyone was chilling

<u>before</u> I left) to give people their forties and the next thing I know Sophie and Andre were in there goin at it. Sorry about walking in on you guys, but nobody fucking warned me. But, just remember, don't get too attached too soon, 'cause that could possibly get to be a really suckey situation... and I don't mean the cock. (Although you should do yo' thang.)

Proof that Tyler is a S-L-U-T:

At the party I slept in the big bed with Tyler and Patty. I was pretty spent so I fell asleep earlier than everyone else. About an hour later I woke up to the sounds of two people in the bed next to me hooking up. I was laying on my side with my back to them, but I couldn't move or they'd have known I was awake and that would've been <u>Really</u> awkward. So, of course once I wake up I can't go to sleep among the sounds of those two ho bags in the bed next to me and I'm stuck not being able to move or speak or breathe to loudly and enduring one of the most uncomfortable experiences in my life. Imagine having to listen to the sounds of people laying RIGHT NEXT to you grunting and sighing and rubbing and... aghhh. So, in the end, she jerked him off and I almost had to go to therapy. Why this was SO wrong: ① I was IN THE BED (I mean at least have some

that sounds really painful -CT

courtesy). ② Patty and Tyler are only friends, not "friends with benefits," or even that close to each other. ③ Tyler said the only reason he hooked up with her was because she was "there."* So basically, he was horny, she had a pussy, and Tyler has ZERO respect for other people. Present company included.

But Courtney's gonna have an asscrack explosion if I don't give her the notebook soon, so I gots to go.

~ Lindsey

The Bed Of Lies

*well you were "there" too, good thing he didn't try to make it a threesome
—CT

Tuesday was Judgement Day.   4/30/03

It was about 10am and we made the fucking dumbass decision to smoke up ~~during the day~~ in ~~plain sight~~ in the playground under the highway near the river. We squatted down behind a pillar in the basketball courts and I held the weed so Sophie could empty out a cigarette to use as paper. I could feel we were going to get caught, and well, then we did. I'm hanging my head towards the ground and I see shiny black boots and I know it's over. I look up and it's like my whole future just flashed before me. He's talking but I have no fucking clue what he's saying, and then Officer Gomez is slapping the cuffs on Sophie, because she was the only one technically holding the weed at that moment. I had just handed it to her a second before, a mere second that probably saved me. I could ~~still~~ feel the impression of Roe's weed jar in my hand from just a moment before, but now I was hastily walking behind Sophie who was hauled to the police van and had to get in the back. Heather and I sat there for a while trying to ~~understand~~ understand everything as Gomez takes down Sophie's phone numbers. He couldn't arrest her b/c she was only 15, but Heather and I had just turned 16, which meant we could have been in a lot of trouble.

Luckily, Sophie's pea-brain thought hard enough to call Rick, her sexy guitar teacher, and have him pretend that he was her uncle, because apparently if he picked her up that would be enough to

haha, best phone convo. exer: GOMEZ - Excuse me, do you have a niece?
RICK - NO.
GOMEZ - A niece named Sophie?
RICK - NO.
GOMEZ - A niece named Sophie who goes to Stuy-
vesant?
RICK - uh... Yes! where is she? Is she ok?
-SPC

let her go. I mean if I had been holding that weed at that moment,
I would have been 16 yrs. old and had no "uncle" to call and
rescue me. It would have been over. Rick came to pick us up two
hours later and all is freedom.

Well when ~~you couldn't~~ you couldn't think my Spring Break could get
any greater, Wednesday happened, the first day of the rest of
my life. Heather and I met Roe around 6-ish and we met Sophie
at her house to smoke up. We were leaning out the window trying not to
get the room messed up and we must have smoked 6 bowls each
and real real fast too. The weed was great, as usual, and hit hard
really fast. Then Lindsey came and we decided to go out and I just
started freaking out. We were in the elevator, which is totally blue and
small, and it started to cave in around me and it was all bad shit
from there. I guess you can't really explain a drug freak-out to
someone until they've had one. It's honestly the worst thing in the
entire world and I couldn't live one ever again if you paid me a million
dollars. The hallucinations are so fucked up that deep in your heart
you know everything is ok and you are trying to shake yourself
out of this mental fuck but your mind is playing so many tricks on you
that you can't even trust yourself. To lose trust in yourself is the
most frightening thing in the entire world because you are battling two

different people. I know that I was screaming that I was going to die and everything, and that might have sounded crazy, but that's how it feels. It's the closest I've ever felt to dying, I guess.

Eventually I realized that I had to call my mom, and that she was going to find out about everything. Basically my mom has no experience with drugs or anything like that so she freaked out and called my sister. She ~~too~~ explained to my mom that I ~~yesterday~~ probably had a bad reaction to the PCP (which weed is cut with a lot), because you guys were ok, and that all we could do is put me to bed. My mom came to pick me up all frantic and she just held me in the cab and took me home to my bed. My parents were real worried and sad and my dad just sat by my bed and held my hand until I fell asleep. It took me until midnight to really come down and for the rest of the week I was really out of it and couldn't sleep and had vicious nightmares.

Once my parents knew I was ok they started in with the guilt. My mom wasn't mad, but she ~~kept~~ kept asking me, "Why would you do that? You almost <u>died</u>!" Ah! She is so naive! Mostly they didn't ground me or anything, they just did the whole disappointed routine, which is much worse. That's the worst part. The looks on their faces. They hugged me a lot and randomly asked me if I was "ok?" and said that they were glad "I'm still here." They're

just worried because they said, "this isn't like you." (ha right)
And my mom was like, "so what else have you done? Is it in the ~~line~~^the
Notebook?" Those questions make me really uncomfortable
because it brings us all into the problem. Sophie, you are lucky
you have "teenage parents"!

So I guess I'm off weed for a while, I DO NOT want a repeat
of last week. Thus alcohol is my new best friend. Possible party
at Julia's this weekend? Yay. Soph, spill the freaky, nasty
details about your blowout •hookup with Andre? Good kisser?
How far did he/you get? Give us the hookup? Julia and Marc
maybe get back together? Lindsey (always out of the loop), he's the
hot SSAC (student social action committee)
guy who will save the world + give us
wet dreams – SPC Thanks... LN

Today that senior Lucas walked by and Carlo Jones asked
him for a cigg and Lucas handed him the one he had in his
mouth, which Carlo then gave to me, and I smoked it, and
essentially ~~we~~ made out with hottie Lucas. Word, here's
proof.

→ the part we both
touched with our lips

Made it through the rain.
Courtney

the
rain
– JB

5/4/03

Word to the lovers and the hip huggers! (random?) Answer: yes! -LN

I'm back from my homework hibernation period and I missed everyone. I feel so out of touch with you guys! I've been working for like 4 hour blocks every night and I still have an 89 average! How??? I'm pretty exhausted (my body is trashed - it's like diseases are bargain shoppers and my body is having a dollar day sale) and on top of all that trying to ~~B~~ eat healthy (excluding ice cream) and trying to find ass (Tori just wasn't receptive, I dropped it), I need you guys right now to be my gossipy, shallow, hilarious, and dependable old buddies. Basically, everything you're good at.

excuse me? well you're ugly-SPC

OOb#1: Possible ass for Julia? So as I said, I'm pretty ready to give up on Tori. I was feeling pretty low, until I was talking to this girl Annie (u know, the really hot one with dreds) and she was like, "Do you know how many people in NFTY have crushes on you?" so I pried more with a skeptical "well, who?" and she said "what about me?" Yahoo! I, of course, being suave, took the opportunity to say "we'll work something out" and then we pecked in like a friendly way. So maybe hit up Annie? I mean I've been wanting a girl, I know she's ~~experienced~~ experienced like that, she's maaad hot, really fun, a NFTY and school friend, and she seems mature enough to be able to handle just a hook up.

B/C there's a cash prize-SPC

Speaking of sex, why do I feel like suddenly there's a mad rush to have sex? It's like the whole world is rushing to get the "dreaded first time" out of the way. I can wait goddammit! Sex is for people in long, healthy relationships... or friendships if you get bored. I do <u>not</u> want to grab the next hot guy I meet and make babies with him, and I feel like everyone else does! I feel like I'm in that movie Bambi in the spring scene when everyone starts falling in love, and I'm the nasty old owl who's all alone and keeps giving everyone weird looks. You know something's wrong when you're that guy.

The lovely virgin
Julia

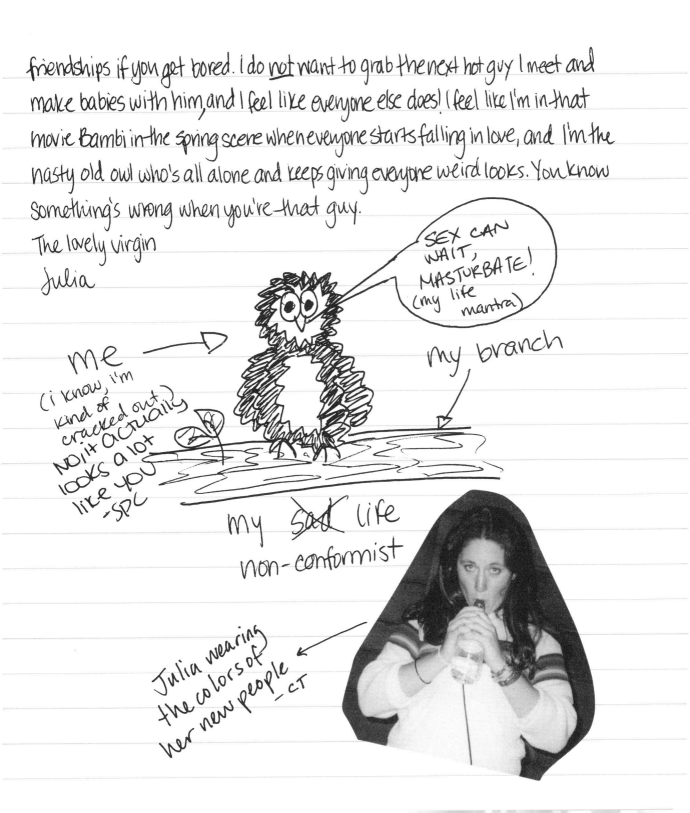

SEX CAN WAIT, MASTURBATE! (my life mantra)

my branch

me
(i know, i'm kind of cracked out) No! it actually looks a lot like you —SPC

my ~~sad~~ life
non-conformist

Julia wearing the colors of her new people —CT

Crackeross Whiteys + Lindsey- so much to write about!

odd#1- Back to the bust. Scary stuff, but I have to say, a part of me felt cool when they put the cuffs on. All I could think was "I feel like 50 cent!.... oh man, I'm the biggest cracker alive!" I always do that- in times of crisis, I can never be scared. I think the dumbest thoughts because I just can't believe the thing is actually happening. But OH MAN, my "pea brain" kicks ass for calling Rick, the best guitar teacher in the world, who was awesome + saved our lives. So we gotta 1) be more careful and 2)... yeah, I guess that's it. Not much else to say about that.

odd#2- Hungarian Hardons. So @ my party, last Saturday, the TV was on + that movie The Ring was playing. Tyler, Heather, Andre, + I took a break from the festivities to watch it for a bit. I was too drunk- like don't-know-what's-happening-drunk, and then somehow I was hooking up w/ Andre. Then those other cats left the room + we hooked up some more, *That was only ONCE.... Sorry! -LN* and also got walked in on a bunch (Thank You Lindsey Rachel Newman). It was so nice b/c that night we slept on the couch all snuggly + sweet. *OMG! exciting!-CT* We've been hooking up ever since, and, as stated by Julia, kissing in school is AWESOME. Yes, Jules, it is cool beans. At Julia's party, I was pretty apprehensive about *how to act around* him @ first, b/c we haven't really established where we stand. But then it was fun, + we got to sleep in the bed together... Julia's bro's bed is tainted! It's nice feeling so comfortable around him, esp. w/ my body. It's like a breath of fresh air. or fresh penis. But yeah, not knowing where we stand = scary. Sometimes I worry he doesn't want to hook up w/ me, so I'm only able to relax when the next kiss comes - as in "whew, ok, now I know I'm not embarassing myself." On the other hand, I'm not sure if I want to go out w/ him. Well... I dunno. It's so confusing. I know I'd be sad if he hooked ↑ w/ someone else, but do I like him enough to date him? Also, I know I can lose interest in a boy like that (aka me snapping my fingers), and I worry a commitment would freak me out + make me lose interest faster. Ah, this is such a catch 22... like the band! Speaking of which, Andre has got to stop wearing that catch 22 shirt every day + investigate the contents of his closet more carefully.

Other Andre news is I kinda want to give him head, but I'm scared b/c I've never done it before.

Hey court, was that really that fun to feel? -JB

hey! I was tired! -CT

Sophie

←why is court wearing a bandage on her hand? she must have been really wasted!

AS ALWAYS, NB. GIRL PARTY Photos!

Julia is our ←little ray of sunshine! I am.

get your hands off my vodka!

True.

Grrrrr

that happens w/ me + my parents all the time
—SPC

Trunk o' Trunk o' burning Love!   5/12/03

word to your mom literally. —CT

OOB#1: Parentals Man, I hate it when I want to talk to my mom and my dad is there and I'm talking about make up or my period or some girl stuff and my dad comments on the conversation and I'm like this is a GIRL conversation and you can't comment. I hate when he just has to come into the conversation even if he doesn't really have anything to say, he just has to be included. And the comments aren't even productive, they're just jokes or shit like that. I mean, I love my dad and all, but some things are just MOM topics, sometimes you just need that special love and support from Mommy. Dads have their own

awww true -CT

special stuff, like hugs, basketball games, making you feel protected, teaching you how to ride a bike, etc. ANOTHER thing about parentals, I hate when parents have these moral expectations and standards for you that they don't even hold for themselves. I say they should Act on what they preach, and then I'll listen to them.

OOB#2: Trunk o' burning love. I just looked in my trunk where I keep my stuff and where I also hide my alcohol, and it made me really happy. I'm talking B-B-Bacardi (two kinds), 40 oz., vodka, some Jack Daniels and some Tequila. The only reason I have all this shit is because at the end of all the parties and chill nights we've had recently, there's always stuff left over and therefore gets taken back to my room to be stockpiled for future events. But now we need

i have a drawer clicked right? —CT

or just for you —CT

to find a new place to party 'cause I heard Sophie's Il Duce fascist super in her building finally busted her. So we need to find that new place so we can use my stash. └→that he did.
                                                      - SPC

    That leads me to my <u>3rd oob</u>: Jesus ——→ (Pronounced Hay-sus, unlike the messiah) New hottie on the radar. He's in my chem class and my homeroom and I always thought he was hot, but now I've recently had contact with him, in labs and such. He's really nice and actually looks you in the eyes when he talks to you as well as just genuinely talks to you about you. It would be really cool if he was friends with people we knew and invited him to one of Sophie's parties (that won't exist anymore). Plan: get drunk and tap that ess.

    <u>Reasons Jesus is hot:</u> (feel free to add)

1. Hispanic . . . . At our school, any kind of diversity is hot. AND I think he speaks Spanish = Really hot

2. Athlete. . . . . Sorry, but that's just an added bonus, even though he's not very good at basketball, but you can't have everything.

3. He's ▮▮▮▮nice, not intimidating or anything

4. He has rhythm. . . . . As a woman of color, I feel like this is very important.

5. They treat girls well. - CT

6. Their mom moms cook good food. - CT

OOB#4: Saturday Sex: Sex scare on Saturday! OK, so on Saturday there was a big hangout/party at Sophie's house (of course) and Sophie and Andre hooked up (of course). What was scary about this time was: I was sitting in the living room with a bunch o' people and Tyler comes in saying stuff like "Sophie just asked me for a condom." And I'm just thinking "no way," 'cause it was so out of the blue, and Sophie hasn't talked about the possibility yet. But, then Dave and Tom say that Sophie and Andre asked them for condoms too. And I'm thinking "they're not gonna have sex... but why did they ask so many people for a condom?" And then I thought, "well, at least I'll win 2 Bucks!" That's right, 2 dollars SCORE!! (for the bet we had that Sophie would have sex before sucking cock; damn we know our friends so well) But later Sophie comes out and tells me 'bout what happened... don't worry, no SEX! Apparently, Andre didn't think it was a good idea for them to "do the nasty" at that time, especially 'cause Sophie was pretty WASTED. But I think it's really cool that Andre was watching out for you and said no on Saturday and didn't want to take advantage of you. me too. —cT

OOB#5: Sexy Andre (is that even possible? Just kidding... but seriously.) PLEASE think about possible sex with Andre before you make any kind of decision. Losing your virginity is a one time thing that you can't take back.

<u>Reasons To Wait (at least for now)</u>

1. You two haven't been "together" for more than two weeks. So far this is just a casual hookup relationship. Having sex will DEFINITELY change it. Are you sure you want that?

I'll said - CT

2. If you aren't ready to have a serious relationship (i.e. you get freaked when people like you. examples: Paul, Hunter, etc... others?) Maybe that's a sign you're not ready for sex either.

3. You were both drunk and/or High at the time. Drugs + Alcohol + Sex = fun <u>or</u> regret.

<u>OOB#6</u>: Tobacco may~~be~~ be whacko, but it works for me:

I've realized that I've become more comfortable with smoking cigarettes, especially because so many of our friends now smoke. This gets me a little worried because I used to feel so adamant about not smoking (for myself, whatever other people choose to do is cool with me) and I thought it was bad for your moral and physical health. But now, it doesn't seem like it's so bad and I worry that maybe I'm compromising my beliefs and I wasn't as much as an independent thinker as I thought. I definitely don't want to be addicted or anything, but is a cigarette now and then so bad?

Aight, I'm OUT.

nope! -CT

Lindsey

P.S. When I told you guys a while ago about Patty and Tyler hooking up, that was meant to stay between us. I just found out that somebody (JULIA BASKIN) told the story to Tom, who told EVERYONE. The reason I care that people know about this is that now Patty and Tyler know that of course the only person who could have told people this story is me. Which makes me look sneaky and like I was talking behind their backs. Which I was, but that's beside the point.

Woa! So much to say,

Oob #1: On that note, Sophie and Andre are such cuties. But you really gotta get that kid off weed. That needs to be something he does before he ends up with no life... So anyway I really respect Andre for not fucking you when you were wasted at a party. He isn't the guy I thought he was (the fuck 'em and leave 'em type). You should consider the fact that sex does change everything and often fucks up the relationship in the bad kind of "fucks up" way, not the good kind. But I'm so proud that

you guys were going to use a condom. That's really mature and smart. Speaking of ~~proud~~ proud that goes into my next piece; When we went to Julia's service at her ~~synagoque~~ synogoque on Friday, I was so proud of her!

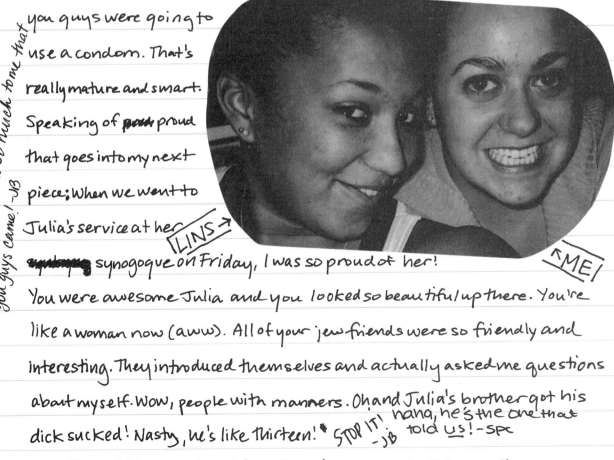

LINS →

^ME

I think it means so much to me that you guys came! -JB

You were awesome Julia and you looked so beautiful up there. You're like a woman now (aww). All of your jew friends were so friendly and interesting. They introduced themselves and actually asked me questions about myself. Wow, people with manners. Oh and Julia's brother got his dick sucked! Nasty, he's like thirteen! ❋ STOP IT! -JB   haha, he's the one that told us! -SPC

Oh and Lindsey should tap Jesus' ass, except all the parties are over.

Ha ha sucks for you bitch! Is this the first guy you've liked recently? Wow, he's lucky... or something nice like that. And why didn't you alert us of his hottness earlier this year.

00b#2: So Sophie's last party. Tear. Too bad I couldn't make it, but somehow sober is good right now. After Julia's service on Friday, Lindsey and I were talking so much about it and I'm so much happier now. When I look back at all the times we've been stoned, it makes me feel dirty. I'm just glad that I realized that, but I guess it took a lot of shit to get to that place. My detoxing has been a religious experience and it just puts a smile on my face. Yay for my self realization! I'm really excited for this summer, even though my original plans were to smoke a lot. Oh well! My parents have laid off, which is good.

Parents. Basically they are fucking superheroes to you when you're a kid, then puberty hits and you realize they suck a lot more than you thought. Parents are just really hard on us because they're mad because their lives didn't turn out the way they wanted it to. Boo-frickin-hoo.

Peace to the Parents of all youse.

Courtney

really? oh wait, yeah -CT   5/27/03

Hey guys —→ lots to talk about. I need to change ~~switch~~ pens. Hold up.

OK, oob#1: last friday, a day that will live in infamy (big ups to FDR!), I
                                    Upper West Side! yeah -CT
chilled w/ Andre, Gabbie, Allie, Dave, etc (the usual UWS kids). Andre walked

me home, b/c I had to be back early—damn those early curfews! After

we met up w/ Roe so Andre could hit up that shizzit for later (damn drug

dealers always ruining our lives) we were at the church on 86th + West End.

we were standing on the church steps kissing, and Andre said "so last week,

when you asked what was going on w/ us, and I gave you some bullshit drunk

answer, what I really meant was will you go out w/ me, because I like you a lot."

WORD! Aww yeah! -CT

oob#~~sex~~: yeah yeah, he respects me, blah blah blah. Basically I was really
                    never a good combination. I feel horrible, however
drunk + really stupid - ~~scribbled out~~
"respectful" it proves him to be, that ① I was that much of a stupid idiot,

and ② that he said no. I know it was ~~good~~ he said no, b/c he knew I was

just drunk and stupid, but I'm still so embarassed. AND he teases me about

it — I know he's just trying to make me feel better about it, but it just makes
                              don't worry about it, he had both of
me feel worse! Ah, I want to cry! your best interests at heart. -CT

oob#what the fuck: So on Sat. night we partied it up. Some (Cour, Allie,

Andre) say I was hitting on Tyler. Others (Tom, Dave, Michelle) say he was

hitting on me. I feel like I was a little, but I distinctly remember feeling like

he was hitting on me and thinking "if Tyler kisses me right now, I won't know what to do. So Dave came over to me + was like "Sophie, Tyler is hitting on you. You need to go over to Andre + kiss him + make him happy." But Andre was really upset + yelled @ me. We haven't ~~never spoken~~ spoken since (it's been like a day), but now I realize that being in a relationship is a BIG deal. I guess I need to devote more of myself to making sure he's happy. I sort of had this idea that relationships are ~~or~~ basically perfect until you break up. Now I'm learning that there will be bumps in the road, but you gotta learn from them + work through them. Whew! I made Andre a mix CD + put it in this big, official-looking envelope, and im gonna give it to him in one of his classes. I love pretending to work for the school. Do you guys think it's a good idea? *yeah, that's really sweet -CT* well too late now, b/c by the time I get this back I will be 26 years old. *shut up. -CT*

Lindsey — don't worry about your dad always wanting to talk about periods w/ you. Maybe he is considering a sex-change operation + wants to get the low down on what being a female is all about. Or he's just ~~crossed~~ nosey. Either way.

Sophie

Next day: Yay Andre + I made up + I'm SO glad. He yelled @ me so much, I wanted to crawl into a hole + die. But @ least I know he cares a lot about me. Even tho we're good now, I get scared b/c we always argue about stupid shit, and I worry that this will be

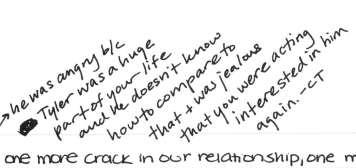

→ he was angry b/c Tyler was a huge part of your life and he doesn't know how to compare to that + was jealous that you were acting interested in him again. -CT

one more crack in our relationship, one more thing bringing it down. (Speaking of crack, CoCo I'm proud you were able to put down the pipe. OK, you weren't smoking crack, but I am proud of the decision you made. It wasn't easy, I know, but I really admire you for it. You have made the decision to put your physical + mental health over social pressures, and that is a really mature thing to do. Power to the people. I know that was kinda cheesey, but I had to say it. What are lesbian lovers for, Court, if not love and support (and a little poon!!?) thanks for that, I'm glad you understand -CT

Right now I gotta focus on the ISSUES OF LIFE: school work, finals, studying, Andre. You guys aren't on the list, b/c I ain't got no issues w/ you. I'm soooo glad we're not fighting. We gotta be strong! . . . or something. We're not offended, we don't need no list to know we're cool. -JB

I'm getting really sick of doing party pix everytime I write about a party, but I'm a slave to routine + I love photos of our beautiful faces so here we go:

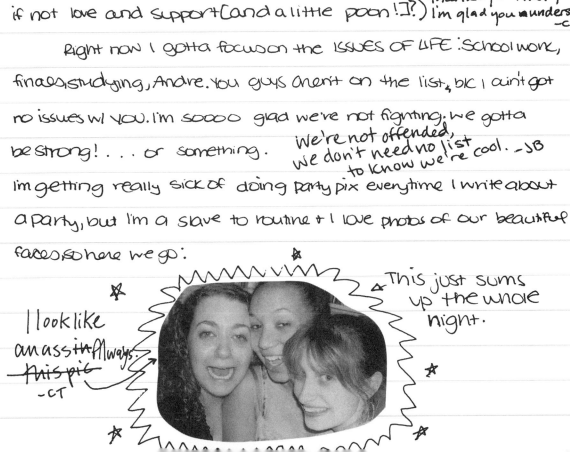

This just sums up the whole night.

I look like an ass in Always. this pic -CT

Lindsey is my name and Sophie's really lame (you   6/5/03
know it's true)

   I don't really know what to write about. No parties in the last
couple of weeks to talk about. So basically without drugs and
alcohol, there are no social happenings.

   OOB#1: This weekend was bad/boring/sad. From
Thursday to Sunday I sat Shivah for my Grandmother with my
family. :C Basically, I went to school, came home, prepared
last minute-kind of for shivah, then lots of people came over,
had evening services with Rabbi in my house (all of which
didn't end till like 11 pm), went to sleep and then got up and
did it all over again, it was sad and draining. I was absent
for a day, and when I came back to school I was just feeling
down and kind of depressed, but then I saw you guys on the
train and youse guys always know how to make me feel better,
so thanks. you're welcome Linds, I hope everything's ok - CT

   I totally missed out on the whole weekend, so we NEED
to have another PARTY/FUN night soon, I haven't done
anything illegal in like 2½ weeks. Oh the pain.
Right after regents, if people will still be here, we have to
have an end of school year PARTY OF THE MILLENIUM,
(or just 2003, whatever...) Now, when I say party, I just

mean fun night. → *I didn't even go to that shit! - CT*

I thought it would be fun! It was so lame. Too lame for words. -JB

Speaking of lame ass shit, I wonder how the semiformal went. Actually I don't, but I'm laughing 'cuz Julia actually went. What adds to the hilarity is that some people payed $20 for a ticket, while others paid 5 bucks at the door. Ha Ha!

P.S. While walking down the hall today, I passed Lucas and his arm brushed my hand!!! For about 3 seconds we were one spirit, one soul, and then I cremed my pants. A lot. It was great.

~ Lindsey

Why didn't I get in on that shit? -CT

Sophie. Dick. -JB

OH my god that boy is god's gift to the world, and his girlfriend is so undeserving! I ♡ you hottie Lucas! -JB

to know way to tell Sophie

P.P.S. - OMG Newsflash! Since I still have the Notebook, I must let you know: Sophie had sex with Andre! I know that bitch like the back of my hand, and Julia now owes me $2 dollars COLD HARD CA$H. We had a bet and I said that she'd have sex w/ him before giving him head. Congratulations on DOIN IT! That's so exciting, our little Sophie is growing up. So now that you're the only one of us who's crossed to the other side, you must give us all the details. *Oh I Will... -SPC*

The heat is coming.   6/6/03
Fuck that.

The term is almost over and I can't wait. I am so tired of sophmore year,
it's so fucking long. By this time in the term I just come home from
school and end up not doing any work and somehow it totally doesn't
matter. There's only 5 days of school left, and then fucking finals. Arg.

   Ooob # UNO: In reference to what Julia said, it does feel like everyone
is having sex lately. Tyler and I were talking about all the people who
suddenly want to fuck. It's funny b/c h.s. kids who are in serious
relationships don't seem to have as much sex as those who aren't in serious
ones! What an interesting turn of events.

   By the way, Congratulations Sophie on having sex with Andre.!!
You are lucky Andre liked you alot, or having sex with him could have
fucked things up alot. Tyler was saying how he felt about having sex
for the first time with Maggie and how it made him feel (= bad).
He just really wanted to lose it to someone he actually loved. He
basically said having sex with her was really miserable because
he didn't like her that much and the physical attraction was not
so hot. Despite how many girls he's hooked up with, he takes sex
really seriously. I guess in the end you just have to find yourself
and then find a person like you... and then have wild elephant sex.

HEY SEXY!

Here are some questions for Sophie to answer about her experience:

① How big was that Hungarian dick? oh... normae?
yes   yes
② Did it hurt / did you bleed?

Oooh, sepia toned. -JB

③ How long did it last? 5 min? No idea.

I am sexy in sepia! -SPC

④ Did you talk during it? not really

⑤ Were you both totally naked? nope

Tupac - "changes"

⑥ What was the setting? (music, lighting...)

⑦ AND THE MOST IMPORTANT QUESTION OF ALL:

   Did you use condoms? OF COURSE!
         him   me... goddamn.
Oh, and who came first, or not at all?

By the way, I'm glad things worked out for you. Thanks.

oob# ultimate fool: Also weird, Tyler and maggie broke up at last! I told Tyler that it was a totally fake relationship. I said, "Did you love her?" "Uh yeah, it was fake. Who knows if I really loved her." I would have thought she would have dumped him b/c she had the
                              she didn't want to admit that. -LN
upper hand from knowing he had cheated on her with 6 girls. -SPC me: like!
How was she so foolish about Tyler and her relationship? Oh well, she's just a lesbian.

   SPEAKING OF LESBIANS:
   Word Julia, you need to give us the scoop on that hookup!

Did she know what she was doing b/c she has her own pussy? Or was it the same as what guys have done?

~~████~~ Sod off dingle berries (British accent),

Court   Chop Chop!
                    -JB

P.S. Speaking of ultimate fools: So a few days ago my favorite teacher Mr. Stein was talking about those girls in high school who read Walden all day, smoke clove cigarettes, sexually experiment with other straight girls and talk about their English teacher who they wish they were sleeping with. These are such pathetic representations of what women are. We DO NOT sit around and talk about our ~~██~~ "feelings" all the time or our "periods" or some fucking poem. These bitches don't even know how stupid they are and how their whole image is manufactured from Urban Outfitters. GET A FUCKING LIFE!! You will probably end up in some coffee house trying to such dick to get your short stories sold. Eat me.

WORD. YES!
              -LN
-SpC

Hmm, if only this were real......

6/7/03

Um wow. So much to talk about. Where do I start?

OOb # Sophie gives a certain someone her flower 🌸: WOW. Holy shit. That's sooo insane! Are you freaking out about this? Do you think about it like all day? Basically, I want the ill low-down Coco. *don't you mean soph? -ct* I just want to say though that I now understand that we have different opinions about sex and what it means *I do think it's a big deal, I just felt ready* to both of us, and I respect that you don't think it's as big of a deal as I do. As long as you're ready for it, safe about it, and comfortable with it, that's all that matters. Oh, and it has to be awesome. Maybe I've just been watching too many chick flicks lately...

OOb # Speaking of movies... Saturday night Linds and I shmoked in the park and then went to see Finding Nemo 🐠. It was amazing! Hilarious! Best movie of my life. Not that I can really remember it. The only part I really remember was buying the popcorn. Oh buttery love. Linds, we're the ill cinema stoners.

OOb # The oob that likes girls... otherwise known as me! Oh my god me and Amie! Ok here's the full story of what happened. So we decided she'd sleep at my house on Friday, we'd "study", go to services at this really awesome temple called the Carlebach Shul on 79th and West End, and chill. While we were walking to the temple she totally admitted she had a crush on me. So my ego was significantly boosted. Later at home, we talked till like 2am, and then I made my move, and it worked! It was so hot! She's just so cool and comfortable to be around, and strangely, it was more fun doing stuff with her than with any other guy. And let me tell you: girls are better at everything. Excellent night. The only thing was we couldn't cuddle after cuz we didn't want my parents to catch us.

The morning was really calm and relaxed, we both ate... breakfast. Caught ya there, didn't I? You guys, I really like her and I can't stop thinking about her! But what does this mean? Am I gay? I don't think so... I mean, I never actually thought I was gay, does that mean I'm definitely not? It's weird and scary to think about if I am and I don't know if I'm quite ready to deal with that possibility. It's just that after girls, guys seem so, well, second rate. I can't even really picture myself with a guy right now. When I told Tori about it, she was so non-responsive, and then on Friday when me and ~~███~~ Annie were chillin on the wall, Tori and her girlfriend were eyeing us. I couldn't tell if it was like a "aww, you're cute" thing or a "are they really serious?" thing. But I feel weird. I'm just really confused. Not that I need to categorize myself, but I just want to know. What am I?

UR BOTH -LN

Ahh! Oh and also, if people find out about this, will guys not be interested in me anymore because they'll think I'm a lez? Or will they be more interested in an obnoxious threesome type way? Uchh... Either way, that would suck. Riding the sexuality carousel is not fun. Well, maybe a little bit.

Your rainbow pal,
Julia

those balls are so huge it looks like a hairdryer. HA! -LN

(The sexuality carousel)

(BOOBS)

By SPC

PS: will you guys make me a shirt that says "LEZ B FRIENDS"? NEVER! -SPC

⊰WOAH⊱ now that I finally have this, I don't know where to begin!
i didn't really...

OOb#Julia eats poon: YES YES OH GOD YES! uh... sorry... anyways... I'm so happy

for you! Do you want a 'ship w/ her? What do you want? About your sexuality

amusement park - today I was talking to Rosa, + she was saying how she's had

feelings for/done sexual stuff w/ girls before, but she doesn't feel bi or lesbian.

I think you're probably mostly straight (c'mon Jules, we know you can't stray

too far from the chicken), but you also sometimes like girls. So like ~~███~~,

~~███~~ but leaning towards boys? I don't want to classify you, b/c I'm

not you (thank God!). You shouldn't worry - guys know you're not only into

girls and they'll keep wanting your sweet sweet ass. mmmm...

⊰OOb#SEX!⊱ To answer your questions, Courtney, before I go into detail,

① The Hungarian hardon measured up just fine, but who am I to know?

② It hurt a lot the 1st time (in the beginning), + yes I did bleed, but the 2nd

time it didn't hurt + even started to feel good. ③ I have no idea how long

it lasted. ④ We didn't really talk except the 1st time, when Andre was concerned

about hurting me. He was so nice + it made me so happy to be w/ him. He was so

concerned about me + how I was feeling, and I could tell it meant a lot more

to him than just getting ass. The 2nd time, my mixed CD was playing, and he

haha was like "I can't believe we're having sex to 'Changes,'" which was ~~███~~

hillarious. ⑤ We weren't both totally naked, which was weird - kind

↙see photo @ end of entry

of lame and teenagerish and not romantic. ⑥ Setting: lights off, but it was evening, so it wasn't too dark. Music: Tupac, Changes. Also some Rolling Stones. ① Of course we used condoms!! good girl! -CT

I was so nervous before he came over, I sat in Joan of Arc park and smoked like 298 cigarettes. I tried to call you guys for some soothing words, but no one was home! Sorry! CT

We were hooking up on the couch when he came over, and then we moved into my room. He stopped and asked me if I was nervous, + then I realized I wasn't @ all anymore. I guess b/c it was so hard to get used to the idea that I was actually going to have sex. I ~~asked him~~ said "no, are you?," + he said he was, + I kissed him to say hey don't be nervous, I like you a lot.

After, we just lay in my bed listening to Simon + Garfunkle "Bridge over troubled waters," and I shed a tear or two. Not b/c I was sad or regretted it at all, but it was just a big release of emotions I think. Also, you guys know I cry over everything, esp. those cheesey movies when the dad hugs the son + says "I love you, son!" and the son says "I love you dad!" Anyway, I feel so much closer to him, but I was shy about saying it. Then he just came out w/ "I'm so glad we did it, b/c I feel so much closer to you, like everyday I get closer to you."

So basically, to recap, ① Sex = cool ② I like Andre a lot + he likes me ③ Julia's mom is hot! Hey!

Andre keeps doing dumb things + then freaking himself out.

He keeps saying "I love you" in a friendly way, not really thinking about it, and then freaking out + saying "Uh... like a dog loves his bone!" What the fuck does that even mean? Yesterday he was telling me about this beautiful city in Hungary he used to go to when he was little (I always forget he's from another country, b/c he has no accent + is totally American b/c he came here when he was so young). He was saying how he wanted to show me all this Hungarian stuff + it'd be so cool if he could take me there, over winter break. Then he stopped dead all freaked out that I'd be freaked out, since winter break is so far away. It was cute, b/c he's so nervous about saying the wrong thing. *Aww what a dork. -CT*

                    -Sophie

PS-Oh my god I went to the gynecologist today! WEIRD! It was a *whew!* woman, thank god. I couldn't handle a guy gyno, esp. after seeing the movie about the guy gyno who molests a patient + then she gets him put in jail + then his wife becomes the woman's babysitter *good movie! -CT* and tries to kill her + steal her family, aka "the hand that rocks the cradle." That would be bad. It wasn't too scary, but I don't want to go into too many gruesome details, except to say that they use this metal thing that is COLD - a shocking refresher, to say the least. But don't worry, guys, my Axl Rose is a-ok and in great shape - a veritable Paradise City if you will. *good one*

Before the appointment, I talked to my mom about going on the pill. Basically it seems like an all around better thing than condoms because A) more effective - no ripping, holes, etc, and B) you don't have to worry about remembering to buy one or stopping the hot + heavy passion to put it on (which SUCKS, by the way, to be like "omg this is amazing... wait... pause... condom... ok back in action). Also, my doc. gave me a prescription for Plan B - I don't want to be in the position of being about to do it, oh no we don't have a condom... hmm, should I just go ahead + take the morning after pill tomorrow? That would just be SO irresponsible. yes! So my gyno gave me a prescription to the pill + I start taking it soon. Now, I feel like this is a milestone. Little Sophie is growing up! It's really strange. Growing up. Sorry i'm not putting this into words better, it's just really strange.

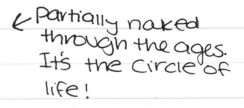

← Partially naked through the ages. It's the circle of life!

PS - please don't take this out + put it on a child porno website. Seriously.

WOW. I get to write the first entry back at school 9/12/03 after the summer. Well, JUNIOR YEAR is here!!! Can you believe we're finally upper class(wo)men? (Except for Courtney who's always low class trash.) It seems like we just graduated from middle school, and now we're half way done with high school. At least that means we'll only be in this hell hole for two more years. And now, this is the year that counts more than anything, it's gonna be so hard to have to buckle down and do really well so that hopefully I'll get into college next year.

And now a poem about Junior Year:

Junior year is now in gear
And no one can spell weird
but have no fear
'cause julia's queer
and Sophie's downing beers
Although Courtney has no idea --r
how ugly her i-d. picture looks.

Yet another school year has begun and so the torture ensues. The one good thing about the new school year: I'M OFF PUNISHMENT! YAY! Yes, just to catch the notebook up to speed, my parents discovered my trunk o' burning love and I was on lockdown for the last few weeks of summer. It sucked. It sucked a lot.

Other than that, my summer was pretty cool. And hot. At the same time. I set a new record for how many days in a row I could be fucked up, and in the most cities. But now back to the sucky reality.

OOB # I don't care : ~~XXX~~ My parents are ruining my fucking life. It's true. I know we say it a lot, but lately it's been barely bearable. Since my parents found my alcohol stash, there has been so much tension in my house. My mom totally doesn't understand anything! At first she was scared that I was drinking by myself. Wouldn't that be sad if I was having parties by myself, drinking Jack Daniels in a corner of my room, alone? (Wow, sounds like I just described Monday - Sunday nights for Sophie Pollitt-Cohen.) Now my mom's just annoying. My parents don't really know how to deal with this (The correct way is to not give a shit.) and I really think they're doing everything the wrong way. Why can't they just fucking realize that I'm sixteen and this is something kids my age do. Instead of acting like they have _no_ trust in me, they should say, "Look, we want you to know that we're not comfortable with your decisions but we can't force you to do anything, so we trust you to be responsible in whatever you choose." If they did this, then everything wouldn't have to be such a big fucking secret and things would just be better. I mean, it's not like I've ever came home drunk (or detectibly so) and they've never seen me out of control, so they should take this into account. I mean, things could be a lot worse. Don't they realize that the more they restrict me the more I'll want to rebel? And don't they realize that I'm basically gonna find a way to do what I want, so I can either sneak around and go behind their backs or be more honest about it. Just because they didn't do shit when they were younger doesn't mean that I'm gonna be the same way.

parents
don't
care.
their
word
is
the
law
—CT

Just waiting for the day I move out,

Lindsey

Oh my lawd it's a new <u>school year</u>!   9/19/03

Actually, we've been at school for like two weeks already but shhh, the notebook doesn't know that. So... things to talk about... ok, well... I'll just write some crap until some things come along →

→ Oooh Oooh I know! **THE BLACKOUT**!!!

That shit was sooooo crazy! I fell asleep alone at my house in the middle of the day with all the lights off. When I woke up I noticed that the clocks were all screwed up and my answering machine was beeping and going all crazy. I didn't realize anything had happened until my sister came home about half an hour later and said NYC had no power. ~~No~~ At first I was really scared that it was another terrorist attack so we knelt down in our living room and listened to the radio. When we turned it on we got the tail end of ... TERRORIST ATTACK and I totally freaked out Yeah but then they were like ... WE REPEAT THIS IS **NOT** A TERRORIST ATTACK. That was a close one.

My sister and I got really excited so we started to think of things to do, like fill pots with water and put them in the bathtub (that's ~~why~~ what they told us to do, I don't know why), get out the candles and go get food

we didn't have to cook because we really had no idea when we'd get our power back on. It was creepy going down the apartment hallway and 15 flights of stairs with just a flashlight, accidentally bumping into people and freaking out. We went ~~inside~~ outside and it was chaos everywhere, cars backed up and people sweating like crazy b/c there was no A/C.

THE SUN

COMES OUT!! (a lot later)

I thought you hated tuna... -SPC

We went to the Korean deli and bought tuna, bread, and water and waited in line in front of people buying beers for block parties. We trudged back up to our house to wait for my parents to get home and see if there was any more news on the radio. We hung out trying not to totally pass out from the heat and my parents came home about five hours later. We all watched the sun set together, which was really creepy because watching the sunset over a dark Manhattan is something you don't see often. My sister and I went out later to get some air and as a car ~~approaches~~ went by its headlights swept across the sidewalks suddenly revealing hundreds of people lying or sitting in the streets like zombies in the heat. I felt like I was in this surreal horror movie, kinda like after the apocalypse in Night of the Comet or in Dawn of the Dead.

I went home and slept in my underwear because of the heat ~~and~~ and I read by book by the light of a candle. I could see the stars outside because, for once, the NYC lights weren't a barrier. Sleeping at night, all I could hear was the silence of the heat and my breath. The next day the power went on, there had been no looting, and the world was back.

That must have sucked, but I was in the asshole of the U.S. → Houston, TX -LN

--- new info ---

OOb#1: Sophie and Andre split-er-oooed! Sadness, oh I mean <u>not</u>!

— that wasn't the (only) reason I broke up w/ him! —SPC

Having unpleasurable sex with that boy was just too stressful on your tang (pootie that is). Word of Wisdom: I know things aren't the greatest they've ever been but he's just taking time to get used to you guys not being together. Break-ups are the super blows to the male ego – let him reinflate. —JB wow way to steal my thunder for my entry. —JB

ool #2: Damn that Julia and her "girlfriend" Annie. What the hell! Why aren't you just going out, not talking about it. You need to make this girl shape up. Ironically, when Julia is dating guys, she's really passive, but when she's dating girls, she's like the confrontational-true... —JB masta! Well good luck working things out with Annie and losing your lesbian virginity (aka she eats you out). Awesome. —JB

Well I'm really sick and in desperate need of Day Quil. Can't smoke or drink until I get better. Means I must forgo the weed (haven't smoked in 5 whole months!) Maybe I'll have some this weekend, I'm a lil nervous about having a bad high again, but I'll probably just have like 3 hits. And then like 10 shots of vodka. Ugh.

woah! good job! —SPC

Courtney

down periscope!

We're upperclasspeople!

9/22/03

HEY NOW, HEY NOW, THE NOTEBOOK'S BACK!

I'm so happy! I've missed this thing sooo much over the summer. It's weird, I know the nbk is somewhat dying down and the use for it becomes extraneous as we become closer and closer, but I still find it to be unique and awesome facet of our friendship. Besides, we get to call ourselves "The Notebook Girls." And on to oobie doobies...

↳ wow, you sound like a bullshit English essay you had to write b/c you couldn't have sex w/ the teacher for a good grade-spc ← word. →

Oob #1: Junior Year. Oy. What a load of work. I'm stressing like woah. I'm still in disbelief that we're upperclass people (see, being a lesbian has turned me gender sensitive). I'm just not mature enough to think about college- I want to enjoy life as a troubled, confused, depressed, self-conscious, overtired teenager!

Oob #2: It was so hard coming back to Stuy from my wonderful summer at camp. No, I won't go on and on about how Jew camp was the greatest experience of my life (though it was) and about how everything and everyone else sucks in comparison (they do, except you guys, you just suck in general). Aside from you and a few other cool Stuy kids, everyone just seems so lame. All these stupid social distinctions and separations, and the fact that there are some potentially cool people I'll never know just because we "run in different circles," it's all ridiculous and unfair. Back in the harsh world of high school, it seems as if everyone exists just to bring you down. And yes, in case you were wondering, it is a Julia-centric universe. I don't know. I miss open communities I guess.

Oob #3: JULIA HAS A GIRLFRIEND NOW! Yes, it's true. Though Coco

omg-I was just reading through old NB entries, ~~oode~~ sp. the one where Julia wrote "I mean, I'm not gay..." That is the fuckin' funniest thing ever, b/c you had NO IDEA of the homosexuality that would ensue!
— SPC

stole my thunder by mentioning it in her last entry - thanks cockmuncher - I'll say it again! Me and Annie are officially an item. I am so happy! Though we had a rough summer (apparently it doesn't work to come into Jew camp with a relationship and see each other literally 24/7), I'm glad we've decided to go back to how things were in June. I think it's better this way b/c now I'm used to the fact that I'm bisexual and I don't need to freak out, I can just enjoy myself. I went to a soup kitchen with her after school (Jews: saving the world, one lesbian at a time) and realized that it's awesome that we can be really close friends sometimes and be really romantic and hot other times. I'm not uncomfortable or self-conscious around her at all, and she actually makes me feel good about myself. It's like we

not like us, we think you are stupid/ugly. - SPC

both understand each other's beauty in a different way. It's hard to explain. I really think this is the start of a good, healthy, long relationship (finally! It's been long enough). Anyways, I'll keep you updated. I know you're dying to know.
Julz Schmoolz

wow, it sounds like a really awesome relationship! rock on julia! - ct

ps: I haven't forgotten about the T-shirt. I still want it.

It's never gonna stop... -JB
no it won't -CT

9/23/03

Hello + welcome to W.U.R.GAY, all the news, all the gay. This just in: JULIA AND ANNIE are one! More on that story right after this...

{OOB#1} Here we are, back at school. New year, lots of changes, namely I'm glad I gave Andre the boot, b/c that shit was getting too stressful. I decided to do it, but we'd already planned that he was gonna come over later this week, and I just couldn't face seeing him, knowing what I was about to do. But we're starting to talk again - he met me after my math tutoring on sunday night so we could talk stuff over. It's always sorta bittersweet when we talk, because it's cool + good but also sad b/c we both know nothing can be the same. He said "it sucks b/c I've always thought you were really good looking, but now for some reason you seem even hotter," and then we laughed b/c it's funny and sad.

{OOB#2} And we're back w/ the top story, Julia is back together w/ Annie! I'm so happy for you + confrontational Proud of how confrontational you were. You're getting cojonas! Just remember the clit. *Word, I was mad confrontational -JB*

{OOB#3} So it was the 2nd anniversary of 9/11. All my feelings about my 9/11 experience center around feeling like I'm not supposed to. When I think about it, I'm sad, because all those people dying is sad, but I feel like I'm not sad enough. At the time, I was scared, but I remember feeling like I should be more scared, should be more panicked, should be crying. I remember when the 1st plane hit perfectly. The whole building (Stuy) shook, but our teacher told us it was probably nothing. He wanted us to focus on homosapiens, not looking out the window. Then a guy came into the room + told us a 747 crashed into the WTC 3 blocks away, maybe by accident; maybe he'd fallen asleep, maybe passed out. Everything was "maybe," because no one had a clue what was going on or what to do. Even then I~~h~~ felt like I should be freaking out, but the whole situation was so bizarre, it was as if it wasn't really happening. In homeroom, some dumbass was like "maybe it's aliens!" and another kid said "stop saying that, I'm <u>really</u> scared of aliens!" At a time like this, that's what you're thinking about? Aliens? When the school evacuated us, and Stuyvesant High School joined the hundreds, thousands of people walking uptown away from the WTC, I remember looking uptown + seeing <u>so</u> <u>many</u> people walking, it didn't even look like people, just an ocean of bobbling heads. Some of the bobbling heads were white, and then I realized they were covered in ash. Everything was such a strange spectacle, ~~that~~ and my feelings were ones of awe—I was so/overpowered by ~~so~~ how weird everything was, that I wasn't really scared. I saw all these businessmen covered in ash from head to toe, and they looked like zombies. I remember turning around to look back @ the WTC, but it was just a huge cloud of dust, like a mushroom cloud, set against this brilliantly blue sky, and it was so beautiful, like the way a volcano erupting is beautiful. And looking into the dust cloud, which was beautiful, too, I could see thousands + thousands of pieces of paper floating to the ground. I called my dad from 23rd st, which is about 1.5 miles from school, 3.5 from home, and he rode his bike down to get me. Waiting for him, I finally got to sit down + collect my thoughts. But I just sat there on the curb, looking @ my sneakers, then the dust cloud, then my sneakers again, and I knew I should be feeling sad or scared or something, but all I could think was "what the FUCK just happened?" When I saw my dad, and he hugged me, I finally cried. In The Things They Carried, Tim O'Brian writes about war: "to generalize about war is like generalizing about peace. Almost everything is true. Almost nothing is true." That's kind of what it was like.

-Sophie

Whatever you feel is right. There is no wrong reaction. -CT

You down with O.P.P? Well, good for you.   10/18/03

Hey ladies! I feel like things are so different now that it's
Junior year. When I flip back and read all the entries in the
notebook, we were such different people back then and life
was so much different. Now we're **2** years older and wiser, with
less (baggage) to hold us down, or maybe more, I can't decide.

Speaking of changes; Julia, how's the sex
change going? ~~xxxxxxxxxx~~ (dicks to chicks)
I think it's really cool that you have so much
courage to openly explore a new side of
yourself and have so much confidence about
it. And I also think it's also cool for you to
not ~~to~~ definitively categorize yourself as
anything, you know, sometimes straight,
sometimes gay, either way, you're

CoCo and Sophie w/ their Baggage · just JULIA.

Even more changes: I don't know what it is, but getting high just
seems like more of a burden now than ever before. Last year
we would get high almost everyday after school, and I still can't
believe we got away with that and that we had so much free time
on our hands. Weed just isn't what it used to be and there's
just so much ^more^ at stake. Don't get me wrong, I still like to party,

emotional
that
is
-ct

who doesn't, but I feel like weed doesn't have the same grip on my life that it used to. That's a good thing. We're actually growing up- SPC

haha that is true -CT Frustration on the guy front. Question: Why do I always { attract the losers? Not just the losers, the weird, stalkerish, socially awkward losers. It's not fair!!

And now onto the neverending saga of the parentals: Lately, I wrote about all the tensions between me and my parents and I had some more to say about that. Someone told me that the reason why child-parent relationships are so messed up in adolescence is so that when you have to "leave the nest," it's easier to separate. This sounds like it makes sense, though recently things have gotten better and chilled out with my parents. Less tension and hard times. Tonight I'm going to a Knicks game with my dad and those are always fun, except when he yells at the refs like he's on the court instead of sitting in the third tier.

Lovin' it,
Linds

P.S. Any new hotties on the radar? Did anyone get more attractive over the summer? And who are the new hot seniors?

P.P.S. - What's happening with Sophie and Andre? I'm so confused, one minute you're together, the next you're not, and then you're back again. Why am I ALWAYS out of the loop?

10/21/03

(P.S. This is going to be an entry of self-realizations so bear with me) So I guess my badass days of smoking weed are over. Oh well, I don't really care anyway. I miss the fast/easy way to get fucked up, but I just care so much about other stuff now. Like Lindsey said, "So I guess you'll just have to make up for it by having a lot of sex." Well freaking out was extra-not-fun so I will Never Ever Ever

good attitude. We know you'll miss it but way to be strong. -JB

weed is not a priority - JB

w/ hot Austrian boys! -SPC

for the observers as well as the participant. -JB

EVER SMOKE WEED AGAIN!

And weird flashbacks really fucking suck. dude it's like you took acid and had a bad trip. -JB

Now that's out of my system, on to the other matters:

oob #1: Aww Sophie and Dre got back together. Except not, but kinda, wait what's happening? Has there been any makeup sex? Well let us in on the scoop?!

Ok, so now that Sophie and Dre are happy together then I would like to address an issue that has somehow permeated our lives for the past two years: Tyler. My theory on Tyler is this: He has everything in the world; he's hot, rich, smart, funny, charming, has a nice family, cool friends, but ultimately is the lonliest person I have ever met in my life. Most of his connections with people are really false, I mean look at him and Maggie. He can't stand more than a few weeks without

But doesn't give a shit about anything. -LN

hooking up with someone, and even when he has a gf he needs attention from other girls (hence the constant cheating). So when Sophie and he became really good ~~friends~~ friends, even though he dated other people, he took out his lonliness on you. He felt this great connection with you but he knew that if you guys hooked up you'd have to jump to a serious relationship, which he obviously wasn't ~~even~~ ready for, so instead of kissing you, he fingered you, which is less "serious." In a weird ~~way~~ way kissing can be a lot more intimate than a blow job and he bypassed that whole situation of intimacy by not kissing you. I think he was afraid you were falling in love with him and he didn't really know what to do about that so he just decided to stop speaking to you for like four months.

Of course in that time you grew as a person and met Andre, which totally changed your life. I think Tyler saw you find someone and he was really jealous of you and how happy and non-lonely you were so when he got the chance he hooked up with you to prove to himself that ultimately he had you. It's like if he could get you to kiss him so intimately then he could prove to himself that you didn't really love Andre. But he was wrong and you came out on top for once. In the end Tyler is still lonely and the shit you went through with him only made you stronger.

I guess it's stupid to spend so much time talking about Tyler and looking at his name one more fucking time in this book is gonna make

★★★ I'm out. ⊕ bitches

Amsterdam 69 (my ACTUAL porn name)
↳ EW. Watching a porn w/ you in it
would be like watching Lindsey's parents
have sex (slightly disturbing, but strangely
~~AROUSING~~) -SPC HEY! -IN

me puke. But the fact is, he represents so many of the guys we've

encountered. They are all lonely and reach out to girls for comfort,

only to throw us aside when they get scared of getting too close, those

ironic bastards. No one will ever be able to resist Tyler, he has a
                                                            PUKE
psycho-sexual hold on just about everything with a pulse, but for his

sake I hope that one day someone cares about him outside the Tyler-
                                                                PUKE
obsessed world.

                                                          yay!
oob#gay: So hung out with Annie... no seriously it was really cool.
                                    well she's a stoner. She needs weed
                                    to do everything. -JB
We needed the weed (for her) to break the ice, but then it was awesome.

She was like, "I never laughed this hard with my stoner friends." Sweet

but also really sad. So many jokes; but then again, things are always
                        I know, it was   so many
awesome with us.   amazing! I laughed so hard, it   funnies
                    was like a month's worth of   -spc
                    sit ups. -JB

OMG it's 7:30am and I'm at school. I told my friend that I would

campaign① for her, but it rained today so I came in for no reason. Speaking

of school: oob#hottie teachers: I know it's weird, but there are actually

mad hottie teachers at Stuy.   ~~teacher~~

                                                the guitar....
                                                -JB
| Mr. O'Brien | (gym teacher - needs no explanation) | Mr. Gray | (~~prep~~ school)
                                                                  boy cute
            ↳ massaged my head in   ↳ looks like a caveman
            the library. LOVE HIm. -SPC   But SEXY!

| Mr. Waters | (gay English teacher cute) | Mr. Joyce | (hairy history teacher cute)
                                                        ↳ we're getting married
                      WORD! -JB   (he doesn't know yet). -SR
| Mr. Stein | (Julia's got my back on this one) | Mr. Klein | (cutie hottie cute)

Wow I really hope no teacher ever finds this and reads that, that would
                            be like the funniest thing ever. ★★★

Footnote:
① campaign: hand out stupid flyers that no one will read so that you
            can win junior ♫ cock-us (caucus) ✦ what?!!?
                                                      -IN

had a snowball fight w/
Lindsey (that girl) tells me
about it EVERY DAY!) -SPC
the eyes.↑
-JB

Hello Dahhlings....

I'll race to the oobs....

10/27/03
*That's never good. 'Cause when you spend a
lot of time with someone who has problems like that, it
starts to mess with your head.
-LN

Oob#1 The lezzie lover: So Annie and I are going pretty well. I called her today and we were talking about her psychiatrist, and I kind of realized she has a lot* of problems and that intimidates me a little bit. Every time I meet someone with heavy duty drama, it turns me off from them. Also, this is like the 2nd real phone convo we've ever had, which could be a bad thing.

Oob#2 Surprise! I just wanted to say thank you to S, C, & L for the excellent surprise party. Everything was so awesome and it was so sweet. I've always wanted a surprise party! It was truly a great night. Blindfolding me from Sophie's house all the way to Lazer Park in Times Square? Getting touched by a freaky weird lesbian sanitation worker along the way? Awesome!

Oob# I'm so proud of Coco: Court, props to you for realizing that weed done you bad. It takes true maturity to realize that though everyone else is doing something, you just have to abstain. I really admire you for that. Also it's not like we even smoke that much now anyway. At least not compared to freshmen year. After we realized that getting stoned is always the same, I guess ive chilled out. And there's so much fucking work this year that it's practically impossible.

thnx jules-ct

true, true -ct

Awww Sophie and Drei Drei making babies. You know, I really do think you make a great couple. Sorry about telling you never to hook up with him at that party. My bad. Oh, and also, just a warning: your lukewarm feelings for him may turn chillingly cold after seeing him in a woman's dress on Halloween.

Signing off, Julz.

HAPPY HALLOWEEN?

Drei Drei clad in drag...

with fat ~~thighs~~ thighs? Oh sweet lord - SPC

OTHER HAPPYs COMING UP:

Happy Hannukah!

Merry Christmas!

hoho ho...

Happy Kwanzaa! THIS HOLIDAY WAS INVENTED IN THE '80s. i DON'T KNOW THE SYMBOL.

AND SOON...

HAPPY NEW YRS!

2004!

"Halloween costume, right...
you wore that shit for real all the time!!
-SPC

My halloween costume. The onsie rules all!! (and makes me look rather shapely as well)

I would really like some cake right now. Since I don't have any, I can only express my desires artistically.
That looks more like pie. Trust me, I'm an expert. -JB   Losers -CT 10-31-03

Hey Doucheys! Man, Douche is such a funny word. I'm so glad to have this notebook!!! we've been writing in this for a long ass time. Alright, simmer down, let's get to the odds.

ood# Chillin' w/ lesbians - Yeah, so we chilled w/ Annie, and I'm glad I got a chance to know her better. Even though we've had big differences/ (b/c you stole her ex, Hunter) -CT
hostilities in the past, I know we've all grown up a lot since Freshman year. She is important to Julia, so she's important to me. Plus, it was cool going to a hookah bar, I'd never been to one. We had fun trying out the different smoke flavors (I esp. liked the rose one),
I did
but NOT enjoy paying $5 for one goddamn Corona. But all in all, I'm glad to have spent some time w/ someone who is mad important to The Baskin. PLEASE DON'T START CALLING ME THE BASKIN. -JB hahha

ood# Andre: Alright, so to get the NB up to speed, things were going along well after the breakup, talking + generally being civil to eachother. Then he found out I cheated on him over the summer w/ Tyler. Sorry I didn't update the NB about that; not much you really need to know. Drunk summer, make-out, the end. In the past, whenever something sexual between us would go down, it would just lead to more weird feelings, unanswered questions, confusion, and drama. But this time, and I know it will be the last time, was like an unspoken end to all the shit in the past. It was almost as if everything had been leading up to the time when we could kiss + have it not be a huge deal. It provided some much needed closure to a roller-coaster relationship that can now be laid to rest. Thank the fucking lord! Anyway, Andre FLIPPED OUT + stopped talking to me (BTW, court, everything you said in that entry about Tyler was exactly right. And I made it through the rain!), even tho he cheated on me w/ his ex-girlfriend *from Hungary – CT* ! But somehow me doing it is bad, but him doing it is *No!* OK. Then a few weeks ago was Michelle's awesome b-day party. That was such a good time! Lots of beer, a great house to chill in, and all our friends were there. Andre came, but of course we didn't really talk to eachother. Then @ the end of the party, he got really sick (stupid boys blazing + drinking too much) + was lying on the couch looking dead while downstairs Dave + Tom got yelled @ by the Parks dept. for God knows what. He looked so sad + shitty feeling, so I asked him, feeling really shy, if he wanted some H2O. I brought him some + sat w/ him on the couch while he drank it + then he reached out + grabbed my hand + we were both looking @ eachother like 'ooh I've missed you!" Then he hugged me + started kissing me, but I kept telling myself not to kiss him, but then all these feelings came flooding back + I missed him so much + then we kissed + it was so

all yeah! –CT

nice. He said "I've missed you so much, this month w/out you has been so awful." We're not officially together now, and I like it like this. He came over last week + we had sex for the 1st time since the breakup. Now Tyler + Tom are saying I'm leading Andre on. But I'm not! I told him I didn't want a relationship + he said he understood. I know he likes me tho, but I like this low-key situation. T+T keeps saying I'm doing something wrong. What do I do? I don't want this to end, but I don't want a relationship. Right now this is so perfect: guy who likes me + I like him (kind of?), chill hookups, hanging out, it's all good. That's even what he said: "chilling + hooking up is good." Ah. Oh no... guys, do I like him? I think I do. OH MY GOD, I like him, and I know he likes me!! Or maybe I don't like him?

the suspense is killing me! -LN

Oh god, it's halloween + he dressed up as a girl! eww I know! -CT

I was thinking about something Julia said/wrote about (aren't those basically the same thing?) a while ago, about ~~giving~~ when she gave head for the 1st time + it was oh-so-exciting. You talked about how it felt kind of empowering, a little of that I-AM-WOMAN thing. I just have so many conflicting feelings: on the one hand, Julia, I know exactly what you mean. There is something empowering in feeling completely in control of the guy's pleasure, and you're the one doing it so COOL BEANS for you. I also feel ~~good or bad~~ *like *wow, I really* love this guy,

if you want that kind of relationship and you told him that, nothing you did is wrong! -CT

he looked better as a girl than you did -CT

I know, and that really upsets me -SPC

and i'm glad to be doing something that's all about pleasing him (tho it can't be like that <u>all</u> the time, if you know what I mean, and I think you do, wink-wink, nudge-nudge, eh eh, mum's the word...OK, i'm done). But then another part of me thinks, OK maybe i'm in control," and hippidy-dippidy for me, but @ the end of the day, i've just got a dick in my mouth, so how empowered am I actually? true whatever. In the end, obviously it's more a feeling of loving Andre + being glad to make him feel awesome than a feeling of being degraded. I don't feel degraded. But I def. think girls giving head @ parties or to guys they don't really know is gross. I think it's a lot more respectable to have sex w/ a guy early on than to give him head, which is cool for me b/c that's what I did w/ Andre. Let me explain. Sex

no wonder you think that's more respectable —CT

is a 2 person thing, but oral sex isn't. oral sex is about one person's pleasure. So when girls give head @ parties, it's disgusting. If she doesn't even know/care about the guy, why is she literally <u>on her knees</u> trying to please him? Sex is different, b/c both people get something out of it. And that's what I have to say about that.

　　　　　— Sophie

PS-guys, the most ridiculous thing happened to me today. So I'm on the train going from SAT prep to Tom's house, and i'm looking in my book, doing some practice math problems (don't comment). The

middle-aged-ish man sitting next to me goes "oh, is this a workday?"
I thought "ok, friendly man, whatever," and said "no it's just an SAT
study day." He starts in w/ all the usual questions grownups ask, what
grade are you in, where do you go to school, what colleges are you looking
@, etc. Then after a long pause, he says "so can I get your number?"
WHAT THE FUCK?! So I said "I'm 16," thinking & "you complete ASSHOLE."
Then he tries to pull all this whole "uh...um...I didn't know" BULLSHIT,
but he should know I've got the mad argumentative logical skills,
which I proceeded to whip out, because he did know I'm 16. So I
said "but I just TOLD you I'm a highschool junior - SATs, applying to
college, remember?" and he was getting really embarrassed, and I
was getting really mad (but also enjoying telling him off) and
going on this whole rampage. After I finished my little speech, there
was a long pause, and I figured he'd gotten the message. BUT NO.
He goes "I don't mind..." Well I just about LOST IT. I said "well I
DO!!!!!" jumped up, and peaced to another car. What a DICK.

that's really freaky. -CT

11/11/03

Hey Guys-

Just got back from Sophie's Christmass tree decorating/eating pie/deep talks extravaganza. You are the only person I know who has a pickle ornament. 'Twas awesome, get it? man, I'm a loser. No one say anything. God I miss this book. I always say it, but combined with the ludicrous amount of time it takes for it to circulate and the nostalgia that I feel looking at it, it's just so sentimental. It's unfortunate that it's ending (not ironic, as Alanis Morisette so easily confuses the two). This is my last entry, but it's 2-pronged. One is a regular entry and the other one, the sappy bullshit, is a few pages forward.   → courtney's requirements for a sexy evening. ~spc HA!.. iN

Oob#1: Sleigh bells and chocolate sauce: Sophie's Christmas extravaganza was so fun! It was nice to see that we can just chill, be ourselves, and never even think about getting fucked up. I love that so much, and above all, it counts as the measure of true friendship. Though it's mad fun and we all need it sometimes, I'm getting really tired of the "good times only if drugs and alcohol are involved." There's more out there than that. Like ~~pro~~ miscuous sex.   Pro (spelling errors)

Oob#2: My love. So for the record, on paper, here's the deal with Annie. We broke up (thank god and good riddance, though I really could've used some jungle love, I even trimmed my tree for it).   another x-mas pun, never too many-ct   We were just tired of the relationship I guess. We never called, never talked to each other, I thought she was being really selfish most of the time, and she probably thought the same of me. We're just too different to be so closely connected. So I was thinking of reigniting the flames with Cole, since I need a rebound and we are really good friends. Thankfully, this NFTY event came along (GOD I LOVE NFTY) and I

↑ b/c they provide you with hot-jew ass_ct

really clicked with this guy ~~Adam~~ and we ended up hooking up. So we'd been having these amazing phone conversations and we chilled at a friend's house like 2 weeks after that, and determined that we were going out. He's just so cute! And he's not agressive or selfish like Annie. He's on the water-polo team at Horace Mann (if I don't see his <u>8 pack soon</u> – he calls it a 6 pack and 2 for free- I'm gonna die). He totally

HOTT-LN

meets the criteria: a) he's Jewish b) he doesn't play guitar but does play piano and c) listens to good music and finally d) has a sweetly hilarious immature south park-like sense of humor. The only thing that bothers me is that I'm kind of scared about the seriousness of the relationship. The label "boyfriend" really scares me since I haven't had one, in truth, since 8th grade. The other day I was thinking about him and I wrote "J+A" on my hand. I haven't done that since the "J+D" days.

I can't pinpoint exactly what's wrong, it's just that now I feel like there's this huge extra thing in my life that I love but I'm so scared that I'm going to mess it up that I don't want to let it get better. I never thought I'd be scared to let someone in. Maybe this

you can do it!!-spc

just goes to show how long its been since I've been committed to someone to the point where they can really hurt me. I guess I always wanted to make sure the person really cared about me before committing, and I haven't really found someone in a while who I believe cared about me like that. I always think people are really ready to break up with me, I need affirmation of their affection, and then I convince myself that I don't want to be committed, and I break it off. Ohhh the issues...

So that's it. I think I'm done with my last real entry. Wow, this is really, really sad. For once I don't feel bad about wasting all this space. My "conclusion" is a few pages ahead.

Peace, Julia

THINGS THAT MAKE CHRISTMAS FUN @ SOPHIE'S HOUSE:

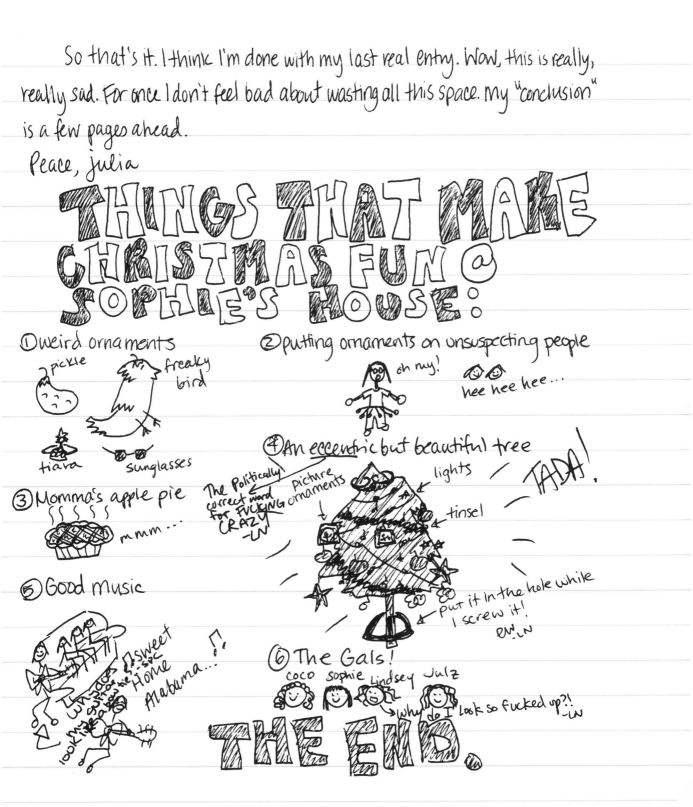

① weird ornaments
- pickle
- freaky bird
- tiara
- sunglasses

② putting ornaments on unsuspecting people
oh my!
hee hee hee...

③ Momma's apple pie
mmm...

④ An eccentric but beautiful tree

The politically correct word for FUCKING CRAZY —LN

picture ornaments
lights
tinsel
TADA!
→ put it in the hole while I screw it! ew. —LN

⑤ Good music
♫ sweet Home Alabama... ♫
looking out my back door

⑥ The Gals!
coco sophie lindsey Julz
→ why do I look so fucked up?! —LN

THE END.

Ay yo! What up! I guess it's now common knowledge 11/18/03 that the notebook is coming to an end and we all need to come to terms with that horrible fact, even though I think it's time we lay this lover to rest. Since this is my last entry, I need to make it good.

And Now for the pictures! (starting on the next page)

~Lindsey

Intrue Lindsey style, there is <u>no</u> actual entry. Lindsey will express herself in pictures b/c often times she doesn't know how to do so in words. She gives us... blank canvases. -CT

12/22/03

Ladies, I don't even know how to start my final entry. So I think I'll just pull a Julia and be a lesbian. I mean, write a regular entry and then write my last entry later.

OOD#1: So about a week ago was me + Andre's 7 month anniversary. (7 months since he first asked me out in May, 1 month since we got back together - he asked me out on what would have been our 6 month anniversary, how cool!) He wrote me this really long, sweet letter + put it, along w/ some flowers, in my locker - he didn't tell me, so when I found them, it was just a big fatty surprise! It just made me realize how much I appreciate him. We said "I love you" for the first time a few days ago, + everytime I say it, I realize how true it is. Even tho we fight, and OH MY GOD DO WE FIGHT, I feel like I've finally "met my match," so to speak (if that makes any sense). We hung out tonight - it's like 11:30pm + he just left. He came overe around 6. My mom was out + it was just a really fun evening. At one point, we were just lying in my bed not really talking, just lying there. And I couldn't get over ~~how happy I was~~ the fact that I was so happy not even doing anything, just lying there. He tells me that I'm his best friend, which makes me happy (b/c that's so sweet and I love him + bla bla bla), but also kinda sad, b/c I feel like shouldn't he have a best friend who's like... one of his friends?

I feel like he doesn't like his friends as much as he acts. He's friendly w/ so many people because he smokes weed w/ them, but is he really friends w/ them? Probably not. Then again, I also have friends w/ whom drugs is really all we have in common.

ooo#2: The big O! Finally, ~~scribbled out~~ I reached the top of the mountain! What a relief and release. Now it's all xxxtra special.

ooo#3: I'm not sure if you guys know, but that kid Ben died. I know we weren't really friends w/ him - if I saw him on the street I would have recognized him + waved. We saw eachother @ parties sometimes. He was pretty close w/ Tom - but I can't stop thinking about what happened. It's making me reconsider a lot of stuff.

He overdosed on heroin. I know this isn't something we or our friends do, but this has made me see our lives really differently. As teenagers, we love to think we're invincible, but we're not. When I think back over the years, I realize we did <u>so much</u> STUPID shit - smoking weed bought from random guys on the 94th st. projects that was usually laced w/ crack and God knows what else, drinking + being wasted w/ ~~strangers~~ guys we didn't really know, getting into random guys' cars, and running around NYC fucked up off our asses @ like 1 in the morning. Thinking back on all that makes me realize what incredibly dangerous situations we were in, and how lucky we are that nothing bad happened, b/c it could have. Something like this - Ben's death - really makes you realize how vulnerable and _mortal_ we actually are.

oo6 3 - Julia, I'm really happy for you + your sexynew Adam lover. He seems like a great guy. And you've gotta look @ his 6 (or 8) pack! You will probably shit your underoos when you see it, so remember to wear your Depends. I always do - CT

I know! -JB

PEACE
- Sophie

Au Revoir!

12/23/03

OK, let me start this entry by saying that everything I will write here is going to be cheesy, corny bullshit.

I don't really know what to say. I didn't want to have to think about it beforehand, because then I knew it would be contrived. I mean, what do you say about the notebook? It will always be a part of our lives. ~~thank~~ That won't change. Fresh~~man~~ year the notebook was a way to form bonds, become friends. But now the notebook means so much more to me. I can't live without you guys. You are my best ~~ass~~ friends, plain and simple. There is nothing we can't share. This notebook is living proof of that and proof of how much we've been through together. Over the last two years, the notebook has been a huge part of our lives, and now it seems like the best time for us to stop writing. It no longer feels like a place of free thought (because of you know what) but a burden to pass along quickly. That's why it's coming to a close.

<u>Personally</u>, the notebook is also really important. I am ~~so~~ <u>not</u> the same person I was three years ago, and neither are you guys. That's a very good thing because we were all douche bags. Looking back on everything, I realized that we all figured ourselves out in this whole mess. We all made some sort of breakthrough in this book and forever we are changed because of it. But even though it's difficult for me to look at the shit we used to write, it makes me more proud of the person that I am today.

Are these sperm?....

and the people that we've become.

Let me start off with myself. A couple of days ago my mom made dinner and she made this shit called Swiss Chard, that I'm sure you guys have never eaten, but it basically tastes like wet underwear. Anyway my mom and I used to fight about it for hours when I was a kid because I'd never eat it, she'd force me to, and I'd have to cave. But when she put it down in front of me I picked up my fork to eat it and then I just stopped and said, No. No fucking way do I have to eat that. I'm seventeen years old and if I don't want to eat something then I don't have to, so throw it out. It was at that moment that I finally realized I was my own person. I was in control, and there wasn't shit anyone could do about it. Over these years I did a lot of shit ~~because~~ because it let me be in control of my life. Sure it blew up in my face eventually, but I did it on my own; I made the ultimate decision about eating or not eating the "Swiss Chard" (aka drugs and everything else we've done, in-case you didn't get the metaphor) Telling my parents everything that happened in this book was the most liberating thing I've ever done, because there is no more lying, no more secrets, and now they know that I've been making my own decisions for a long time now and I'm not a little kid anymore.

And the best part about figuring all this out in the notebook is that I can see how you all came to the same realizations that I did, just through different ways. Look at you guys:

Julia, you grew up under the roof of a synagogue that most people ditched after their bat mitzvah party but you stayed with it because you believed in it. You made the jew-thing your own and met all these amazing people and learned all this stuff about life. You also broke away from all those traditions and dated girls, something I don't think many other people would have expected from you. You made all those decisions based on your heart and not what your parents or anyone else wanted for you. That's an amazing accomplishment. We always joke that you are gullible and a bit of a push-over (humanitarian pussy - A name I ~~have~~ invented) but there is no way a push-over would have chosen a life that isn't exactly the easiest to live, which is really.

And Sophie, you met that guy. That fucking first guy who breaks your heart and you'll never forget for the rest of your life. Seriously, everyone has that one guy who either never liked you as much as you liked them, or the one you loved from afar, or the guy you dated who treated you like shit, but since he was the first one to fuck with your heart, that's why it hurt so much. For most people it takes years to get over him, trust me I know. You pretend to hate him but it still really bothers you, and you date other guys but you still can't forget what happened. He knows who he is to you, and he takes pleasure in that, which hurts even more. For every relationship after that it'll never hurt as much as that first asshole, but eventually you have to forgive him for being an idiot and forgive yourself for getting so wrapped up in him. Tyler thought he owned you but you wouldn't let that last forever. You met the first guy to break your heart, but you were also lucky enough to meet that other guy. Your first love. That's pretty fucking awesome. Tyler isn't a problem anymore because you made the decision to forget him and let Andre in. That's really mature.

Yo Lindsey. When I first met you there was ~~you~~ this whole "Lindsey's really shy" image and WHAT ~~$~~ THE HELL IS THAT? ~~E~~ ~~people~~ ~~Mmmmmmmmmmmmmmmmm~~ ~~As~~ ~~HELL~~? Those people don't fucking know you because you are like the _last_ person I would call shy. Since freshman year you have totally broken that image of yourself, with us and with everyone else, and finally shown your individuality to others. You also opened up to people about what you feel and your opinions. There wasn't any more running to the pizza place at lunch and ditching Lindsey time because that's not what best friends do. You made the friendships count by letting people in to that mysterious mind of yours, and not being afraid that we'd all think you were stupid. You also proved yourself on the court (god that sounds lame) and I was so proud to be your friend when I heard all those guys in the back of the gym talking about how hot Newman's game was. That's definately a Michael Jordan moment, not Shaq making the fucking front page because he's ~~obvious~~ a freaking ogre.

Ok so now that the tears are definately flowing it's time to finish my entry. The truly sad thing about the book being over is that it will never be here to see us graduate, go to college, get married, have babies, die, you know the whole "life cycle" thing. Wow I just summed up our lives in one sentence. ~~deeply~~ Creepy. We've made an amazing record of our lives for the past two years and luckily we will never forget it. I love you guys and I love the Notebook.

Final Peace Out

CoCo, Court, C-love, etc. or just plain Courtney

GOOD BYE NOTE BOOK!!

12/24/04

I think I'll start this entry off with the same warning Courtney used: this will probably be the cheesiest entry I will ever write, but I gotta say what I feel, you know, keep it real, so deal with it.

Well, I guess this is my last notebook entry... EVER. The rest of my notebook entries will be entered in the book of life (too cheesy? Ok, I'll tone it down.) I just gotta say that I love you guys so much, I don't think I could ever make it through high school without all of you. Through the good times and the bad, I've learned so much from all of you and I hate to admit it, but I think I've become a better person because of knowing youse guys. If anything has taught me to open up and share myself with other people, it's this lined piece of trash. The notebook will forever be more than just a bunch of bound pages. For me, it has become something so much more. The notebook is something that has helped me grow and change in the last three years more than anything else in my life. It has become a beloved fifth friend and a place that I could bring all of myself and all my baggage and be a better person for it. I have to say it's been liberating. Not to mention the crazy communication skillz we got from this whole experience. Every disagreement we have is talked through and resolved. It's weird that we never really fight, and every argument we have is resolved before we part. It's almost sickening how well we get along with one another.

I just read through all the final entries and I'm just about bawling.

Flipping through this book is kind of like seeing your life flash before your eyes. It may sound a little dramatic, but drama is one thing far from lacking in this little journal of ours. Despite all the drama, the real value of the notebook is apparent to me now more than ever. Being able to reflect on your life and yourself in this unique way is amazing. I have to say that, as Courtney has said in the past, we were all douche bags back then. Now, while I'm not usually one to judge anyone (i.e. myself, you bitches can go to hell) it's totally true. But, as I always say, everyone is a douche bag when they're younger, and if they think they weren't, then they definitely still are a douche bag. We can all look back on ourselves (and one another) and point out times when we weren't the best versions of ourselves, but, if nothing else, be better people for it. But I guess that's what adolescence is, a series of painful self realizations and awkward moments, all for the purpose of learning about yourself so that you can grow and become a better person and better understand life. I'm so glad I've had our friendship to make this process a little easier to bear, and at the same time, experiencing this together makes our friendship stronger, so I expect us all to be friends for the rest of our lives. Unless I win the lottery, in which case, you bitches are dead to me. But until then, I love you guys more than life itself... or something like that.

This is what I think of the Notebook Girls:

COURTNEY: The most insightful person I know. If you analyze someone or a situation, I always know to listen to you, 'cause you're ALWAYS right! How do you do it? You are such an understanding and intuitive person. Somehow what should be 15 minute phone conversations with you always end up lasting hours. What can I say, I love it. No doubt, you keep it real, even if it might hurt someone's feelings, but as you've taught me, it's better to be faced with something unpleasant and fix a situation than to pretend like nothing's wrong and ultimately do more damage.

Things I ♡love about Courtney:

★ Walks REALLY slowly ★ know everything about everyone (even things you didn't know about yourself) ★ is really funny ★ can sing her balls off ★ was the STAR of Junior SING! ★ Can draw a picture of a vagina surprisingly realistically ★

JULIA: The one we love to walk all over. Just kidding, really, you are one of the most thoughtful, genuine and nicest people I've ever met. Something I will always admire about you is that you're nice to everyone, maybe even a little too nice sometimes, but you are who you are and you don't let anyone change that fact. You're friendly and loveable: the proof of this is the fact that you're friends with EVERYBODY (even some douche bags that don't deserve the awesomeness that is Julia) and I've seen many a boy get sucked into that Julia-ness and definitely fall in love.)

Things I L♡VE about Julia:

★ is a humanitarian pussy ★ never knows what's going on ★ has a hilarious sense of humor ★ can always take a joke even if it's about her mom ★ is gay, sort of ★ is a good (lap) dancer ★

SOPHIE : One of my oldest friends and no doubt one of the most special. We've had some damn good times since sixth grade and I can't wait for the new hilarious times we'll have in the years to come. There are so many instances when we don't have to say anything cause we can practically read each other's minds. Life with Sophie is always an adventure and I'm glad I could stick around for the ride. Also, we definitely have the best song and dance routine this town will ever see.

Things I L♡VE about Sophie:

★ Always has her cellphone and planner on hand to organize SOMETHING ★ has dance parties with me in the middle of the street ★ thinks everything is about her ★ rocks out on the guitar ★ is cracked out and all over the place yet really anal retentive and organized all at the same time ★ loves poop jokes as much as the next girl ★

Well, my last entry is now coming to an end, so I guess I have to say goodbye to the notebook for the last time.

So just to sum up:

1. We know each other like the back of our proverbial hands
2. The notebook is Amazing
3. We'll be friends till the end (or until I win the lottery)

But, as they say, "Papa was a Rolling Stone," so I gotta Roll...

~Lindsey

MERRY CHRISTMAS!

12/25/03

So guys, this is entry #last.

I've been avoiding this entry for as long as I can. Drawing pictures in the back, flipping pages, I just can't let go. Though, as Coco mentioned, the nbk has become a burden and it's time to lay it to rest, I still can't bear to put down something that makes me smile every time I read it. This is really our lives here, in the purest, truest, though not cleanest form.

I have to say thanks to all of you, first of all. Though I'm not nearly done growing or learning about myself, you guys have helped me discover who I am. I'm not afraid to stand up for myself, or for what I believe in anymore. I've learned that it's OK to be ridiculous, and who cares if I embarass other people, life is too short for it to be about someone else. This nbk has given a new definition and meaning to the term "talk out your issues." We've tossed around quite a few in here. Sometimes, the only way to solve a problem is to pine over every agonizing detail. I feel like saying goodbye to the notebook equals saying goodbye to the notebook girls, but if anything, our relationship has progressed independently of the notebook, and it will always be there. And I think, when it all comes down to it, that's the most important thing. That through 2 years of our lives, we've attained bonds that some people never find. For the cost of a composition notebook, we probably created some of the best friendships we'll have. I can't tell you how happy it makes me to know that I'm never alone, that you guys know me from the inside out. I think the notebook helped us learn from each other even more, because we look back at our lives on paper (wow that sounds weird) and realize how many colossal and monumental mistakes we made (developing commitment-phobia, being obsessed with the "coolness" of drugs and fucked-up-edness to name a few) and how we've moved from them.

In terms of each of you, I've definitely noticed us grow. Soph, in the beginning of the notebook didn't you say you were afraid you'd have an affair with a married man when you were older because you couldn't handle real relationships? And now, out of all of us, you're the only one who's kept up a successful and serious one. Linds, you totally changed from shy on the outside, comedian on the inside to just all-around wonderful goofy gal. You're more open about your style and your opinions and just your personality in general. Court, well, you started taking showers, so you don't smell quite as bad (just playin). Seriously, you've managed to help guide us through all of our issues, and you seem now to always know what's best for you, and have the maturity to make good decisions, even if they're hard.

This is so sentimental! When I try to explain the notebook, people don't even get how much it means to us. They don't realize that opening this book is like breaching some secret code, it's trespassing into a time capsule. I can't even begin to say how grateful I am that all this has happened. This book has helped me sooo much (thank god, I was the lamest person I've ever met back in the day). In a nutshell (is that the same as a ballsac? Can I say "in a ballsac" from now on?) I guess I should thank the notebook for existing. We're just really lucky to have this, and to have each other. My pen is my sword.
I'm done bitches! Julia

12/24/03

I don't even know how to write a last entry. How do I sum up our friendship in just a few words? Trying to do so will just trivialize everything, so I'm just gonna make this short + sweet (like me!)

You guys have been everything for me. Whenever life seems too crazy, too wierd, too scary, or too sad, I know I can count on the 3 of you to help me work everything out.

Everyday I learn from you, whether it's Courtney's medical facts (like the difference between canker sores + herpes - yay, I don't have a herpes!) or Julia + Lindsey's Jewish history + their patient explination again + again the difference between Reform + Conservative Judaism. I've also learned about love, friendship, family, and a whole lot about myself (namely that I'm a big cracked-out princess, as Courtney put it best).

I never feel as at home around anyone other than you 3. No one understands me so perfectly. I'm always amazed by how little we have to explain or say outloud - we always know exactly what the other means. I can say anything and trust that you all understand. No one else could read my handwriting either.

Looking through the notebook, I realize how much I~~am~~ (and you three) have changed. When I read those Freshman year entries, I (and you three!) sound like such a little kid. Over the course of nearly 3 years, I feel like you~~;~~Julia, Courtney, and Lindsey - have helped me grow and change so much.

This wasn't as profound (i.e. long + cliched) as everyone else's final entry, but I just don't want to drag out the end anymore. It's ~~sad~~ to say goodbye, but as The Doors said, "the ~~time~~ to hesitate is through." It's been an amazing experience, so peace, ladies. Here's to notebooks and friends. I know I'll never experience anything like the ones here ever again.

—Sophie

PS- Julia + I had this idea of each of us keeping a diary, but like sharing them + then... wait. NO. Time to move on.

How the notebook was born!

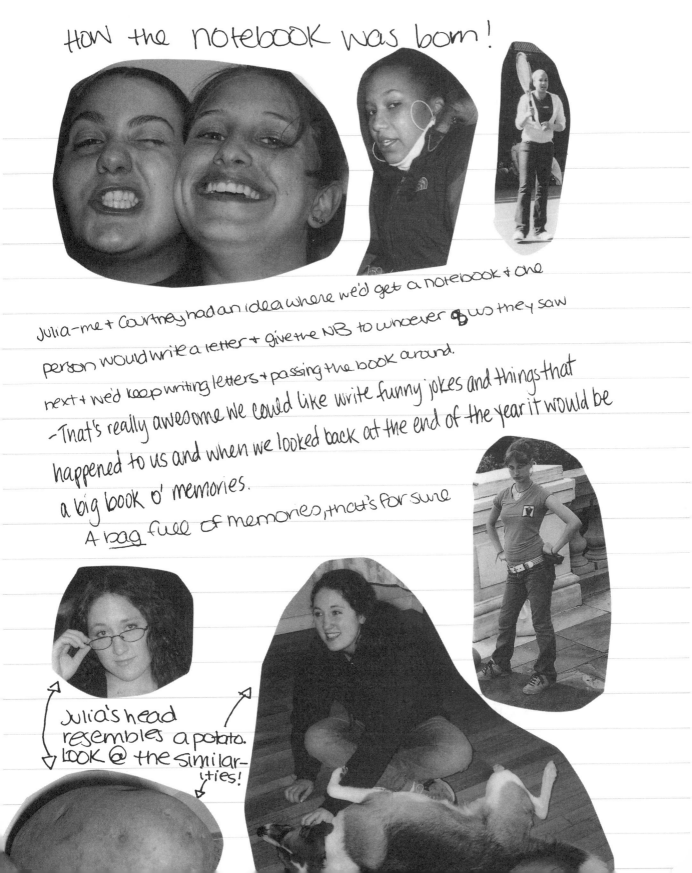

Julia - me + Courtney had an idea where we'd get a notebook + one person would write a letter + give the NB to whoever ⊕ us they saw next + we'd keep writing letters + passing the book around.

- That's really awesome we could like write funny jokes and things that happened to us and when we looked back at the end of the year it would be a big book o' memories.

A bag full of memories, that's for sure

Julia's head resembles a potato. LOOK @ the similar- ities!

♪♫ BAND CHART ♪♫

ROCK ON!

Your Name	Band's Name	Why they're cool
Courtney	White Stripes	b/c they're ex-married and make all the music
Julia	Blues Traveler	Because it's blues and classic rock and folk style all blended and it has awesome lyrics
Sophie	Queen	Their songs are amazing, funny, and just put you in a really good mood (they rock the cheesey guitar solos). You want to jump around your room in your PJs.
Lindsey	Shit Inc.	Because I love shit.
	SOPHIE YOU RETARD	
Lindsey	BOB Marley is Awesome!!	

COCO's life of Pain, by sophums

"Oh man. first day of calculus. This is scary, the class is supposed to be so hard!"

ABCDEFGHIJKLMNOPQ

$\frac{d}{dx} x^2 + 2 = 7x + x^3$

BLAM $\int x^4 = ?$

teacher He
baseball bat

ABCDEFGHIJKLM

$\frac{d}{dx} x^2 + x^2 + 2 = 7x +$
$x \to nx$

welcome to calculus. BITCH.

The Notebook Dictionary
(words frequently used by the 4 beauties)

① <u>Douche</u>: n. asshole, nerd, idiot, funny person, funny looking person, general weirdo

adj. "That was so douche" stupid, dumb, corny, you should die, don't ever speak to me again

② <u>Cracka</u>: white ass whitey

③ <u>wanker</u>: like douche but dumber

④ <u>Jewish</u>: The thing you can blame for all of Julia's problems & reasons why she can't chill Friday nights

⑤ <u>cocktapus</u> - noun. A mythical beast w/ <u>mad</u> cocks all over the place. Also used to describe a guy being all sloppy and <u>way</u> too excited trying to hook up w/ you.

⑥ <u>To casual</u> - verb. To hook up w/ someone repeatedly and regularly but not be an official couple. see - Sophie + Andre right now, Zoe + Brody

⑦ <u>Black Out Wasted</u>: noun, adj. Pretending that we will get really fucked up at some mythical awesome party, and ending up walking the streets all night, being cold and ending up hanging out with people we don't actually want to see

Say it ain't so—Weezer
Tears in heaven—Eric Clapton
Brick House—The Commodores
Yeah—Usher
Pressure Drop, 54-46 Was My Number—Toots + the Maytals

and being home by 11:00.

ex. adj: "Hey guys, let's get black out wasted tonight!"

⑧ smoke ~~~~~ marijuana: the fun (and sometimes painful) thing we do any day of the week (aka smoke up, blaze, hit that shit, pack the pipe, smoke weed/tree/bud/herb/blunts/a jay/ganja) ↓

Songs of the Notebook Girls:

You Shook Me All Night Long—AC/DC ★ Oh! Darling, Down Let Me Down—The Beatles

Last Kiss—Pearl Jam ★ Beautiful—Xtina ★ Toxic—Britney Spears

Knockin' On Heaven's Door—Bob Dylan ★ Bohemian Rhapsody—Queen

Walk This Way—Aerosmith/Run DMC ★ The Oscar Meyer Weiner Song—Unknown Hotdog

Sweet Home Alabama—Lynyrd Skynyrd ★ Under Pressure—Queen w/ David Bowie

Journey to the End—Rancid ★ Just a Friend—Biz Markie ★ Crossroads—Cream

The Theme to Welcome Back, Kotter ★ Changes—2pac ★ U+Me—2gether

Runaway—The Real McCoy ★ You make me feel like a Natural Woman—Aretha Franklin

No Woman No Cry—Bob Marley (and The Fugees) ★ Should I stay or should I go—The Clash

Faith—George Michael ★ Moulin Rouge Soundtrack ★ Little Wing—Jimi Hendrix

Wake me up before you Go Go—Wham! ★ Sweet hometown Jamaica—Toasters

What I got, Santeria—Sublime ★ Black Dog + Over the Hills and Far Away—Led Zeppelin (Tangerine + D'yer M'ker)

Build Me Up Buttercup—The Foundations ★ She's got a girlfriend now—Reel big Fish

Here I go Again on my own—Whitesnake ★ Sweet Child O'Mine / Welcome to the Jungle > Guns'n Roses

Fill in who you chose, they don't have to
be *hot*, but could be hook-up-able)
— CJT

funny how we bend the rules b/c there aren't
enough guys — JB

☒ = Sophie will
tap
— SPC   yeah
right! CT

Hot guys at our school: a masterpiece brought to you by courtney

Lets fill in the obvious:

① Tyler (good looking and charming)

☒ ② Omar (Indian Prince — hot and really profound — might just be all the acid he's on)

③ Marc (likes music *and* is mad good at sports)

I discovered him in my freshman Bio class... a thank you. — LN

Then:

④ Andrei   what?! mentally yes
but physically? — JB   ⑱ Ari Simon

⑤ Paul (sadly) Barf. — LN   ⑲ Cam

☒ ⑥ Shane West-look-a-like   ⑳ Malik (hot hot hot) hot.

⑦ Hot Irish Kid   ☒ ㉑ James (senior) SPC

⑧ Sean   ㉒ Jesus
(Hay-sus)
for all you gringos

our friend,
Petey the
pube!
— SPC

⑨ Tim

☒ ⑩ Amos (junior with mohawk)

☒ ⑪ Arlo

☒ ⑫ Micky (gay guy with beaded bracelets)

⑬ ??? Come on, we can break 15 — JB
↳ Hot Senior in SSAC (Lucas) — SPC YES. — LN

☒ ⑭ If stoner mick wasn't so stoner + short, then maybe — SPC Death! — JB

⑮ Rob (yeah, yeah — CT) NO NO NO NO NO NO! — SPC

⑯ Other Micky, sometimes, if his eyebrows were fixed.

☒ ⑰ Nino — no matter what you say, those ghetto Russians always
get to me! — SPC

The Many Shades of Sophie (and Andre)
by the ultimate in cool → Courtney
Andre kiss me!
Don't touch me!
Andre didn't call me!
Boohoo Andre
OMG Andre Loves me!
So I was talking to Tyler last night...
Andre doesn't appreciate me!
If Andre dresses up as a woman for Halloween I will never have sex with him again
then he did
Awesome!
Is he hooking up with Zoe because I will kill him!
Awesome!
LOVE FOREVER!!

♡ ♡ ♡ ♡

PAGE DEDICATED ♡

♡ TO THE FACT THAT

♡ JULIA HOOKED UP ♡

WITH DAVE FRIKIN

BERGER!!! (11/1/02)

♡ ♡

NO wonder...who could
resist this? ⟶
~~~?
-SPC

WORDS of WISDOM

← owl-ct

"I feel like blind people are always watching me." —Julia

"It's like an Odyssey when you're stoned, a WEEDESEY!" —

Julia + Courtney when blazing haze

Sophie's mom — Garibaldi's soldiers were known for their beautiful, romantic, red shirts.

Sophie — So they were gay?

mom — Yes. A hundred thousand homosexuals came in and united Italy.

"Yo, let's take my cat's ear medication." —Sophie

"Hey little girl, want a quarter? WELL I AIN'T GOT ONE!" —Some homeless guy

A homeless guy's sign: Please help me. Ninjas killed my family. Need money for karate class.

Lindsey — "My mom's on a history book-kick!"

Courtney — "Well my mom's on a crack-kick!"

"The only thing worse than bad beer is ~~warm~~ chugging bad beer." —Lindsey

"Tyler, can you put your fuckin socks on, you look like Frodo Baggins." —Sophie

"Ohh, that says Museum-Of-Art, not museum-o-fart. That makes more sense." — Me (Julia)

Lindsey — "Wow, these questions are really easy, they like, give you the answers." Zoe — "Lindsey, we're on the answer page."

WORDS OF WISDOM CONT'D...

A really nasty looking guy walked into class and said "Am I late?" And I said, "No. But you sure are ugly." -Lindsey

"Whenever I think of Squanto, I just think of an Indian shitting a piece of corn." -Julia

Proof of fat Julia is: She pulls out the trundle bed, gets on it and it just collapses. -Lindsey

Lindsey-"Wow, if there's ten people, and everyone pays ten dollars we'll have like...a thousand dollars!"

After a contemplative silence...

Julia-"But ten times ten is a hundred"

Lindsey-"Damn I'm taking the PSATs tomorrow."

"What's a carnie? Is it some kind of bird?" -Julia

"Is it dangerous to run with an umbrella?" -Julia

"Wow. I'm stupid." - Julia

"Do chickens have a patella?" -Lindsey

SPC-You don't know Jack Shit!

LN-who's a Jack shit?

I love you -Paul

"If I was funny, I'd have something to say right now." -Julia

SPC-Can I draw a picture of you?

JB-
No. Last time you drew a picture of me, you drew a butt w/ shit coming out!

THIS IS WHAT HAPPENS WHEN SOPHIE DON'T GET NO SLEEP: "Kenyan people always win the marathon... Back in Kenya a lot of people don't have shoes." - Sophie

WORDS OF WISDOM STUYVESANT STYLE

—"Fronting is an automatic ZERO!" - Mr. Greenberg

—"Europeans suckle anti-semitism from their mothers' teets!" - mr. Green-borg

Kid in my Economics class - "since we're ~~cuddon~~ not on the gold standard anymore, isn't the gold in Fort Knox just the government's jewelry?"

Ec. teacher - "I guess... the government's jewelry that it keeps in a secret, dark place, + doesn't show anyone."

Sophie (in my head!) - So basically, it's the government's clit ring.

— In response to a student who asked to write the homework on the board:

"I said ~~no~~ NO. You cannot write it on the board. What happens next year, in college, when you ask the professor, 'Can I write it on the board' and he says 'Can you NOT be in this class?" - Ms. Green

— "The Nanny' has problems. Math has solutions." mr. Puerta

— Health teacher - "What are some derogatory names for girls?"

The class - "Dirty cum guzzlers!!", "Carpet munchers!!", "Lumberjack pussy-lickers!"

Some girls in my class - "You're a ho."

Other girl - "Hey that's my last name."

WORDS OF WISDOM con'td... again

- Health Teacher: "what are some consequences for calling girls hurtful names?"

Some kid in class: "They cut off all their hair and become lesbians."

Il worda di Wisdoma della ~~La~~ Bella Lingua (aka
(my)
here's the funny shit that goes down in Italian class)

[Ti amo = 'I love you' in Italian]

Mr. Finestra: "Ti amo." This is a good phrase to ~~know~~ learn so that you
can always talk to your cat.'

- "You hate mondays? I hate my bus driver."

- 'I'm bad, I'm bad. But I am NOT michael Jackson.'

- "I have a joke. Do you cry when you eat?"

- "If you're very wealthy, you have more holes in your blue jeans than money can buy."

ABOUT THE AUTHORS

Julia, Lindsey, Sophie, and Courtney are all native New Yorkers who graduated from Stuyvesant High School. They currently attend Washington University in St. Louis, Cornell University, Wesleyan University, and Princeton University, respectively. Although there is no more notebook being passed along, they admit to having taken out their own group e-mail on the Internet; they make time for their studies in between entries.

Julia

Lindsey

Sophie

Courtney